HOW TO DO RESEARCH

SAGE was founded in 1965 by Sara Miller McCune to support the dissemination of usable knowledge by publishing innovative and high-quality research and teaching content. Today, we publish over 900 journals, including those of more than 400 learned societies, more than 800 new books per year, and a growing range of library products including archives, data, case studies, reports, and video. SAGE remains majority-owned by our founder, and after Sara's lifetime will become owned by a charitable trust that secures our continued independence.

Los Angeles | London | New Delhi | Singapore | Washington DC

HOW TO DO RESEARCH

15 Labs for the Social & Behavioral Sciences

Jane F. Gaultney
University of North Carolina, Charlotte

Hannah D. Peach
University of North Carolina, Charlotte

Los Angeles | London | New Delhi
Singapore | Washington DC

Los Angeles | London | New Delhi
Singapore | Washington DC

FOR INFORMATION:

SAGE Publications, Inc.
2455 Teller Road
Thousand Oaks, California 91320
E-mail: order@sagepub.com

SAGE Publications Ltd.
1 Oliver's Yard
55 City Road
London EC1Y 1SP
United Kingdom

SAGE Publications India Pvt. Ltd.
B 1/I 1 Mohan Cooperative Industrial Area
Mathura Road, New Delhi 110 044
India

SAGE Publications Asia-Pacific Pte. Ltd.
3 Church Street
#10-04 Samsung Hub
Singapore 049483

Acquisitions Editor: Leah Fargotstein
eLearning Editor: Katie Bierach
Editorial Assistant: Yvonne Mcduffee
Production Editor: Kelly DeRosa
Copy Editor: Diane DiMura
Typesetter: C&M Digitals (P) Ltd.
Proofreader: Jennifer Grubba
Indexer: Jean Casalegno
Cover Designer: Anupama Krishnan
Marketing Manager: Susannah Goldes

Printed in the United States of America

Library of Congress Cataloging-in-Publication Data

Gaultney, Jane F.

How to do research: 15 labs for the social & behavioral sciences/Jane F. Gaultney, University of North Carolina, Charlotte, Hannah D. Peach.

pages cm
Includes bibliographical references and index.

ISBN 978-1-4833-8512-9 (pbk.: alk. paper)

1. Psychology—Research—Methodology. 2. Social sciences—Research—Methodology. I. Peach, Hannah D. II. Title.

BF76.5.G384 2016
150.72'1—dc23   2015029289

This book is printed on acid-free paper.

MIX
Paper from
responsible sources
FSC® C014174

16 17 18 19 20 10 9 8 7 6 5 4 3 2 1

BRIEF CONTENTS

DETAILED CONTENTS

NOTE TO INSTRUCTORS

This lab manual has grown out of activities developed over many years of teaching Research Methods. It is intended to supplement traditional textbooks in research methodology. Our goal was to create a lab manual that was useful for a variety of disciplines in social sciences. To that end, we have featured articles and examples from a broad spectrum of social sciences. While the activities were developed for use with undergraduates, we have included advanced material at the end of each lab that will make the manual useful for early graduate students as well. We want to help students make the leap from learning *about* research to learning *how* to carry it out. We don't expect most undergraduate students to produce publishable research at the end of this class—if we can just get them to be a little excited about the possibilities of doing research and an appreciation of what constitutes good research, then we've accomplished a lot. Although some of my colleagues find it a bit strange, Research Methods lab is one of my favorite classes to teach. Not only do I love research, but this course allows me to do more hands-on teaching than is possible in a large lecture course, and students make so much progress throughout the class.

Each lab features a different area of social sciences. Labs begin with an objective so you can quickly determine the topic(s) to be covered in both the basic and advanced (If You Want to Go Further . . .) sections. This is followed by a target article that illustrates the focus of the lab. Each lab includes background information and an assignment. The instructor can choose to use canned data we've provided (along with illustrations of the output) or use the suggested activity to collect your own data. Note that students will need access to *Statistical Package for the Social Sciences* (IBM® SPSS® Statistics*) to use the step-by-step instructions. A student version can be purchased if students don't have access through your institution. Questions that check students' understanding are embedded throughout the lab (along with answers so students can get immediate feedback). The more advanced sections also follow this

---

*SPSS is a registered trademark of International Business Machines Corporation.

pattern. Students are reminded each time they analyze data to check for anomalies in the output that may signal a data entry error. **(Eyeball your data.)**

The labs have been arranged to be consistent with the steps students take to do a term-long research project, all the way from coming up with a topic to producing a finished, APA-style paper. You can present them in any order that is most useful to your students or pick and choose the ones most relevant to your discipline.

We've included links to a variety of online resources. Links, of course, are notorious for being broken. In each case, we also included a suggested search term that can help you quickly find an alternative site. As we become aware of broken links, we'll post updated ones on the SAGE website.

We'd love to hear your experiences in using the labs, and we're always interested in coming up with ways to improve them, so please share your thoughts with us.

ACKNOWLEDGMENTS

To all the students who have survived our class in Research Methods: See, you really could pass the class and even excel! I hope you're proud of how much you learned and accomplished.

To Paul Foos, who said, "You have already written a lab manual; it can't be much more work to publish it." Yes, it can. Thanks for the encouragement.

To Vicki Knight of SAGE Publications, who very patiently guided us through the publication process.

The authors would like to thank the reviewers who helped shape the contents of this lab manual.

- Brian V. Carolan, Montclair State University (Education)
- Mary Siegrist, Regis University (Health Services Administration)
- Gwen Urey, California State Polytechnic University, Pomona (Urban and Regional Planning)
- Alexander Jakubow, New Mexico State University (Government)
- Norbert Elliot, New Jersey Institute of Technology (Humanities)
- Diane L. Verrill, St. Gregory's University (Social Sciences)
- Stephen Sammut, Franciscan University of Steubenville (Psychology)
- Stanley Chinedum Nwoji, Trinity Washington University (Graduate and Business Studies)
- Thomas V. Frederick, Hope International University (Marriage and Family Therapy)

Jane F. Gaultney (jgaultny@uncc.edu)

Hannah D. Peach (hpeach@uncc.edu)

NOTE TO STUDENTS

This *How to Do Research: 15 Labs for the Social & Behavioral Sciences* methods lab manual contains exercises that reinforce concepts presented in many Research Methods textbooks. One can learn *about* research methodology from the textbook, but the only way to learn to *do* research is ... to do it. These exercises are intended to supplement your textbook and to cement concepts presented in class rather than teach new material. I want to help you add "knowing how" to "knowing about." Do you remember when you first learned to drive? You read the drivers' manual, you learned about how a car operates, you memorized the road signs and driving laws, but learning to drive required getting in a car and practicing. Knowing *about* driving was important but wasn't the same thing as knowing *how* to drive.

You will need access to *Statistical Package for the Social Sciences* (SPSS) to use the step-by-step instructions in this manual. A student version can be purchased if you don't have access through your institution.

An open-access companion website for this book at study.sagepub.com/labresearch includes the Excel and SPSS data sets you'll need to follow along with the book, as well as web resources for each lab and selected SAGE journal articles.

We realize many of you may not have looked forward to taking Research Methods with a lot of joy. Some of you have been avoiding it for years! Many of you do not expect to have a career as a researcher and question why you should spend so much time learning skills you don't plan to use. This class is still useful for you! Our job is to give you the tools you need for future research, graduate school, or for life as a consumer of research. What you learn here, although sometimes tedious or difficult, actually benefits you (as opposed to merely making you miserable!). Perhaps it will help if we point out to you some of the skills you can develop or improve through these assignments.

I don't plan to attend graduate school or to pursue a career in research. How do I benefit from this?

First of all, you already are a researcher. What would you do in preparation for buying a car, adopting a new pet, deciding where to live, what kind of career you'd like? You'd probably start by doing some background research—tracking down information, reading reviews, considering the options, deciding on a direction to take and then acting on your decision. These assignments should help you develop sharper skills for something you'll be doing all your life.

✓ There are some skills you've developed through this class that can apply to many other occupations and to living in general. These are skills you can feature (and document) when you apply for many types of jobs. For example, there's always a need to be able to write in a coherent, integrative, analytic manner. Practice at writing is never wasted.

✓ You will always be a consumer of research. The material you've learned about and the practice you've had with critical thinking will allow you to evaluate research results you encounter in daily life. You will be able to recognize and challenge the conclusions of pseudoscience ("Nine out of ten doctors agree . . .").

✓ Hopefully, you will be a lifelong independent learner. There are still a lot of learning opportunities ahead of you. Some of the skills you acquire in this class will promote this.

✓ In many types of jobs, there is an advantage to being able to identify a problem, come up with a way to evaluate or solve the problem, collect data, then organize, analyze, and report on the data. Sell your ability to do these things when you apply for jobs.

✓ Think about all the time management you have to practice to complete this class—this is a useful skill throughout life.

Finally, we hope that you will discover the fun of doing research. Research is somewhat like a treasure hunt—you never know what you're going to find! We wish you the very best as you continue your college training.

Jane F. Gaultney
Hannah D. Peach

ABOUT THE AUTHORS

 **Jane F. Gaultney** is professor of psychology and a faculty member of the Health Psychology PhD Program at the University of North Carolina at Charlotte. She has taught Research Methods for many years (never mind exactly how many), and uses the labs in this manual as teaching tools on a regular basis. She received a PhD in psychology from Florida Atlantic University. Her current research program looks at sleep and its association with cognitive, behavioral, and health outcomes.

 **Hannah D. Peach** received a PhD in health psychology from the University of North Carolina at Charlotte, where she currently teaches in the Psychology Department. Her research examines associations between sleep characteristics and health outcomes, particularly among adolescents and emerging adults. As a health psychologist, she encourages a healthy work–life balance among her undergraduate students (especially for those currently enrolled in Research Methods!).

PART I

Before You Collect Data

LAB 1

Finding a Topic, Finding Resources, and Critically Reading Appropriate Articles

Objective

The purpose of this lab is to help students choose a topic for an individual research topic, find appropriate sources, and suggestions on what to look for when reading research articles.

Target Article

Kenrick, D. T., Keefe, R. C., Gabrielidis, C., & Cornelius, J. S. (1996). Adolescents' age preferences for dating partners: Support for an evolutionary model of life-history strategies. *Child Development, 67*(4), 1499–1511. doi: 10.2307/113171

Which seems to make more sense to you—an older woman dating a younger man, or an older man dating a younger woman? You're likely to choose the latter configuration. Is it just a western cultural thing, or is it a common pattern throughout the world? According to Douglas T. Kenrick et al. (1996), it appears to be common in many cultures. Evolutionary psychology suggests that this aspect of human behavior may have evolved because younger women are likely to be more fertile than older women, and therefore are more attractive to older men. If fertility rather than age is the determining factor, then adolescent males should be attracted to slightly older women, again for their greater fertility relative to teenage girls. The authors interviewed over 200 adolescents ages 12 to 19, as to their date preferences. As predicted, males indicated that although they'd be willing to date someone slightly below their age, they preferred to date someone older than themselves. Adolescent females, however, indicated they preferred to date someone their own age or slightly older—as was also true among older females.

"More and more, I identify with Mrs. Robinson."

© iStock.com/andrewgenn

FINDING A TOPIC

Your instructor may ask you to complete a research assignment during this term. The labs in this manual are designed and organized to help you carry out your project. All you are doing at this point is identifying a topic—not a hypothesis or methodology (those will come later). For example, you might choose "false memory in sleepy and rested college students," "health in marginalized youths," "social stigma and obesity," or "social patterns in the XYZ cultural group."

Where Do I Find a Topic Idea?

The topic for your research project should be something that really interests you. It's going to be a lot of work, so it will be best if you like your topic. Begin by thinking about areas of your discipline that have interested you as you studied them in other classes. Skim through different relevant textbooks, looking for a small *subheading* (a major heading probably covers too broad an area for your project) that looks interesting. Once you have several topic ideas in mind, do some reading about each one. You can read about them in textbooks (perhaps your instructor, your library, or your peers have textbooks you can peruse) and in journals. For example, in a chapter on biological bases of behavior

JSTOR

you see a section on emotions and a subheading on cross-cultural similarities/ differences in the expression of emotions. If that interests you, then look for more information.

Use a search engine such as PsycINFO, PubMed, or JSTOR to help you locate journal articles relating to your topic. Search the Internet for websites that relate to your topics (remembering that some websites are more reliable than others). Use these sources to help you narrow down your topic to a manageable size. For example, I opened JSTOR and entered "older adult and aging" and got over 800 pages of titles. I then added "older adult and aging and independent living" and whittled it down to fewer listings. I then tried "older adult and aging and independent living and geography" and got a more focused listing of articles. Tightening the focus, I then tried "older adult and aging and independent living and geography and quality of life." Now I'm down to a manageable number of listed articles, so I can start reading through titles and abstracts to narrow down my choice even further. At this point, you aren't reading articles in detail; you are just skimming to get the general idea of the article in order to refine your topic.

Other Sources

When I refer to URLs in this manual, I will follow it with relevant search terms in case that link is broken. Updated alternate links can be found on the website that accompanies this manual at study.sagepub.com/labresearch.

1. With your instructor's guidance, look online.

   a. Check out the demonstrations such as those at https://implicit.harvard .edu/implicit/demo/ {suggested search term *implicit attitudes*}.

   b. You can go to http://www.about.com/#s2_ to search for your topic {suggested search term *about your discipline*}, then type in your field of study (e.g., about psychology, about sociology, about communications studies, or even something more specific like dating practices) in the "learn about" box.

   c. Go to Multimedia Educational Resource for Learning and Online Teaching (http://www.merlot.org/merlot/index.htm; click *communities* and choose your discipline; suggested search term *Merlot education*).

   d. Check out the home page of your discipline's professional organizations (e.g., American Psychological Association, American Sociological Association, American Economic Association).

   e. Another resource available on the Centers for Disease Control and Prevention website is http://www.cdc.gov/ViolencePrevention/pdf/ YV_Compendium.pdf. This is a collection of violence-related attitude and belief assessment instruments. Even if a test is intended for a specific population (such as adolescents), you may be able to adapt it or find something similar for other populations. Remember that younger college students might still be considered adolescents or emerging adults. For a list of several cognitive assessments, check out http://freecognitivetests.yolasite.com/. You may find a topic that interests you even if you don't want to use one of these instruments.

2. Is there an aspect of some area in your field that has always puzzled or intrigued you? What topic caught your attention in your introductory course? This could be your opportunity to answer your questions. What can you find about that topic in the literature?

3. Your instructor may have a collection of idea starters—ask what is available.

4. Look through journals relevant to your discipline. Just read the titles in the Table of Contents and see if you get inspired.

Keep a list of topics that catch your attention as you search. Narrow down that list to your three favorites and then explore those three in more detail. Your instructor may wish you to submit one or more topic ideas for approval.

Reality Check

If your instructor is going to have you collect data on your topic at some point down the road, you may need to keep in mind some of the realities of your situation as you choose your topic. For example, unless you have Institutional Review Board (IRB) approval you will want to avoid involving protected populations (such as children or prisoners). In other words, don't choose to study pro-social behavior in 4-year-olds unless you plan to go through the IRB approval process. You may also need to avoid animal research—don't go there if you don't have access to an animal lab.

Not all research topics are created equally. There are some perfectly interesting topics that aren't amenable to scientific study. You may be convinced that watching sunsets is a cure for stress, but there may not be any scholarly research available. If you can't find anything about it in the peer-reviewed journals, then pick something else. If, however, you *do* decide to collect data on sunset watching, let me know and I'll volunteer to be a participant!

Courtesy of Jennifer Hrncir

It's OK to change horses in midstream. You may get started on a topic and decide it is a dead end or just not something on which you want to spend a lot of time. In that case, change topics (unless, of course, it is the day before your paper is due) to something more productive.

WHAT ARE THE STEPS OF A RESEARCH PROJECT?

Now that you've identified a topic, what happens next? It might be useful to write in a date when each of these steps should be started and completed. Don't feel overwhelmed by all that has to be done for a research project. Take one step at a time. This lab manual will assist you with some of these steps.

1. Review the literature. Read about your topic in professional journals and scholarly books. This will be the basis for your literature review paper (which becomes the introduction section of your final paper).

2. Develop a research question. If you are proposing a quantitative design, develop a hypothesis based on a relevant theory.

3. Design a study that will adequately test your hypothesis or address your research question. This includes identifying the design you'll use, who your participants will be, the materials you'll use, the exact procedure you'll follow as you collect your data, and the statistic(s) you'll use to analyze your data. If you do a thorough job on this you will have much of your Method section written.

4. Submit your study to an IRB. In some cases, your instructor may serve as the IRB for a classroom project.

5. Collect data.

6. Analyze and interpret your data.

7. Interpret your findings. What are some alternative explanations for your findings? Why should the reader care what you found?

8. Report your findings. You may do this by means of a poster, orally in a presentation, or in written form (or perhaps all of the above).

9. Use your findings as a springboard for the next project. OK, so maybe you won't have time to do another project for this class, but it is a good exercise to always be thinking ahead to the next project.

TRY IT YOURSELF

Look through the sources indicated above and generate a short list of possible topics. It might be a good idea to indicate where you found each topic so you can go back to it later. Write a short paragraph describing each of three potential project topics you'd like to explore. Put the topics in order of interest. Be as specific as you possibly can. For example, "memory and napping" is more specific than "sleep." The more specific you are, the more your instructor can give you specific feedback. Don't

try to develop a hypothesis or research question yet. Once you settle on a topic, begin collecting peer-reviewed source material.

TIPS FOR FINDING SOURCES

Note: The following information is somewhat generic and may or may not reflect sources available to you through your library. Information specific to your library will be most useful for you. Find out if your library offers classes on how to find research sources. If such instruction is available to you, take advantage of it.

1. Evaluating Websites: If your instructor permits it, look at relevant websites. Be cautious, however, that you are looking at a credible website. For assistance in evaluating websites see http://guides.library.uncc.edu/ENGL_Web_Evaluation {suggested search term *evaluate website academic*}.

2. Locating Articles: Databases and indexes will vary by library and by discipline, but some general issues are:

A. **Selecting the appropriate database:** There are many databases to choose from but not all of them are appropriate for a particular discipline or topic. There are interdisciplinary databases such as Academic Search Elite (that include areas such as psychology, literature, education, business, politics, sociology, the sciences, etc.), PubMed, JSTOR, but also discipline-specific databases such as PsycINFO. The examples given here use PsycINFO.

Many times students are tempted to skip the academic search engines and search via Yahoo or Google for the information they need. If you are looking for older or open-access articles, this can be a good approach. However, you want only peer-reviewed scholarly sources. Using a general search engine will give you a lot of links you can't use, and you have to be able to distinguish the usable from the rest. There is a great deal of interesting, helpful stuff on the Internet, but in most cases, it hasn't met the scientific standard of peer review. The peer-review process is a method for ensuring that what gets published has been carefully thought through, properly carried out, and appropriately analyzed and interpreted. Published peer-reviewed articles and information have been scrutinized and critiqued by experts within that field of study, so the peer-review process acts as a filter that prevents substandard or incomplete research from being circulated. Websites and non-peer-reviewed journals could give you anything from high-quality information to useless or inaccurate information.

B. **Selecting appropriate terminology:** Most disciplines have their own vocabulary, so using the correct terms is important. Students need to learn the terminology of their discipline. This is especially important when searching a database like PsycINFO that uses APA-defined terms. If you are not successful in searching a particular term, check to see if the organization's website has a thesaurus of search terms. If you still aren't succeeding, look for terminology in textbooks or ask instructors for suggested terms.

C. **Developing appropriate search strategies:** Once you have search terms, you will need to create a strategy that will provide relevant results. This is where the use of Boolean (or logical) operators and "nesting" play a part. You can combine terms so the *logic* retrieves entries that are very specific to your topic. For example, if you are interested in the development of self-concept, click on the Advanced search tab in the search engine, then specify terms, linking them using *and, or,* or *not.* If you are interested in self-concept in children, you could enter *self-concept* as a subject and *children* as a subject, linking them with the word *and.* This would limit your results to just those dealing with self-concept and children, as opposed to self-concept at any age.

D. **Selecting appropriate types of materials:** You should use peer-reviewed and scholarly materials in your literature review. This includes articles published in a professional journal as well as chapters in books that have undergone a peer-review process. Some databases (like Academic Search Elite) provide an option to limit a search just to peer-reviewed and scholarly literature. Other databases do not provide any option and students have to know the difference. In that case, your instructor can steer you toward appropriate journals.

E. **Database features:** Each database has options and features that can assist the student in retrieving the desired results. Think about exactly what you want, and then see if the database lets you limit your search based on your needs. For example, Academic Search Elite includes articles in popular magazines, newspaper articles, and articles in peer-reviewed and scholarly journals. You can set the limit to the type of publications you want. It also allows you to specify the time period to be searched (e.g., articles published since 1999), what fields (subject, keyword, author, etc.) to be searched, and whether or not to limit the output to just what is available full text (if the database offers that). This last item is tempting since students often want only full text. They don't want a citation that they then will have to find in print or will have to order through interlibrary loan. However, if they limit the search just to full text, they may be missing important articles. Be willing to actually go into the library and find the hard copy of a particular journal. Other features may include (1) English-language materials; (2) limits on the type of sources, such as journals, rather than books, chapters, or dissertations; (3) population (human, animal); (4) dates to be searched; or (5) empirical research, for example.

Since I mentioned publication dates, consider whether your instructor wants you to use articles from a specific time period. Some may want you to use

only sources published in the last five years, while others might want you to focus on a specific time period. There may be times when you want to trace the evolution of a topic from its origins to its current state. In that case, some of your sources may be older.

Don't overlook search engines that are specific to other related disciplines. For example, you might search PubMed if you were studying health psychology. Consider whether your topic might also be of interest to researchers in criminal justice, communication, business, education, and so on and then check out their sources.

© iStock.com/YuriBBS

HOW TO READ AN ARTICLE

OK, so you've found your article. Now what? There is a method for reading an article critically. You are now going to work through an online tutorial that will make this method explicit. Go to http://www.psych.ualberta.ca/~varn/Kenrick/Reading.htm and work through points to look for in each section of a research report {suggested search term *critical read your discipline research*}.

Start with "Questions to Consider" in the tutorial and go through each section of the paper, answering questions as you go (click on the green check marks). First, read the section in the original article, then read the online comments about that section and answer the questions.

Here are some points to consider as you read about a study. Some of these questions may require more knowledge than you have at this point, and you will not be able to answer them. They are included here just to let you know that they are important considerations.

Introduction

Who wrote the article and in which journal was it published? When you write, just identify the authors as Kenney, LaBrie, Hummer, and Pham (2012) the first time you refer to the article, and as Kenney et al. (2012) thereafter.

What was the research question or hypothesis (some studies will have more than one)?

What background information was cited that led to the formation of this question? Was the background adequate to justify the question?

Does the research address an important issue?

Method

Who were the participants, and how were they recruited? Are they appropriate for this particular research question?

What design was used for the study? Is the design appropriate to address the research question?

What measures were used? How were they operationalized?* Do they measure what the author really wants to measure (in other words, are they valid)?

What ethical issues apply to this study? Were they addressed?

Were any extraneous variables identified? How were they controlled?

Results

What were the main findings of the study?

Do these results address the research question or hypothesis?

Were appropriate statistical analyses performed and correctly interpreted?

Discussion

What conclusions did the author draw from the results? Are the conclusions justified based on the results?

How do these findings relate to the literature (e.g., do they confirm earlier studies? Contradict? Raise new questions?)?

To what extent can the findings be generalized?

 * *Operationalized* refers to defining an abstract construct—like self-esteem or depression—in terms of a behavior that can be observed and measured. For

example, anxiety is abstract and can't directly be observed, but feeling anxious can raise one's heart rate. You can operationalize anxiety as a rise in heart rate as compared to a baseline.

Put It Into Practice

Go ahead and begin collecting articles that pertain to the topic you've chosen. Use keywords to search a relevant search engine for articles related to your topic. Obtain the entire article, not just the abstract. Read the article (not just the abstract!).

CLOSURE

Consider the advice of Mark Twain: "The secret of getting ahead is getting started. The secret of getting started is breaking your complex overwhelming tasks into small manageable tasks, and then starting on the first one." This lab manual teaches one aspect of your final project at a time. Don't worry about all the assignments you have for this class. Just organize what you need to do into smaller steps and do one small step at a time.

IF YOU WANT TO GO FURTHER . . .

Secondary Analyses of Large Data Sets Available Online

We discuss (here and in other labs) some realistic considerations for designing your own research project, such as access to populations, feasibility, ethical considerations, and the benefits of a large sample size. You may have a very interesting research question to ask but cannot feasibly collect the data yourself. Fortunately, researchers sometimes can answer such questions using *secondary data*. Secondary data, also known as archived data, refers to information that was collected by someone else or for a purpose other than your current research project. These data can include censuses, government-funded research projects, large-scale university projects, and more. Secondary data sets can provide you with large sample sizes, longitudinal data, and measures that you otherwise would be unable to collect.

For example, let's say a student is interested in examining if parent–child interactions during adolescence can predict psychological well-being in adulthood. Let's also suppose this student wants longitudinal data. Unless the student plans to spend 10 or more years collecting data during their undergraduate experience, he or she will need to examine other options for answering this research question. The student could instead analyze data from the  National Longitudinal Study of Adolescent Health (Add Health), a longitudinal study funded by the National Institute of Child Health and Human Development that followed a nationally representative sample of 7th- through 12th-grade students for many years. This data set includes information for over 10,000 participants regarding a host of different social, economic, psychological, and physical variables. This data set is publicly available (http://www.cpc.unc.edu/projects/addhealth) and would allow the student to examine longitudinal relationships between parent–child interactions during high school and measures of well-being during adulthood (while still graduating on time!).

Using secondary data can be beneficial to researchers but is by no means an "easy" way to conduct research. A researcher must carefully review codebooks to understand what variables are included in the data set and how they were measured and should always consult with his or her university IRB (or the instructor in the case of class assignments) before analyzing previously collected data. Many archived data sets are available for use by students and researchers; some are free, while others cost money to access. In addition to the Add Health data set, below are examples of available data sets that can be used to answer social science research questions.

The Panel Study of Income Dynamics: http://psidonline.isr.umich.edu/

National Longitudinal Survey of Youth: http://www.bls.gov/nls/home.htm

Youth Risk Behavior Surveillance System: http://www.cdc.gov/HealthyYouth/yrbs/index.htm

Wisconsin Longitudinal Study: http://www.ssc.wisc.edu/wlsresearch/

Behavioral Risk Factor Surveillance System: http://www.cdc.gov/brfss/

A list of publicly available databases for aging-related secondary analyses in the behavioral and social sciences can be found at http://www.nia.nih.gov/research/dbsr/publicly-available-databases-aging-related-secondary-analyses-behavioral-and-social.

http://www.wpclipart.com/

You may also search for databases related to your topic at the Inter-university Consortium for Political and Social Research website (http://www.icpsr.umich.edu/icpsrweb/landing.jsp) or at http://www.apa.org/research/responsible/data-links.aspx {suggested search terms *secondary data available online your discipline*}.

What about those of you who are interested in qualitative data? There are resources available to you, as well. For example, in the lab on qualitative research, we make use of data on reasons why teachers left the field of teaching (http://www.indiana.edu/~educy520/sec5982/week_5/qual_data_analy_ex1.pdf) {suggested search term *qualitative data analysis exercise*}.

> **Assignment:** Find publicly available datasets from your discipline. Try searching on *publicly available data* _____ (fill in the blank with your discipline). List at least five sources of data you might be able to use in your future research. Find the user's manual for the data from one of those sources and look at the variables available to you. What are some research questions that could be addressed using the data?

Let's try an example. Your instructor may want to modify this assignment to use another data set. Look at the *Youth Risk Behavior Surveillance System* (YRBSS). Choose Youth Online Interactive Data Tables. You can look at statistics on safety and health topics by clicking a category on the right.

SOURCE: Centers for Disease Control and Prevention (CDC). *1991-2013 High School Youth Risk Behavior Survey Data.* Available at http://nccd.cdc.gov/youthonline/

For example, look at consumption of soda by state and separately by gender.

Want to get fancy? This is a bit more complicated. From the YRBSS home-page, I clicked Data Files and Methods. I downloaded the ASCII data file for 2013 and saved it to my computer as a .dat file. I opened SPSS, a statistical package for the social sciences, and then clicked FILE, NEW, SYNTAX. The use of syntax (verbal instructions) is an approach to using SPSS, and gives the researcher more control on how analyses are run than is possible using the point and click method. I opened the SPSS Syntax file for 2013. I copied the syntax and pasted it in the blank syntax file. I edited the syntax in three places (once in the beginning, twice at the end) so that the file name and location matched the name and location of the data file, and then saved it. I saved the syntax file to the same location as the data file then clicked the large green triangle (run file) in the top tool bar. This created an SPSS data file on my computer. I then downloaded the User's Manual to see what each variable measured, and from "variable view," I typed out a more informative variable name for those that interested me (for example, *seatbelt.use*). I then can run analyses of the variables of interest to me. Since this is early in the lab manual, you may not yet know how to conduct the various statistical tests. That's OK; just hang on to these sources of data so you can use them later.

LAB 2

How to Write a Literature Review

Objective

This lab is intended to introduce how to write literature reviews. Before you launch a new research project you need to know what has already been done in that area. The lab will focus on APA style since this is used by writers from many social sciences, but your instructor can guide you to the style preferred within your area. Additional material will consider some elements of good writing and ways in which scientific writing differs from prose or creative writing.

Target Article

Veil, S. R., Buehner, T., & Palenchar, M. J. (2011). A work-in-progress literature review: Incorporating social media in risk and crisis communication. *Journal of Contingencies and Crisis Management, 19,* 110–122. doi: 10.1111/j.1468-5973.2011.00639.x. Retrieved from http://online library.wiley.com/doi/10.1111/j.1468-5973.2011.00639.x/pdf {use title of article as a suggested search term}.

Suppose for a moment that you are a public official with responsibility to an area that is in the path of an out-of-control fire. Your job is to get an urgent, short, coherent message out to thousands of people to warn them to leave the area immediately. How will you do that effectively? Or perhaps you are a citizen in an area that is undergoing tremendous political upheaval. In order to control the situation, the government has cut off radio and television broadcasting. You want the outside world to know what is happening. Assuming cell phone and electricity infrastructure are still working, how might you give the world a blow-by-blow account of what is happening? One way that has been tried is to make use of social media. This article describes research on the use of social media in crisis communication. It ends with a list of best practices to use social media for this purpose.

© iStock.com/ runeer

THE LITERATURE REVIEW

The job of a literature review is to teach readers about known material on your research topic. There's no point in designing a study if you don't know what's already established.

1. Read before you write—Prior to writing a literature review, you have to know what is in the literature. This sounds pretty obvious. Don't even try to write until you have become familiar with the findings already published in the literature. Use scholarly sources. By "scholarly" I mean peer-reviewed articles or chapters from peer-reviewed books.

2. Outline and revise—Now that you have some knowledge base, begin to outline the most important points you noticed about the topic.

3. Keep experimenting with and refining your outline until you have a guideline in place for writing. You could organize your topic chronologically or topically. For example,

   Chronological organization:

   I. Early theories about ability to delay gratification

   II. Shift from behaviorism to cognitive processing explanations

Table 2.1 Choosing Your Sources

Source	Can You Use It?
Journal of Personality	Yes
Reader's Digest	No
Edited book with scholarly chapters	Yes
Popular press book (one published for the general public)	No
Websites	Check with your instructor

III. Recent explanations for delayed gratification

IV. Purpose and hypothesis of present study

Topical organization:

I. Typical sleep problems in young children

II. Associations between children's sleep patterns and

A. Child's characteristics

a. ADHD

b. Internalizing

c. Diet

B. Social context

a. Maternal depression

b. Neighborhood and socioeconomic status

III. Purpose and hypothesis of present study

The purpose of the target article described above is to present a digest of the relevant literature rather than report original research (it is a *literature review* rather than a research report). Look at the complete article and think about how this literature review is organized. The authors made this easy for you by using headings and subheadings. Notice they write about how their sources make similar points; it is not a series of descriptions of individual articles.

1. Write your *first draft*. Do some of the work for the reader by giving an overview of your topic. Your goal is to write an organized, concise overview of the topic. Don't focus on one study per point; synthesize the information in a logical way. Identify themes, points that have contradictory findings or conclusions, and identify gaps in the literature.

©iStock.com/Pashalgnatov

2. This is where you introduce your individual project. The end of your review should summarize the main points that emerged from your review and suggest the next step or steps in solving the problem. Tell the reader the purpose and hypotheses (or research question) of your project. You want to lead your reader to agree with you that the project you are about to describe is the next logical step.

3. Write **MANY drafts** of your paper. Ask for feedback. Rewrite. Check to be sure you have used correct formatting for your discipline. This brings us to the activity for this lab.

APA STYLE

Many social sciences use American Psychological Association (APA) style, so this lab will give you some practice with this approach to formatting. First, you need to get an idea of the purpose and details of the APA style.

1. **Explore:** Open http://flash1r.apa.org/apastyle/basics/index.htm and proceed through the tutorial {suggested search term *APA style tutorial*}. Look for additional websites that cover some specific details. For example,

   a. Additional information about citing electronic resources: http://owl.english.purdue.edu/owl/resource/664/01 {suggested search term *APA cite website*}.

   b. When there is no author for a Web page, the title moves to the first position of the reference entry: http://www.apastyle.org/learn/faqs/web-page-no-author.aspx {suggested search term *APA online sources*}.

Note: Double check your instructor's advice about using websites as sources.

    c. Now go down to the link titled *Frequently Asked Questions*. Explore the information in this file. Return to it when you are writing your literature review.

    d. For those of you who prefer videos, see http://psychology.about.com/od/apastyle/tp/apa-format-instructional-videos.htm {suggested search term *APA format instructional video*}.

2. **Practice: Write these on a reference page (*Reference* is a Level 1 heading) in correct 6th edition APA style.** List them alphabetically by first author's last name. You can use the examples in the tutorial as a guide. Remember to add the digital object identifier (doi) which will begin with "10." If you have trouble finding it, go to crossref.org, guest query, scroll down then type in first author's last name and title {suggested search term *find doi*}. There is no punctuation after the doi. The answers are included at the end of the lab, but don't peek until you've tried these on your own!

    a. Book: http://www.amazon.com/Implementing-Public-Policy-Introduction-Operational/dp/1412947995 (use most recent publication date) {suggested search term *Implementing Public Policy: An Introduction to the Study of Operational Governance*}

    b. Book, corporate author: http://jasmine.uncc.edu/search~S0?/Xgraduate+study+in+psychology&SORT=D/Xgraduate+study+in+psychology&SORT=D&SUBKEY=graduate%20study%20in%20psychology/1%2C28%2C28%2CB/frameset&FF=Xgraduate+study+in+psychology&SORT=D&1%2C1%2C {suggested search term *APA graduate study book*}. Date of publication may vary depending on which edition you cite.

    c. Chapter in edited book: http://www.amazon.com/SAGE-Handbook-Qualitative-Geography-Handbooks/dp/1412919916 {suggested search term *The SAGE Handbook of Qualitative Geography*}. There is a chapter in this book titled "*Policy, Research Design and the Socially Situated Researcher.*" The authors are Kari B. Jensen and Amy K. Glasmeier. It is on pages 82 to 93. Look at the copyright page inside the book for most recent date. (Don't be fooled by my use of title case and italics in the title—the format is different in the APA-style reference.)

d. Article: http://jfi.sagepub.com/content/23/1/138.full.pdf+html {suggested search term *Linkages Between the Work-Family Interface and Work, Family, and Individual Outcomes*}

e. Website: http://www.nursingworld.org/MainMenuCategories/ThePracticeofProfessionalNursing/NursingStandards {your instructor can give you a search suggestion that is germane to your area}

f. If your library allows you to search for full-text online articles, try to find this article by going to your library website. You may need to sign in to the library site in order to access full-text articles online. Follow the proper path to find the library's electronic link to the journal *Child Development*. You are looking for an article published in 2003 (vol. 74, issue 2) with the first author of Sadeh. Write the reference entry for this article. Remember to include the doi. Even if all you can access is the abstract (which should be easily available via many search engines), you can still find the information you need to write out the citation.

IF YOU WANT TO GO FURTHER . . .

Writing "Good"

Writing clearly and correctly is a valuable skill in any career and is essential to succeed in graduate school. Your institution may have a writing center that can help you strengthen your writing. Take advantage of the service, even if you think you are a good writer. The APA publication manual details some particular points of writing that are common mistakes.

Grammar: Read the pointers about grammar at https://owl.english.purdue.edu/owl/section/1/5/ {suggested search term *Purdue owl grammar APA*}. Then try some of the exercises at https://owl.english.purdue.edu/exercises/2/.

Next, think about the details of punctuation, looking at the list of punctuation pointers listed at https://owl.english.purdue.edu/owl/section/1/6/ {suggested

©iStock.com/LeeDaniels

search term *Purdue owl punctuation APA*}. You can practice at https://owl.english.purdue.edu/exercises/3/.

After you have carefully considered these pages, pull out a paper you wrote for an earlier assignment. Review your punctuation and grammar carefully. Make a list of punctuation and grammar errors to avoid or best practices to remember.

Scientific Writing

You have, no doubt, written many essays, position papers, book reports, maybe even short stories or poetry in your college career. The papers in which you report research, however, are an entirely different category. Many years ago (many, many years ago) a popular television show was *Perry Mason*. Fictional Perry was a prosecuting attorney who solved crimes and convicted criminals. He had a famous line. When a witness was reporting opinion or supposition, he would remind the witness that the job of the witness was to report "just the facts." That applies to scientific writing, too. The job of a literature review is to summarize and synthesize information already in peer-reviewed, published literature. It is not the time to present your opinion, judgement, or fun-filled tidbits of information. Scientific writing is formal and presented in a standard format. OK, it is a bit stuffy and less entertaining than less formal writing styles, but that's how it is. Your goal is to state information as precisely and accurately as you can. Try to find the simplest, clearest way to say what is needed—it doesn't make your paper sound more intellectual to use unnecessary verbiage, big words (unless, of course, the big word is the most appropriate), or lots of synonyms. I once had a student who wrote a paper then looked up synonyms for most of the words in the text. Because the synonyms didn't carry the same connotations as the original word, I had no clue what the

©iStock.com/Izabela Habur

student was trying to say! Look at the published articles from journals in your area. What do they have in common? Use them as a guide for your own writing.

For additional pointers on scientific writing, see http://writingcenter.unc.edu/handouts/sciences/. There are a number of links to facets of science writing available from http://www.theguardian.com/science/series/secrets-science-writing {suggested search term *science writing*}.

REFERENCES

American Psychological Association. (2011). *Graduate study in psychology.* Washington, DC: Author.

Hill, M. & Hupe, P. (2014). *Implementing public policy: An introduction to the study of operational governance* (3rd ed.). Thousand Oaks, CA: Sage.

Jensen, K. B., & Glasmeier, A. K. (2010). Research design and the socially situated researcher. In D. DeLyser, S. Herbert, A. Aitken, M. A. Crang, & L. McDowell (Eds.), *The Sage handbook of qualitative geography* (pp. 82–93). Thousand Oaks, CA: Sage.

Professional standards. (n.d.). Retrieved from http://www.nursingworld.org/MainMenuCategories/ThePracticeofProfessionalNursing/NursingStandards

Sadeh, A., Gruber, R., & Raviv, A. (2003). The effects of sleep restriction and extension on school-age children: What a difference an hour can make. *Child Development, 74*(2), 444–455. doi:10.1111/1467-8624.7402008

Voydanoff, P. (2002). Linkages between the work-family interface and work, family, and individual outcomes: An integrative model. *Journal of Family Issues, 23,* 138–164. doi:10.1177/0192513X02023001007

Note: the issue number (2) in the Sadeh et al. (2003) citation is optional. Also note that the year of publication may differ for a few of the sources. The publication year listed here was current at the time of the lab manual was written.

LAB 3

After the Literature Review

Theory→Hypothesis→Design→Analysis→Results→Interpretation

Objective

This lab will describe the typical flow of logic in the research process and how this cyclical procedure allows scientific research to be a self-correcting field. The process of developing a hypothesis, then selecting an appropriate design, and writing the Method and Results sections of your paper will be discussed. You will then practice using a theory to produce a theory-based hypothesis. Additional material includes cultural considerations in research.

Target Article

David, D. H., & Lyons-Ruth, K. (2005). Differential attachment responses of male and female infants to frightening maternal behavior: Tend or befriend versus fight or flight? *Infant Mental Health Journal, 26*(1), 1–18. doi:10.1002/imhj.20033. Retrieved from http://www.ncbi.nlm.nih.gov/pmc/articles/PMC1857276/pdf/nihms-13963.pdf {suggested search term title of article}

How do we respond when we're stressed? Most of us have heard of the fight-or-flight theory in which our bodies physiologically prepare to handle a threatening situation (this evolved because we needed this response to fend off a predator or run away as fast as we can—assuming we can outrun a tiger!). A more recent stress theory, called the tend-and-befriend model, suggests that females may engage in nurturing behaviors and establish and maintain social relationships to cope with stress. Researchers suggest this may be an evolutionary behavior in which tending to offspring and befriending those around during times of stress increased the likelihood of survival. Based on this theory and the theory of attachment style, Daryn H. David and Karlen Lyons-Ruth (2005) hypothesized that male and female infants would show different responses to frightening scenarios. Results from a study of 65 mother–infant pairs supported their hypothesis, which not only provides evidence for tend and befriend, but expands the theory to document female stress responses as young as infancy. The results also bring to light information that should be considered when interpreting infant attachment behaviors toward their mothers in a clinical setting.

THE LOGIC BEHIND THE RESEARCH

Before we go further, let's establish what we mean by "theory." A theory isn't a mystical, scientific treatise. It is simply an explanation for something. You develop and test theories all the time, so you are already functioning as a scientist. For example, you might observe that your significant other is mad at you. Why? You might theorize it is because you have spent a lot of time studying lately rather than spending quality time with that person. You test the theory by inviting your amore to join you doing something fun. If harmony is restored, the evidence supports (but doesn't *prove*) your theory.

This is important: In this lab, we hope to show you the progression from theory (an explanation) to hypothesis (a prediction based on the explanation) to design to choosing an appropriate analysis to reporting your results and eventually interpretation of your findings. In other words, your hypothesis should be based on a theory. Your hypothesis determines what design you will use and how you will analyze your data. Your choice of analysis will determine how your results are presented, and your results will lead you to interpret your findings.

©iStock.com/sturti

Theory→Hypothesis

All research begins with a question, but how do we arrive there? You've spent time reading lots of articles related to your topic of interest. You've likely come across a variety of *theories,* which are tentative explanations of why and when phenomena occur. Good, clearly stated theories typically relate known information and enable us to make predictions. When researchers develop a theory or come across another researcher's theory within their field of interest, they can use that tentative explanation to inform a specific hypothesis.

For example, in the targeted article above, the tend-and-befriend model connects together information regarding evolutionary theories of human behavior, stress theories, and biological research connecting the hormone oxytocin with certain social behaviors and relationships. The theory, or "model," while broadly theorizing that females are more likely than males to cope with stress through nurturing social behaviors, allows for more specific questions to be asked, such as whether or not female infants show more affiliative behaviors (i.e., behaviors to improve union or connectedness with another) toward frightening maternal behavior. The hypothesis has used a particular theory to inform the question at hand, but narrowed down a prediction about (1) a specific population (female infants) and (2) a specific stressful environment (frightening maternal behavior). The researchers then designed a study that would provide the type of data needed to answer their questions, then analyzed and interpreted the results (was the hypothesis supported or not?). These results of the study can then inform the original theory. The significant results suggest that the theory can be applied even to babies.

Similarly, what if the results had been negative, indicating male and female infants did <u>not</u> differ in their responses to the fearful situation? This information could be used to *revise* the original theory, modifying pieces of the explanation that appear to be inaccurate or have no evidence to support the claim.

This is what we call the *self-correcting nature* of science. When researchers use existing theories to generate novel hypotheses, the resulting evidence for tested hypotheses can improve theories and correct false theories and inaccurate information. The research process is cyclical.

One nice thing about science is that the end of your research report is not really an end to the fun! Once you have interpreted your results and modified (if needed) your starting theory in light of your findings, you use the modified theory to generate new hypotheses and start the process over.

Figure 3.1   The Circle of Research

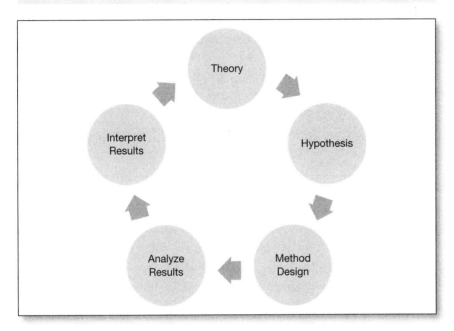

It is noteworthy to recognize that the research process does not always occur as cleanly as this. Science should be a self-correcting process whereby researchers replicate studies to confirm the accuracy of existing theories as well as test novel hypotheses, yet replication research is less likely to be published. Journals often want to publish "exciting" and novel findings, so publishing the exact same study that either confirms or contradicts prior findings is less likely to be accepted. Further, researchers may move backward in the cyclical process if methodological issues arise or hypotheses are not supported. While we should be aware of potential messiness within our research field, the logical flow of research should follow the process of generating a well-informed hypothesis, then testing out that exact hypothesis using an appropriate study design. This ensures good, clean data—data we can trust has provided us with true evidence for our hypothesis. This process may be different for qualitative research or in an area that has little published research.

Researchers may move through this process many times to refine theories. For example, Martin Fishbein and Icek Ajzen proposed the theory of reasoned action in 1975, a theory suggesting beliefs, attitudes, and intentions can predict behavior. After much research was conducted to test hypotheses generated by this theory, Ajzen (1991) revised the theory by adding in the notion of behavioral control. The revised model, called the theory of planned behavior, is a widely used theory for predicting a variety of behaviors. More recent studies (e.g., van der Linden, 2011) using the theory to test hypotheses about charitable giving have suggested further revisions to the theory. When executed correctly, the research process can provide incredible information!

TRY IT YOURSELF

In most labs, we will give you canned data to practice with, but in this case, data won't be useful.

Producing a theory-based hypothesis takes a little creativity and a good literature review. Hypotheses should be worded as statements of prediction and describe exactly what the researcher expects to find.

Step 1: We're going to try this. First, we want to come up with a hypothesis that is a logical outgrowth of a theory. To practice generating a theory-based hypothesis, spend some time looking up the theory of planned behavior using the following websites (or others you find):

- http://people.umass.edu/aizen/index.html {suggested search term *Ajzen theory planned behavior*}
- Azjen (2011): http://www.tandfonline.com/doi/pdf/10.1080/08870446.2011.613995 {suggested search term *The theory of planned behaviour: Reactions and reflections*}

Step 2: Next, choose a specific behavior that could be predicted by the theory—perhaps smoking cigarettes (or stop smoking), teeth brushing, or teaching practices, for example. Search for at least five articles related to the theory *and* the behavior you chose. Consider the following questions:

- What research has been conducted?
- What research *hasn't* been conducted? This may be suggested in the Discussion section of the articles, or it may be something you noticed.
- Who were the participants in the articles you found? Could you examine your behavior and the variables of the theory in a new or special population (i.e., a particular gender, racial/ethnic group, age range, job type, etc.)?
- Is the theory missing any important pieces of information?
- Has research considered possible confounding variables that could be influencing results?

Figure 3.2   The Theory of Planned Behavior

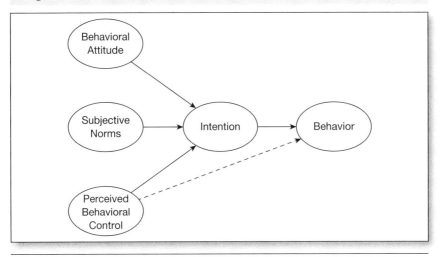

SOURCE: Ajzen, I., 1991, The theory of planned behavior, *Organizational Behavior and Human Decision Processes, 50*(2): 179-211.

Step 3: Based on your literature search, develop a theory-based hypothesis. Word the hypothesis as "I predict . . .," then provide a brief paragraph of how and why you arrived at this hypothesis.

Here's an example using the steps listed above.

Let's illustrate this process.

Step 1: Learning About the Theory

I did some background reading on the premises of the theory of planned behavior. The theory suggests that a person's attitudes towards a behavior can predict, explain, and modify that behavior.

Step 2: Choosing a Specific Behavior

I searched for research on the theory of planned behavior and sleep {searched terms *The theory of planned behavior* AND *sleep* in TITLES in a search engine}.

Articles Found:

Knowlden, A. P., Sharma, M., & Bernard, A. L. (2012). A theory of planned behavior research model for predicting the sleep intentions

(Continued)

(Continued)

and behaviors of undergraduate college students. *The Journal of Primary Prevention, 33*(1), 19–31. doi:10.1007/s10935-012-0263-2

Kor, K., & Mullan, B. A. (2011). Sleep hygiene behaviours: An application of the theory of planned behaviour and the investigation of perceived autonomy support, past behavior and response inhibition. *Psychology & Health, 26*(9), 1208–1224. doi:10.1080/08870446.2010.551210

Lao, H. C. F., Tao, V. Y. K. & Wu, A. M. S. (2015). Theory of planned behavior and healthy sleep of college students. *Australian Journal of Psychology*, online version retrieved 9/25/15 from http://online library.wiley.com/doi/10.1111/ajpy.12094/full.

- What research has been conducted?

©iStock.com/Vesna Andjic

The three studies I found examined variables from the theory of planned behavior (attitudes, subjective norms,* perceived behavioral control, intentions) as predictors of sleep hygiene behaviors, sleep duration, and sleep quality. Some of the variables were significant predictors, with some of the research showing subjective norms were the strongest predictor of intention, and another study found perceived behavioral control was the most salient predictor.

  *A "subjective norm" is a person's perception of a given behavior that has been influenced by the judgement of people who are important in that person's life.

- What research *hasn't* been conducted?

  The majority of the participants in the study were White participants, while one was about Chinese students. I did not find research in my mini-lit review about other minority populations and if findings could be applied to them.

- Who were the participants in the articles you found? Could you examine your behavior and the variables of the theory in a new or special population (i.e., a particular gender, racial/ethnic group, age range, job type, etc.)?

All of the studies examined college students at either Midwestern universities, a Chinese university, or an Australian university. What about other populations like noncollege-age students or older adults? Does the theory of planned behavior apply to children, and if so, would we see similar findings? Also, college students may have a unique "job," so it would be interesting to test if predictors are as strong (or stronger) in adults with less flexible hours.

- Is the theory missing any important pieces of information?

     Some of the studies also examined additional predictors such as scores on a response inhibition task, past behavior, social support, and self-efficacy. Could these be incorporated into the theory or captured by the existing variables?

- Has research considered possible confounding variables that could be influencing results?

     Socioeconomic status was not measured in any of the analyses—perhaps this serves as a confounding variable related to the theory of planned behaviors variables as well as the sleep outcomes.

Step 3: Develop a Theory-Based Hypothesis

Word the hypothesis as "I predict . . .," then provide a sentence of how you arrived at this hypothesis.

I predict that intentions and perceived behavioral control will be significant predictors of sleep hygiene behaviors in middle-age adults. I arrived at this hypothesis because the three studies I found showed that these two variables were the strongest predictors, and none of the studies examined populations other than college students, so I am hypothesizing similar findings in a slightly older population.

Try It Yourself Within Your Discipline

Instead of developing a hypothesis informed by the theory of planned behavior, find a theory within your chosen topic area. Search for articles specifically on your chosen theory and your topic of interest.

Generate three theory-based hypotheses related to your topic and chosen theory. See the questions presented above to assist you. You won't necessarily include all the hypotheses you generate in the research you actually carry out.

THEORY→HYPOTHESIS→DESIGN→ANALYSIS: METHOD SECTION

©iStock.com/Avesun

You have learned how to write a literature review, and you now know how to generate a theory-based hypothesis for your research project. Following your literature review will be the Method and Results sections. In the upcoming chapters, you will learn about a variety of different methodological approaches. You will also master different statistical techniques for testing different types of research questions. When writing your Method section, you should include descriptions of the following in your paper:

1. Participants

What participants will be included in your study and how many? Provide demographic information on the study sample such as average age, number of males and females, racial/ethnic background, and other information relevant to your topic. Decide on your inclusion (people or other units of analysis who can participate) and exclusion (those who can't participate) criteria. How will you recruit participants? Will they receive an incentive? What percent of people whom you asked to take part actually provided data?

2. Measures/Materials

This section will look slightly different depending on your discipline and the nature of your study design, but here you will provide information regarding the materials, measuring systems, or equipment used to gather information in your study. This section will allow readers to understand *how* variables were measured and, for quantitative data, what scores on these measuring tools mean. For survey materials (see Chapter 7), you will provide citations for published questionnaires or protocols, as well as scoring information and examples of survey items. Tell the reader about the established reliability and validity of the instruments. Enough information should be provided here that a reader could find or duplicate all materials if desired. In some cases you may create your own stimuli or measures. Describe what they measure, how and why you created them, and how they were scored. If they are based on published work, describe how you modified the measure.

3. Procedure

   Describe the exact sequence of events of the study here in as much detail as you can. Your readers should have enough information that they could replicate your study if desired. Describe how participants were recruited, the setting of the study, what information participants provided, what behaviors or activities they engaged in, if participants were assigned to different groups, if any experimental manipulation took place, and how participants were debriefed, if necessary.

4. Study Design (or Plan of Analysis)

   Either here or elsewhere in your paper, explicitly describe the research design you chose to test your hypothesis and explain how you used the appropriate statistics (or whatever approach is appropriate to your research design) to analyze the resulting data.

THEORY→HYPOTHESIS→DESIGN→ANALYSIS→RESULTS

When writing a Results section, the statistics provided will vary *based on the type of data collected and analytical plan chosen to test the hypothesis.* If you are reporting quantitative data, you'll provide descriptive data for your targeted variables, then report statistics for your chosen analysis along with a brief sentence stating whether or not findings supported the hypothesis. What details go in a Results section? It depends on your choice of design and statistics. Each lab offers a sample results section appropriate for that type of analysis, so we won't go into more detail now.

If you have used qualitative analysis, your results will look very different from those generated by quantitative analyses. The lab on qualitative research refers you to an example of how such results might be reported.

THEORY→HYPOTHESIS→DESIGN→ANALYSIS→RESULTS →INTERPRETATION

Once you have your results, you'll need to interpret them for the reader. Assume your reader is educated, but not necessarily an expert in your topic. You will need to help the reader understand what you found, why it was important, how it relates back to the theory, and so on. Interpretation will be covered in a later lab when we discuss what information should be included in a Discussion section. Stay tuned . . . coming attraction . . . .

IF YOU WANT TO GO FURTHER . . .

Cultural Considerations

We've suggested throughout this chapter the importance of considering *who* (or *what)* is in our study and how broadly a theory can be applied. Once a theory has been proposed, it is important to test theory-based hypotheses across demographic and cultural groups to examine if phenomena vary by cultures (or not!). *Culture* describes a distinct system of behavior patterns, customs, beliefs, and a way of life that are characteristic of members of a particular society, group, place, or time. A researcher must describe *who* the appropriate participants are through defined criteria, such as a particular geographic location (for example, former Soviet republics), organization (such as Women's Studies Departments at state universities), or way of life (such as homelessness). Once the cultural group has been defined, a researcher can identify unique questions to answer about this group of people, design and implement methodology for data collection, and interpret the results in a culturally appropriate and unbiased manner (at least, that's the goal).

For example, in 1971, Paul Ekman and Wallace V. Friesen set out to show that facial expressions and specific emotions (such as smiling with happiness)

are similar in all cultures. In other words, they tested whether specific emotion-generated expressions were common to all humans or only to specific cultures. They used careful methodology to collect data without exposing other cultural influences to the targeted linguistic-cultural group of the South East Highlands of New Guinea. Their findings suggested that facial behaviors associated with particular emotions are consistent in different cultures. By testing hypotheses within many cultures and generating the same results, converging evidence supports the theory of universal facial expressions of emotion. This improves the external validity (look it up!) of the findings which determines how they can be generalized.

©iStock.com/g-stockstudio

While some theory-based hypotheses test phenomena across cultures, other research focuses on one cultural group to examine the unique aspects of that particular culture. Ethnography, a branch of anthropology, is an area of research that focuses on cultural phenomena. From an emic approach, the goal of ethnography is to examine societal groups *from the perspective of someone within the group being studied.* Thus, ethnographic research is a cultural interpretation from the viewpoint of an "insider." Ethnographic studies are designed to collect data in such a way that the researchers impose as few biases on the data as possible. Their goal is to generate information about social interactions, customs, behaviors, perceptions, and meaning that naturally occur among the cultural group being studied. To accomplish this, ethnographic researchers often become participant–observers within the culture in order to gather the most accurate information about cultural norms and practices.

A famous example, although later criticized for possible inaccuracies, was anthropologist Margaret Mead's *Coming of Age in Samoa* (1928) study, in which she immersed herself in the Samoan culture for nine months in order to study the development of youth and attitudes toward sexuality within the natural settings of Samoan society. While Mead reported interesting findings that young Samoan women enjoy a carefree, sexually active adolescent life, her work was later challenged by Derek Freeman (1983), who claimed the Samoan teenagers played a joke on Mead and lied to her during interviews. This highlights the importance of *reflexivity,* the idea that researchers who become socially and physically immersed in the field must be "reflexive" and continually explore ways in which their involvement may be influencing or informing the research. Participant observers must consider how their presence within the cultural setting could determine behavior, interpretation of language and behavior, and meaning within the culture of study. Participant observation can be time intensive in that it requires researchers to commit to long-term immersion within the culture.

Compare this approach to the etic approach, which focuses on the outside researcher's perspective. Observations of a particular culture are made and interpreted from the viewpoint of the scientist. This approach looks for phenomena that transcend culture.

Considering ethnography is a research approach rather than a specific data collection technique, many methods of collecting qualitative or quantitative data can be employed, such as field notes, interviews, secondary data, and surveys. Regardless of methodology, all collected information is analyzed to identify logical patterns, describe relationships, and contextualize information within the wider economic, political, and social environment. Ethnographic techniques and findings can be applied in a variety of areas, such as informing public policy, healthcare and medical services, marketing decision making, behavior change, and education reforms to name a few.

It's not as easy as you might think!

This doesn't sound too bad; if I want to find whether some behavior, belief, trait (or whatever is being studied) is culture specific, I just replicate it with participants from another culture, right? Hold on—there's more involved than that. For example,

1. Language is an obvious consideration. You'd like to collect data using the culture's primary language. Translating your material is not enough—it is best to have it reverse translated (translated back to the original language to make sure nothing changed in the translation process).

2. You must consider whether your measures are appropriate for the new culture yet still measure whatever it is you want to compare. In order to target the same concept in very different cultures, you may have to come

up with different measures. In that case, you're going to have to demonstrate that you chose the best measure for that culture and that it measured the same thing as the original study.

3. Learn about the culture before you make any assumptions. It's best to partner with research professionals who are from or very knowledgeable about the new culture to help you appropriately design your study and materials and interact respectfully with the new participants.

©iStock.com/scanrail

There are many other cautions that apply here. My point is that cross-cultural research is very valuable information, but must be done with great care and forethought in order to be credible. OK, so that's true for any research—just apply it doubly here!

TRY IT YOURSELF

To better understand the science of studying culture, examine a review of best practices in cross-cultural research within your discipline. This may be found in a journal article or a textbook. For example, those of you who study organizations could look at

Schaffer, B. S., & Riordan, C. M. (2003). A review of cross-cultural methodologies for organizational research: A best-practices approach. *Organizational Research Methods, 6,* 169–215. doi:10.1177/1094428103251542

Ethnographic Evaluation and Analysis Questions

Now find a cross-cultural research report from your discipline or one of interest to you. Answer the following questions regarding your chosen study.

1. What "culture" is being studied?

2. Who are the participants? Sample size?

3. What is the overarching question of the research study?

4. What strategies are used to become "immersed" in the culture (if applicable)? How does the researcher gain the trust of the participants?

5. How are data recorded (i.e., video tape, sound recorder, handwritten notes, typed field notes, etc.)?

6. What are some challenges in obtaining accurate data? Are there language barriers or possibilities of misinterpretation?

7. How does the researcher ensure minimal bias on the data?

8. How might the presence of the researcher within the cultural setting influence participants' behavior?

9. What patterns emerge within the data (i.e., behavioral patterns, cultural customs, etc.)?

10. Are there unique economic or political influences that should be considered within the particular location and time frame of data collection?

11. How might the researcher's own personal beliefs influence interpretations of the data?

12. What are the results (or expected findings) from the data? How can these findings be applied?

PICK A CARD, ANY CARD . . .

Pick any cultural group of interest to you and choose an aspect of the culture to study. Be creative and specific—perhaps you are interested in child-rearing practices among Mexican American mothers or would like to examine attitudes toward violence within the hip-hop culture. Once you have defined your cultural group and research question, design a study in which you will become a *participant observer.* Describe how you will immerse yourself in the culture and collect data on your topic. Brainstorm on possible ways that your presence within the culture or personal beliefs could influence or bias the data. Because you will not actually be conducting this study, describe the patterns and results you *anticipate* finding and consider why these results are important.

Here are the full citations for sources used in this lab:

Ajzen, I. (1991). The theory of planned behavior. *Organizational Behavior and Human Decision Processes, 50*(2), 179–211. doi:10.1016/0749-5978(91)90020-T

Ajzen, I. (2011). The theory of planned behaviour: Reactions and reflections. *Psychology & Health, 26*(9), 1113–1127. doi:10.1080/08870446.2011.613995

Ekman, P., & Friesen, W. V. (1971). Constants across cultures in the face and emotion. *Journal of Personality and Social Psychology, 17*(2), 124–129. doi:10.1037/h0030377 Available at https://www.unimuenster.de/imperia/md/content/psyifp/aeechterhoff/wintersemester2011-12/vorlesungkommperskonflikt/ekman_friesen_constantsemofacialexpr_jpsp1971.pdf

Fishbein, M., & Ajzen, I. (1975). Belief, attitude, intention, and behavior: An introduction to theory and research. Reading, MA: Addison-Wesley.

Freeman, D. (1983). *Margaret Mead and Samoa.* Cambridge, MA: Harvard University Press.

Mead, M. (1928). *Coming of age in Samoa: A psychological study of primitive youth for Western civilization.* New York, NY: W. Morrow.

van der Linden, S. (2011). Charitable intent: A moral or social construct? A revised theory of planned behavior model. *Current Psychology: A Journal for Diverse Perspectives on Diverse Psychological Issues, 30*(4), 355–374. doi: 10.1007/s12144-011-91

LAB 4

Ethics of Research

Objective

The purpose of this lab is to introduce some ethical considerations for researchers. The role of the Institutional Review Board (IRB) in protecting human or animal participants is introduced, along with the need for informed consent. Additional material on preparing a proposal for the IRB is discussed.

Target Article

Haney, C., & Zimbardo, P. (1998). The past and present of U.S. prison policy. *American Psychologist, 53*(7), 709–727. doi: 10.1037//0003-066X.53.7.709

A copy of this article can be found at http://www.csdp.org/research/haney_apa.pdf

This is a review article prompted by a famous social psychology experiment conducted by Philip Zimbardo at Stanford University in the early 1970s. This isn't a research report; it is a review of related research and consideration of its implications for prison policy and reform. Read this article and an overview of the experiment at http://www.prisonexp.org/ and then briefly describe the ethical dilemma that emerged (unexpectedly) during this study, and

©iStock.com/AlbanyPictures

how the experimenter handled it. Can you think of any recent examples of the social dynamics that became apparent during this experiment? You can see a video about this study at https://www.youtube.com/watch?feature=player_embedded&v=sZwfNs1pqG0.

HOW TO TREAT PARTICIPANTS (HUMAN OR OTHERWISE)

It sounds obvious that participants should be treated well when they take part in a study, but without rules, this may not happen. In most institutions, you must receive the approval of an IRB before beginning any experiment that involves collecting data from humans or animals. This has not always been the case. At one time, researchers could design and carry out their experiments without any oversight. However, a number of events convinced people that oversight is a good thing. Read the following and identify several historical events that helped convince scientists that research using human subjects must be regulated. Name at least three.

http://www.und.edu/instruct/wstevens/PROPOSALCLASS/MARSDEN &MELANDER2.htm

The Belmont Report established ethical principles of research with human subjects. The first principle is **autonomy**, which includes participants' rights to understand what the experiment is about, to give informed consent, to withdraw from the study at any time, or to decline to take part in the study without consequences. The second principle is **beneficence,** the concept that participants should expect that they will be treated humanely, and it is the responsibility of the researcher to minimize risks and to justify any unavoidable risks. This principle also addresses whether the project should include vulnerable populations. The third principle is **justice**—participants should be selected and treated fairly. Some individuals are afforded extra layers of protection, such as children, those who are cognitively not able to give informed consent, and prisoners. There are similar requirements for the treatment of nonhuman species.

Read the article by Robert Rosenthal (1994; cited below) and identify at least three ways in which researchers might act unethically. The principles described apply to many different disciplines in addition to psychology.

Rosenthal, R. (1994). Science and ethics in conducting, analyzing, and reporting psychological research. *Psychological Science, 5,* 127–134. doi:10.1111/j.14679280.1994.tb00646.x

For a "Chronology of Human Research" by Vera Sharav see http://www .mnwelldir.org/docs/history/experiments.htm {suggested search term *Human Experiments: A Chronology of Human Research*}.

How to Treat Human and Animal Subjects: Training

It is vital to understand the ethical principles that underlie fair treatment of human and animal subjects before pursuing a research project.

Many institutions require researchers to complete formal training in the ethical principles and guidelines of protection and treatment. Complete your institution's IRB-approved tutorial (if one is available) on protecting human or animal subjects.

If your institution does not provide coverage for this or other training, your instructor may be able to direct you to appropriate resources. Other possibilities include

https://phrp.nihtraining.com/users/login.php (registration is free)

http://www.nyu.edu/ucaihs/tutorial/ (your instructor can assign specific chapters)

http://grants.nih.gov/grants/policy/hs/training.htm

A human subjects tutorial indicates that participants should have the opportunity to give informed consent. Use the consent form format recommended by your institution or search for *IRB consent template* online. Note that some cases (such as observation in a public place without personal contact with participants) may not require consent, and other situations (such as an anonymous online survey) may require consent notice rather than signed consent. Your instructor can direct you to resources appropriate for your project.

After you have completed some form of training on human or animal protection (e.g., tutorial or module), identify ethical issues raised by the studies described in the three sources listed below {suggested search terms are the topics or titles}.

1. How did the experimenter deal with the ethical issues?

2. Should more have been done to protect the participants? If so, what?

3. Was the information gained worth the risks?

4. Is this a study that simply should not have been conducted because of ethical concerns? If you were on the IRB reviewing this protocol, what would have changed?

Warning: Some of these videos display strong emotional content. You may simply read about the experiment online if you do not wish to view the videos.

©iStock.com/stevenallan

Study 1: Harlow's Monkey Study on Attachment: https://www.youtube.com/
watch?feature=player_embedded&v=OrNBEhzjg8I.
    Background: http://www.pbs.org/wgbh/aso/databank/entries/bhharl.html

Study 2: Milgram Obedience Study: https://www.youtube.com/watch?v=fCVlI-
_4GZQ

Study 3: Facebook study of emotional contagion:http://www.forbes.com/sites/
gregorymcneal/2014/06/28/facebook-manipulated-user-news-feeds-to-create-
emotional-contagion/

Figure 4.1   The Institutional Review Board Process

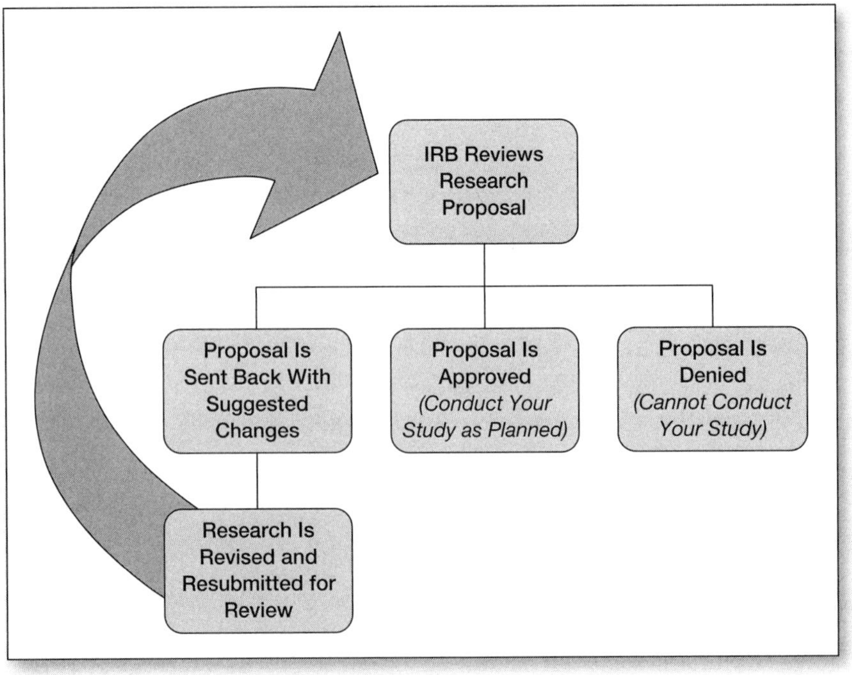

SOURCE: http://study.com/academy/lesson/irb-institutional-review-board-lesson-quiz
.html

How to Treat Human and Animal Subjects: IRB Approval

Now that you understand the ethical principles that guide human or
animal subjects research and why this type of oversight is needed to ensure
fair treatment, let's learn about the process of applying for and receiving

approval by an Institutional Review Board (IRB). As you have learned, historical events such as the Nazi medical experiments, the Zimbardo prison experiment, and the Milgram experiment contributed to the development of a required review board whose role is to ensure that human or animal subjects are properly informed of the nature of a study (in the case of humans) and are treated fairly. The IRB committee requires detailed information regarding the researchers conducting the study, the design of the study, the information being collected about or from the participants, and what the researchers plan to do with that data. If you are a researcher applying for IRB approval, you will be asked to explain the purpose of your study, how you will recruit participants to join your study, and who the participants will be. You will provide the information given to participants to ensure informed consent, the questions or actions you will require of the participants, any potential risks or harm that participants may experience during your study, and whether you will be compensating participants for their time or effort. If your study or experimental design requires deception, you must justify its use and provide documentation of debriefing in which you explain the true nature of your research project once the study is over. You will also describe what you will do with the participants' data after the study is over, how you will ensure the privacy of that information, and how you will analyze the data. Detailed information regarding the application process is available at http://research.uncc.edu/departments/office-research-compliance-orc/human-subjects/application-process {suggested search term *IRB application* or search for research compliance information at your institution}.

Depending on the nature of your study design, your research will require one of three different types of IRB review: exempt review, expedited review, or full review. Exempt review is used for studies in which there are no risks to participants, such as coding instances of violence in publicly aired televisions shows. Expedited reviews are given to studies in which no more than minimal risk is experienced by participants. A full review, in which the entire IRB committee reviews the study protocol, is required for research involving greater than minimal risk to participants. This could include research involving sensitive information or methodology, as well as research with a vulnerable population such as children or prisoners. For more information regarding the types of different IRB reviews, as well as other frequently asked questions about IRB approval, visit your institution's website on research compliance or search *types of IRB review.*

THE ETHICS OF REPORTING OF RESEARCH

How Do I Know If It Is Plagiarism?

Created using wordle.net

You already know that when you turn in a paper that claims to be original writing, it must not contain any plagiarized material. In order to avoid plagiarism, you have to know exactly what it is. Using the instructions below, write a brief paper on plagiarism. The aim of the paper is to teach the reader what plagiarism is and how to avoid it. The following are instructions for the plagiarism paper: Write a two-page paper (title page, two pages of *original* writing, reference page) on plagiarism. Use 1-inch margins on all sides, left justification, size 12 Times New Roman font. Use the following sources (or others recommended by your instructor):

http://ori.hhs.gov/avoiding-plagiarism-self-plagiarism-and-other-question able-writing-practices-guide-ethical-writing sections on ethical writing and plagiarism {suggested search term *avoid plagiarism*}

Isaacs, D. (2011). Plagiarism is not OK. *Journal of Paediatrics and Child Health,* *47*(4), 159. Retrieved from http://www.readcube.com/articles/10.1111/ j.1440-1754.2011.02050.x

See the APA *Publication Manual* or check https://owl.english.purdue.edu/owl/resource/584/01/ {suggested search term *APA cite electronic source*} to find the proper way to cite your electronic source(s).

Your library or research office may have resources on plagiarism you can use.

Other Ethical Issues

Even though we won't go into it in detail, there are other ethical concerns in research. For example, Internet research ethics is a growing topic of interest. Over the last few decades, we have witnessed enormous advancements in technology and communication. Through the Internet, we can now video chat with loved ones who live across the world, maintain online friendships through social media, and seek unlimited sources of information at the click of a button. However, these advancements require unique ethical considerations regarding the use of the Internet for human subjects research. Researchers must consider ethical obligations in protecting the privacy of subjects within "public" Internet sources, online deception, the assurance of confidentiality or anonymity of data obtained online, and the protection of minors (how do we really know who is on the other side of the computer?). See http://plato.stanford.edu/entries/ethics-internet-research/ for further discussion of "Internet research ethics" {this can be used as a search term}.

Additional ethical concerns involve the processes before, during, and following data collection. For example, there are ethical and unethical ways to collect, analyze, and report your data. If you have promised your participants confidentiality or anonymity, then you have an ethical responsibility to make sure you carry out that promise. If you heard someone talking about their research idea (or perhaps reviewed a manuscript for a journal), then you cannot use that idea without crediting the originator. To see what the APA has to say about the ethics of research and publication, see section 8 at http://www.apa.org/cthics/code2002.html or ask your instructor to direct you to information on ethical standards within your discipline.

©iStock.com/kutubQ

Closure

Tips for Avoiding Plagiarism

1. Close all sources when you write. You aren't likely to copy something you can't see.

2. Taking notes: Make notations in your own words, making sure you have written down complete source information, including the page number. If you do use a direct quote in your paper (you should use these sparingly), you must put it in quotation marks, and indicate the source and the page number. Look up use of direct quotes and secondary sources in the APA *Publication Manual.*

3. Identify the source of the ideas or findings and summarize in your own words what was said. Using the author's words while changing a few is still plagiarism. Some sources define plagiarism as any use of four or more contiguous words.

4. Reference the source of anything that is not common knowledge. For example, you don't need to document the source when you state that plagiarism is not acceptable in professional writing; you *do* need to cite the source if you claim that 40% of student papers submitted in college courses contain plagiarized material. BTW, I just made up that last statistic for the sake of providing an example.

©iStockphoto.com/ dane_mark

IF YOU WANT TO GO FURTHER . . .

The Role of the IRB

IRB committee members play a vital role in protecting the rights of research participants. All IRBs are required to comply with policies set forth in Title 45 of the Code of Federal Regulations Part 46 (45 CFR 46). This Code of Federal Regulations is available at http://www.hhs.gov/ohrp/policy/faq/irb-registration/requirements-for-irb-membership.html {suggested search term *IRB regulations*}. IRB committees are supposed to meet the following requirements: (1) select a board of 5+ members of different backgrounds, (2) select a board comprised of both men and women, (3) include members with scientific and nonscientific areas of interest, (4) include 1+ members who are not affiliated with the university or institute, and (5) ensure no members have a conflict of interest with the project under review. Many IRBs include physicians or veterinarians (as appropriate). These requirements and other frequently asked questions are available at http://www.hhs.gov/ohrp/policy/faq/index.html {suggested search term *frequently asked questions about human research*}.

In thinking about how we can meet the ethical guidelines of human research (i.e., respect for persons, beneficence, justice) in all research projects conducted at a university or institution, answer the following questions:

1. If you were *submitting a research proposal* to the IRB, what university or committee members would you want to be on the IRB reviewing your application to make sure you properly protected participant rights?

2. If you were a *research participant* in an experiment involving deception, who would you want to be on the IRB committee reviewing the experiment to ensure your rights were protected?

3. If you were serving as *an IRB member*, what would you look for in a research proposal application to ensure the following?

   a. Participants are fully informed of the nature of the study

   b. The benefits of the study outweigh the risks

   c. Participants are compensated fairly for time or effort

   d. Participants recruited for studies involving deception are properly debriefed

   e. Anonymity or confidentiality of data are protected

©iStock.com/Leontura

PREPARING A PROPOSAL FOR THE IRB

While the broad requirements of who an IRB committee should include are federally set, IRBs are not actually government entities. IRBs may differ between universities in relation to standard procedures and requirements, the turnaround time for reviews of applications, and who from the community or institution actually serves on the IRB. Considering variations among IRBs, we can understand that the exact application process and required documentation will also differ from university to university. Take a look at the sample IRB applications from various universities {suggested search term *sample IRB applications*}:

https://www.csusm.edu/gsr/irb/application_samples.html

http://www.sjsu.edu/faculty/weinstein.agrawal/urbp298_SampleIRB Proposal_Mathur.pdf

http://www.elon.edu/docs/e-web/org/percs/Example%20IRB_application %20Ethnography-1.pdf

http://community.pepperdine.edu/irb/content/expedited-education-sample-application.pdf

Find out whether your IRB provides example applications within your discipline. Your instructor may have an example to show you. While the formatting and specific requirements differ, all IRB applications require information regarding (1) who the researchers are (i.e., you and any other faculty or students who will conduct the study or have access to the data), (2) the purpose of the project, (3) the participants of the study, (4) the procedure of the study and any risks or benefits to the participants, (5) survey questions or equipment used, and (6) how participant data will be protected and analyzed.

TRY IT YOURSELF

As a future researcher, submitting a research proposal to the IRB is a skill you want to perfect. Try searching *institutional review board* in your university website search bar. Spend some time becoming familiar with your university's IRB submission process. Peruse links to frequently asked questions, application timelines (Does the IRB meet on certain dates? How long does the process take for reviewing exempt, expedited, and full review projects?), training requirements, and contact information for employees and representatives who may be able to assist you throughout the process.

Finally, locate the actual Word or PDF application document for submitting a proposal. It can be overwhelming to look at all of the information and paperwork you must provide—but don't sweat it! Take a few moments to skim, section by section, the information being asked. Your name and contact information . . . piece of cake! Information about the purpose of your study . . . you know this by now! Details about the exact procedure and who you want in the study . . . these types of questions will force you (or rather, gently encourage you) to really spend some time making decisions about the methodology of your study and how you will ensure participants are treated fairly and respectfully. In all honesty, the IRB application process can be time consuming, but once you've accomplished this, a major chunk of the Method section of your project has been completed!

Here are some helpful hints for a successful IRB application:

1. Details, details, DETAILS! The more information you can provide, the better. Pretend to be an IRB member; if you were reviewing an application, you would want as much information as possible to ensure you understand the exact nature of the study. Including all details of the study during the first draft of submission will speed up the process by eliminating delays that may occur if the IRB requests additional information from you.

2. Do you know another student, advisor, or faculty member who has submitted an IRB application before? Ask them for suggestions on the process or if you can take a look at a prior application for an example of a successful submission. Just remember, no plagiarism from a prior study—this is your unique, wonderful project!

3. If an advisor or instructor cannot assist you with any questions you may have about the content of your application, contact a representative at the IRB office on your campus. While employees are likely very busy, a concise email or phone call with questions can save time in the long run with back-and-forth questions about your application.

©iStock.com/JulyVelchev

WHAT TO EXPECT ONCE
YOUR PROJECT HAS BEEN APPROVED

Once your research project has been approved by the IRB (congrats!), be prepared to keep records of all documentation. A paper trail of signed informed consents, completed surveys, receipts for purchased equipment, and any other relevant documentation is essential. But wait—what if you later add a research assistant to your experiment sessions or decide to include an additional survey in your questionnaire? Most IRBs have a standard procedure for IRB amendments, in which you can submit changes to the application midproject. You cannot implement any changes until the amendments have been approved, but it is a relief to know if problems or changes occur, you do not have to start from scratch. Finally, when your project has been completed, your IRB may ask you to submit termination paperwork, information about the participants in your study, and any protocol issues or amendment changes that occurred, so have those materials handy. Be sure to follow all require-

ments for storing original surveys and paperwork for a specified amount of time, and verify how you must handle storage of electronic databases and future analyses of the data you collected. As long as you follow IRB requirements, also consider storing your data in several locations—if a computer crashes or a water pipe bursts in your lab (yes, this happened at my university!), you want to be sure you have a backup copy of all your data. Better to be safe than sorry!

PART II

Collecting Data—Research Designs and Tools

LAB 5

Qualitative Research

Objective

The purpose of this lab is to introduce qualitative research as an alternative or complementary approach to quantitative research. Some qualitative methods are described, and the concept of coding is introduced. It concludes with a consideration of issues relevant to the decision to use qualitative, quantitative, or both approaches (mixed methods) for a given research area. Additional material includes further discussion of content analysis and the introduction of grounded theory.

Target Article

Edin, K., & Lein, L. (1997). Work, welfare, and single mothers' economic survival strategies. *American Sociological Review, 62,* 253–266. Available from http://pages.ucsd.edu/~aronatas/Edin_Lein_PS.pdf

How do mothers on welfare manage to survive, and how do they feel about getting a job? Interviews of 379 mothers in four cities in the United States suggested that neither welfare nor a low-wage job is adequate to provide for themselves and their children. These mothers use a variety of strategies to manage, depending on where they live and how much of a social safety net they have. Some of these strategies are more conducive to finding a job than others. While many of the mothers wanted to depend on a job rather than welfare, the type of survival strategy used and the costs of having a job (such as clothing, transportation, child care) made the transition difficult. This study analyzed the content of interviews to arrive at these conclusions. The result was descriptions of themes common in the interviews. This produced qualitative rather than quantitative information. Could the researchers have gotten the same information using quantitative methodology? Probably not.

©iStock.com/Bradley Hebdon

QUALITATIVE RESEARCH: WHAT IS IT, AND WHAT DO YOU DO WITH IT?

Much of the research you may have come across has probably been quantitative—something that can be reduced to numbers and analyzed using inferential statistics. Sometimes, however, a question is better answered with qualitative data—verbal, descriptive information. This is often a good approach if studying a complex or targeted situation (e.g., specific people in specific circumstances), especially when a lot is not already known about the phenomenon. You might create transcripts as you interview many different people from many different perspectives then take that massive amount of data and look for patterns by coding it. You might use qualitative data to develop a grounded theory in order to clarify issues for future research.

Different disciplines may value one type of research or the other (or perhaps both) depending on the types of research questions pursued by that discipline. Whether you use quantitative or qualitative research depends on the question you want to ask. If you want to know whether children who experience an after-school tutoring program perform better on standardized tests or have higher self-esteem, then you are asking a question that can be answered with numbers. You can collect a test score (or self-esteem score) for each child in the experimental group (the ones who participated in the tutoring program) or a control group (children who are as alike to those in the experimental group as possible but who were not tutored). You can describe the resulting information using descriptive data (for example, group means, frequency distributions, variance from the mean) then compare group means using an inferential statistic such as a *t*-test. However, if you want to understand the *reasons* parents sought out the tutoring program for their children, or what barriers they experienced that made participation difficult, then you are asking questions that need descriptive, qualitative data. You might interview parents or children to find out how they felt about their time in the program, or hold a focus group to find out what community members would like in an after-school program. Some research questions may best be addressed by using both approaches to come at the same issue from different directions. Both quantitative and qualitative research approaches are valuable and can be used to build new knowledge in many fields of study (see Table 5.1).

Let's start by considering comparing the two types of research.

Although Table 5.1 is about human participants, there are other sources of data. Both qualitative and quantitative approaches to research can study people or animals, but either may also study data such as books, stories, artifacts, history, symbols, or archived data (for example, arrest records in a particular area). The difference is not so much in the source of the information, but in the nature of the research questions and resulting data.

Examples of Qualitative Research Methods

The type of qualitative design used will vary across disciplines, and researchers from a variety of disciplines might make use of the same methodology for different purposes. For example, someone in history or communication might use document content analysis, someone in social work might create case studies, researchers in anthropology or sociology might utilize ethnography, and so on. A few illustrations are listed here, and several of these will be emphasized in this lab and in others. In each case, the to-be-analyzed material consists of descriptions rather than numbers.

Observation—The observer systematically records information gathered via a variety of senses. In some cases, the observer wants to remain unnoticed so as not to influence the behavior of the target (naturalistic). In other situations, however, the observer may be neutral, in which participants are aware of the observer, but interaction with participants is not featured (for

Table 5.1   Comparison of Qualitative and Quantitative Research

	Qualitative	*Quantitative*
What are the overarching goals?	Interested in holistic, contextual (focus on the big picture) issues. The underlying philosophy assumes that people create their realities based on the totality of their experiences.	This focus is reductionist (studies the details). The underlying philosophy holds that phenomenon can be broken down and studied using the scientific method.
What is the end product?	Qualitative data can be quite varied and may report language, themes, signs, and meaning.	Measures are expressed as numbers.
Are the data analyzed?	Even though qualitative research doesn't produce numbers, it can nonetheless be analyzed. Analyses should be rigorous, systematically planned, and clearly described. Examples include coding or documenting themes.	Yes, it can be analyzed using descriptive and inferential statistics.
Why would I use this type of research?	Qualitative data might be used to explore a new field. If little is known about a research area, then qualitative data may be used to get enough information to generate theories that can later be tested. Qualitative research can be used to try to understand questions that came up during quantitative research. It can be used for program or policy analysis.	Quantitative analyses test hypotheses generated by existing theories.
How are the participants chosen?	Participants/cases can be purposefully selected because they represent some desired characteristic, and they may not be representative of a larger population.	Ideally, participants are chosen randomly. The sample should match the population it represents as much as possible.

(Continued)

Table 5.1 (Continued)

	Qualitative	*Quantitative*
Does the researcher interact with the participants?	The researcher becomes part of the data collection process. The researcher doesn't need to interact with each participant in the same way, but can modify the protocol to take advantage of unexpected directions.	Interaction is limited; the researcher does not want to influence the participants' responses. Once the research protocol is started, all participants must experience the same procedure; the experimenter can't change midstream.
Strengths	Qualitative data is good for generating new theories and hypotheses. It does a good job of establishing content validity (Does my instrument measure the construct it is supposed to measure?). Qualitative research allows for greater diversity of responses and can explore unexpected outcomes.	With appropriate sampling, quantitative methods provide results that are representative. With appropriate instruments, this approach can produce reliable measures with some degree of precision. Results can be concisely summarized as figures and tables.
Weaknesses	Qualitative data is usually difficult to graph or display in mathematical terms. The results may be bulky and difficult to summarize concisely.	This approach can't explore unexpected outcomes. If the experiment doesn't go as planned, some data may have to be discarded or it may be necessary to start all over again.

example, standing on a street corner recording information about people who pass by). Alternatively, the observer may become a participant in the observed setting, such as Margaret Mead did. She became part of a Samoan culture to observe the lives of adolescent girls in this culture from the perspective of an "insider." Ethnography makes use of observational research as well as interviews.

Interviews and Focus Groups—An interview is a situation in which the data collector asks specific questions of participants in hopes of understanding their perspective. It goes a step beyond just observing. It may be unstructured, semi-structured, or structured. In qualitative research, the interview is something like a conversation. A structured interview is something like a verbal questionnaire, while an unstructured interview is very open (for example, "What did you experience as a teenager emigrating from another country?"). Although the interviewer has a goal in mind, an unstructured interview can take different directions for different people. Interviews may also be used for case studies. A focus group is a discussion or group interview about a specific topic for the purpose of data collection. Examples of focus groups include understanding customer response to a new product or evaluating how members of a community respond to a neighborhood initiative. Just for fun (really—you'll laugh), look at an early version of a focus group: https://www.youtube.com/watch?v=eh6mCImeylE {suggested search term *focus group Wizard of Oz*}.

©iStock.com/Neonci

Case study—A case study is an in-depth study of a single individual, often including data from multiple sources all aimed at gaining an in-depth understanding of that person or phenomenon. It might collect quantitative data (for example, scores on an achievement test or a personality inventory) or qualitative data (for example, asking the person to describe their impressions of growing up during the Depression). A qualitative case study is useful to determine why or how a person behaves in a certain way and the context in which this takes place. It provides a great deal of detailed information about an individual. One could also conduct a case study of nonliving subjects, such as an organization or event.

Content Analysis—Likewise, content analysis may collect qualitative, quantitative, or a mix of data. It may record information about manifest (the surface, obvious content) or latent (underlying meaning) content. The researcher decides in advance what the unit of the analysis should be. The researcher uses some type of coding system to record data about the "meaning units" (words/phrases/text that are related in some way). Coded information is used to identify main ideas or themes about the verbal or written material that are interpreted in some way. For example, someone in a health-related field might use content

analysis of intake interviews for new patients with a substance-use disorder to better understand the factors that lead to seeking help for this condition. Someone in criminal justice might use it to analyze transcripts of trials.

Mixed Methods—Qualitative research may be used as the only approach to research, or the information may be reported along with quantitative analyses (multimethod research). Likewise, several qualitative methods might be used together. For example, someone might do content analyses of interviews from case studies and integrate the information into a single report.

TRY IT YOURSELF—CANNED DATA

For those who would like to try their hand at qualitative content analysis, first watch a three-minute video on coding at http://www.methodspace.com/video/eppi-centre-and-ncb {suggested search term *video code qualitative data*} then see the interactive exercises at http://www.sagepub.com/schuttisw7e/study/resources/schutt_7e_activities/engines/index.htm {suggested search term *qualitative data interactive practice*}.

Choose "Qualitative Data Analysis" then "Research in Context" (or another area if your instructor chooses to do so). Take the quiz and answer the questions. You can go to http://www.sagepub.com/upm-data/43454_10.pdf to look for answers.

Another possibility is to go to the following website and see teachers' reasons for choosing a career in teaching. Following the instructions, categorize the verbal responses listed at http://www.indiana.edu/~educy520/sec5982/week_5/qual_data_analy_ex1.pdf {suggested search term *qualitative data analysis exercise*}.

TRY IT YOURSELF—COLLECT YOUR OWN DATA

One way to collect data might be to decide on a behavior to observe and then work individually or with a group to collect observational descriptions of the behavior. Discuss how you could summarize the findings into meaningful units. Similarly, your instructor could direct you to written material to code and analyze.

Another approach could be to form a focus group using a semistructured or structured interview. A focus group is a type of discussion group that might be formed for the purpose of finding out people's opinion of, beliefs about, or attitudes toward something. It might be an idea (e.g., How successful do you think a teen pregnancy center would be in this neighborhood?), a product (e.g., a new laundry detergent), a program (e.g., reactions to a new neighborhood safety program and clients' perception of how effective it is), an advertisement (e.g., How does this commercial make you feel about the XYZ product?), and so on. You can pick the participants who are in the best position to give you useful feedback. A focus group usually takes place in a familiar setting (e.g., a community hall, church, temple) rather than in a research laboratory. The discussion is interactive; the experimenter may have a list of specific questions to ask, but ultimately the direction of the discussion is determined by the group members. It is a way to get valid information about a certain population that allows for diverse responses, finding out what people really think, or discovering new directions to be explored. Focus groups allow collection of a great deal of data in a relatively quick, low-cost manner. Don't get too excited, however—once you have the data you will need to process a large amount of verbal material, so a qualitative approach doesn't mean a quicker or easier research project.

In the present suggested activity, you will use focus groups to generate suggested pedagogical practices to facilitate learning among college students. Form groups of four to six people each. Decide who will play the roles of facilitator (the experimenter) and recorder (or, if everyone agrees, record the session and transcribe the recording later).

In this lab, we're going to use a focus group to identify factors that help college students learn. We'll start with forming focus groups to generate ideas, then code the resulting suggestions, and think about whether any conclusions can be drawn from the data.

Roles

1. Facilitator: One person should volunteer to be the facilitator. A focus group facilitator should be able to deal tactfully with outspoken group members, keep the discussion on track, and make sure every participant is heard. After a participant makes a long statement, try to sum it up in a sentence or two.

©iStock.com/wdstock

a. Make sure there is a recorder keeping notes or the discussion is recorded.

b. Tell the group the objective and ground rules for the discussion.

c. Ask the questions one at a time. Encourage everyone in the group to respond in some way to each question. If the discussion takes a new direction, go with the flow. Explore the ideas that emerge.

2. Recorder: Another person should be the recorder and keep a record of suggestions and answers to questions.

Information above based on http://www.cse.lehigh.edu/~glennb/mm/FocusGroups.htm.

Focus Group Objective: Which classroom or instructional conditions best facilitate learning by college students? Let's suppose there are few, if any, theories about this topic. We won't start with a hypothesis; we're exploring, not trying to test anything.

Ground rules

1. Every group member participates.

2. Treat each other with respect.

3. Avoid debate. This is the time to share your opinion, not to try to persuade someone else to your viewpoint.

4. Offer your opinion openly. What is said in the focus group stays in the focus group. That being the case, please don't discuss the statements of specific individuals outside of this group.

Questions

1. In which college class you have taken thus far have you learned the most? Why did you learn more in that class than in others?

2. What are specific things that instructors do, avoid, or provide that promote learning?

3. What specific strategies or techniques (actions or materials) are most effective at helping you learn?

The following figure is intended to illustrate the coding process for the comments collected from the focus group. I've started with individual comments then coded the information as a step on the way toward developing a grounded theory.

Once you have all the comments recorded, look for patterns in the ideas the group generated. This can involve several types of coding: open, axial, and selective. Open coding involves categorizing the ideas, looking for patterns. One way to do this is to put each idea on an individual card and sort through them several times to see if you can come up with any themes, trends, or patterns.

Once you have identified patterns, look for links among the categories. Do any of the themes group together logically? This next step is called *axial coding*.

Finally, selective coding takes the groups of categories and tries to determine how the groupings relate to core concepts.

This figure is just an example of how qualitative data might be coded; your results may be very different from this. That's fine. Let the data lead you.

Figure 5.1   Coding Qualitative Data

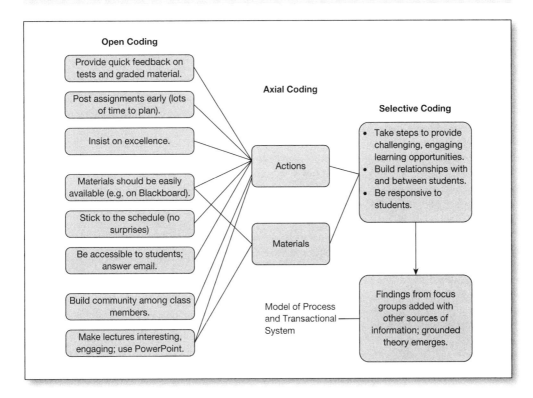

This is a very brief introduction to the idea of coding. Entire books could be (and have been) written on coding techniques and considerations. One example of a resource is http://www.sagepub.com/books/Book237888 {suggested search term *qualitative coding manual*}.

Things to Consider for All Types of Research

To gather objective data, we need to use methods that are as free from any bias as possible. While our measures or coding are unlikely to be completely free of bias, the researcher or coder needs to make a great effort to remove as much subjectivity as possible. One way to do this in the example above is to define categories very specifically. If you are uncertain of how to categorize a datum (the singular form of data), refer back to the definition of the categories rather than to your opinion.

A related issue is reliability between raters. This is addressed in the lab on survey research, but how might it apply here? Let's say there are multiple people who are coding. You want to make sure that everybody would code a datum in the same way (i.e., you have inter-rater reliability). There are several ways you could do this. You could have everybody code all the data. When disagreement between raters occurs, you could require them to discuss the issue until they reached consensus or perhaps put it to a vote. Alternatively you could have all raters code the same subset of data independently then check to see whether they coded each datum the same way.

I've Done the Coding—Now What?

©iStock.com/alexsl

Write about your findings and conclusions. Describe the process you used to collect and code the data. There is not just one right way to do this; think about how to present your data in a way that is easy for others to follow. There are many examples of qualitative research reports within your discipline. Your instructor can direct you to an example or take a look at one of the papers available at http://www.nova.edu/ssss/QR/QR13-1/index.html {suggested search term *The Qualitative Report* and choose a specific issue}.

IF YOU WANT TO GO FURTHER . . .

Content Analysis

As described above, another type of qualitative research is to analyze written or spoken content rather than conversation. Let's think about that a bit more in depth for a moment. One can focus on the concepts that occur (Are they present? How frequently do they appear?), or one can go an additional step by considering how the concepts relate to each other. For example, I could look through editorials in newspapers from a specific era and record how many times reference was made to contemporary political parties' slogans. I could then look to see whether such references were intended as sarcasm. Computer programs are available to help researchers code the material.

In both cases, the researcher would start with specific research questions and identify appropriate sources. The researcher has to decide on the unit of analysis. For example, would the research question best be addressed by looking for specific words, phrases, or idea units? Will concepts be considered only if specific criteria are met (e.g., the word *scandalous* must be used) or will the criteria be looser (e.g., any reference to shocking behavior)? How will you decide whether a unit qualifies as a target concept? In other words, what are your inclusion and exclusion criteria? When you come across unexpected material, will you ignore it or alter your criteria?

Once you have the data, it must be analyzed. Some of your findings may be expressed quantitatively, such as indicating a certain idea appeared, for example, in 30% of the sources. Other times, it may make more sense to describe the findings verbally. Either way, be cautious in your interpretation of the results. OK, that last statement applies to any research, not just content analysis.

For additional information about analyzing qualitative data look at the following source:

Thomas, D. F. (2006). A general inductive approach for analyzing qualitative evaluation data. *American Journal of Evaluation, 27,* 237–246. doi:10.1177/1098214005283748 Available online at http://www.researchgate.net/publication/224029397_A_general_inductive_approach_for_analyzing_qualitative_evaluation_data {use title as suggested search term}.

©iStock.com/Devonyu

Relational analyses may focus on the linguistic features of the material or create network models of the ideas in the material. This could be a visual representation of the concepts and their interrelationships. For example, a researcher may want to represent psychological relationships (such as what emotion or worldview appears to be implied by the material), whether ideas appear to be closely or more distantly related to each other (this may be indicated by the spatial representation of the concepts in the network), or whether concepts can be grouped together in "metaconcepts" that are implied by commonalities in the concepts. This approach reflects ideas adapted from cognitive science and models of artificial intelligence. For an example of this and other approaches to coding see the website below. Exhibit 10.6 is an illustration of a network model.

http://www.sagepub.com/upm-data/43454_10.pdf_{suggested search term *network model concepts image*}.

If content analysis is important in your field, take a few moments to practice this. Decide

1. What is your research question?

2. What is appropriate source material? Your instructor can suggest a suitable document to analyze.

3. Does your research question lead you to ask questions about the presence of concepts or should you look for relationships among concepts?

4. How will you code the material? Define the criteria for your coding decisions.

5. Decide how you'll analyze the resulting data.

6. Do the coding. Analyze the coded material.

7. Interpret your findings. What patterns or concepts emerged? What do these mean in terms of better understanding the field?

Alternatively, it may be most appropriate to perform content analysis on something other than text. For example, you might analyze children's drawings to gain insight into their perceptions of and attitudes toward older adults.

WHAT'S THE POINT OF ALL THIS QUALITATIVE INFORMATION? DEVELOPMENT OF A GROUNDED THEORY

Remember, we started the section on focus groups by pretending to explore a new research area, so there aren't (in our make-believe scenario) any theories to generate hypotheses to be tested. Ultimately, the goal is to develop a theory of good classroom practices. Remember, a theory is just your explanation for why something happens or why it is the way it is. A theory that evolves in this manner is a grounded theory because it is rooted in the experiences and perceptions of people who are closely involved with or affected by the phenomenon under investigation. You may need to look at other studies on your topic (you may have described these in your introduction) along with your findings and develop an explanation for the pattern of findings. If there are no published studies on your topic, be very careful about developing a theory based on one study. You use inductive logic (drawing a conclusion from multiple observations) to develop this theory. Your theory should be modifiable (sensitive to change as new findings are reported) and specific enough that researchers can generate hypotheses to test the theory.

Develop a theory of how the music composer for the Harry Potter movies used music to enhance the action on the screen. You can read about an exercise to do this in

Messinger, A. M. (2012). Teaching content analysis through Harry Potter. *Teaching Sociology, 40,* 360–367. doi:10.1177/0092055X12445461.

This can be found online at http://tso.sagepub.com/content/40/4/360.full .pdf+html {suggested search term *Teaching content analysis through Harry Potter*}.

You can view the scenes described in the article from a purchased copy of the movie or find the individual scenes posted online (there may be commercials). For example,

Practice scene:

Opening scene from *Harry Potter and the Philosopher's Stone*

   https://www.youtube.com/watch?v=O6cddFuTPBA

Scene to code:

Opening scene from *Harry Potter and the Goblet of Fire*

   https://www.youtube.com/watch?v=6Ug8Q8xedx0

COMMUNICATING THE RESULTS

Research that is not communicated is research that is lost. Your data do no good if you don't share your findings. The type of qualitative project you use will dictate the format of presenting your data. One example is listed below. Your instructor can direct you to articles within your discipline that can serve as models.

Ellett, A. J., Ellis, J. I. Westbrook, T. M., & Dews, D. (2006). A qualitative study of 369 child welfare professionals' perspectives about factors contributing to employee retention and turnover. *Children and Youth Services Review, 29,* 264–281. doi:10.1016/j.childyouth.2006.07.005

LAB 6

Case Studies and Single-Subject Designs

Objective

The purpose of this lab is to introduce study designs with one participant, distinguish between case studies and single subject designs, and conduct your own single subject study using behavior modification. Thinking about the opposite end of the sample size spectrum, additional material addresses issues relevant to epidemiology, such as prevalence, incidence, mortality, morbidity, sensitivity, and specificity.

Target Article

Ahearn, W. H. (2003). Using simultaneous presentation to increase vegetable consumption in a mildly selective child with autism. *Journal of Applied Behavior Analysis, 36*(3), 361–365.

©iStock.com/matka_Wariatka

Behavior Modification—Would You Like Ketchup With That?

This single subject study is of a teenage boy with autism and mental retardation who would not eat vegetables. The experimenter paired presentation of vegetables with the presence of condiments such as ketchup, mustard, and salad dressing. The design used was ABABAB, in which A was baseline (no condiments) and B was the experimental phase (condiments present). The adolescent ate more vegetables when they came with condiments.

CASE STUDY VERSUS SINGLE-SUBJECT DESIGN

Some research studies involve only one participant, including case studies and single subject designs. Case studies are non-experimental in that no manipulation occurs; the researcher simply observes an individual and the natural occurrences of his or her life or interviews the individual to gather information about his or her life. This type of research can gather quantitative data but also allows for the opportunity to obtain descriptive and rich qualitative information, often regarding a rare event, a representative event or individual, or a unique physical or psychological characteristic. Case studies can be retrospective, in which a participant is observed after a particular occurrence has taken place, or prospective, in which an individual is measured before and after experiencing a particular occurrence. An example is the infamous retrospective case study of Phineas Gage, an American railroad worker who survived a rock-blasting accident in which an iron rod was driven completely through his head. The head injury destroyed most of Gage's frontal lobe, and case study observations of Gage's cognitive function and changes in his personality and behavior yielded invaluable information about the different areas of the brain and their functions. You can search *Phineas Gage image* or go to http://psychology.about.com/od/historyofpsychology/ss/phineas-gage-images.htm to read more about him.

Case studies can provide important information about a specific or rare case, or an occurrence that cannot be ethically obtained in an experiment. Because observations are of an individual behaving in his or her normal state and natural surroundings, case studies have high ecological validity, or close approximation to the real world. However, case studies may not be representative of the wider population, and these studies can be time consuming and difficult to replicate. Case studies may study nonhuman subjects, as well. For example, you may do a case study on Woodstock as an event marking cultural change (ask any former hippie), or of the XYZ company, or a composition of some type.

From the collection of Jack and Beverly Wilgus

Single subject designs, on the other hand, are experimental in nature. This design investigates the effectiveness of an intervention on a single participant, typically measuring the participant's performance before treatment (the A phase), during treatment or intervention (B), and after treatment or in the absence of the intervention (back to condition A). You can repeat the A and B phases multiple times. For example,

AB

ABA

ABAB . . . and so on.

An advantage of this design is that multiple observations and interventions of one individual allow for comparisons of conditions *within* the participant instead of across individuals or groups. The participant essentially serves as his or her own control, and this design in turn provides useful feedback on the progress and effectiveness of a treatment. Single subject designs are more generalizable than case studies and can be more easily replicated because they are conducted in controlled environments. However, patterns still may not be representative of the wider population, and patterns may be skewed by carry-over effects (in which results from the previous phase or treatment carry over into the next phase) and order effects (in which the order of the treatment and nontreatment phases affect the results).

WHO USES BEHAVIOR MODIFICATION?

©iStock.com/delectus

One approach to treatment may be to modify a patient or client's behavior. Behavior modification has been used to change children's behavior, although at times, a parent may tell you it usually works better with other people's children (Calhoun, Cann, & Terry, 1987)! It has been used to deal with unnecessary crying at night by infants, potty training in toddlers, children with behavioral disorders, troubled teenagers, and so on. And we all know that children can be very successful at modifying the behavior of their parents! Of course, behavior modification isn't limited to humans. It is also used to train pets and working or performing animals.

Calhoun, L. G., Cann, A., & Terry, W. S. (1987). An overview of research findings in the behavioral sciences: The laws of psychology. *Journal of Polymorphous Perversity, 4,* 3–4.

More Information on Self-Modification

Are you interested in behavioral methods for treating eating disorders? There is a 2004 issue of the journal *Behavior Modification* that is devoted to that topic (see volume *26*[6], 2004). For further information about self-modification programs, consult one of the sources listed below or a similar publication.

The journal *Behavior Modification*

Hersen, M., Rosquivst, J., Gross, A. M., Drabman, R. S., Sugai, G., & Horner, R. (Eds.). (2005). *Encyclopedia of behavior modification and cognitive behavior therapy.* Thousand Oaks, CA: Sage. doi: 10.4135/9781412950534

Volume 1: Adult Clinical Applications

Volume 2: Child Clinical Applications

Volume 3: Educational Applications

TRY IT YOURSELF

You will now conduct your own single-subject design using a behavior modification study. In this lab, you will serve as your own participant. You are going to use behavior modification on yourself to change some behavior. Is there a bad habit you'd like to stop or a good one you'd like to begin or increase? Here's your chance! Choose a behavior to increase or decrease and decide on an appropriate punishment (to decrease a behavior) or reward (to increase a behavior) that you will apply to yourself. The end product of this lab will be a poster describing your project and the results. Your instructor will give you the details regarding length. This lab will take a few weeks, so you may need to start it early. As in earlier labs, I'll provide canned data, in case it is not possible or feasible to collect your own data.

Canned Data

Let's pretend that you wanted to increase the number of minutes spent studying. You measure your baseline study time for three days, then for one week, you give yourself five minutes of video game time for every 30 minutes you spend studying. After a week, you suspend the video reward but continue to measure your study time (an ABA design). Here are your findings:

Total minutes spent studying

Baseline day 1	45
Baseline day 2	37
Baseline day 3	23
Intervention day 1	30
Intervention day 2	35
Intervention day 3	45
Intervention day 4	60
Intervention day 5	50
Intervention day 6	73
Intervention day 7	59
Back to baseline day 1	52
Back to baseline day 2	61
Back to baseline day 3	64

What is the average for the first baseline period?   _____

What is the average for the intervention period?   _____

What is the average for the return to baseline period?   _____

Comment on any pattern(s) that emerged from your data. Do you think the intervention was successful? What conditions might affect the longevity of any change? For example, if you decreased the number of cigarettes smoked per day, what environmental or personal conditions might be needed to prolong that change?

IF YOU WANT TO COLLECT YOUR OWN DATA . . .

It's All About You

Follow these instructions to conduct a self-modification study for at least one week. Note that you will report data using an ABA (baseline, intervention, return to baseline) design. The intervention (part B) should last at least one full week. After you have observed your own behavior, you will put together an oral presentation or a poster to describe your results. You will be eyeballing and describing the data rather than running an inferential test. Compare the frequency of the targeted behavior from the first baseline days, the intervention days, and the second set of baseline days. Put your results into a graph or table. In order to provide some background information, you may need to do a little reading on the topic, so you may need to find a relevant article or a section of a textbook to help you bone up on the subject. For example, if you want to stop or decrease smoking, use an appropriate search engine and search for articles on *behavior modification smoking* or similar wording.

Procedure

Pick a behavior you want to change. It can involve either beginning or increasing a desired behavior or ending or decreasing an undesired behavior. Be very specific. Choose something that is observable and measurable. For example, "improving my health" is vague; "decreasing the number of cigarettes smoked per day" is specific.

Decide on your motivation. If you want to increase a behavior, think of a meaningful way to reward yourself. If you want to decrease a behavior, think of a punishment (for example, denying yourself TV time or keeping a rubber band on your wrist and snapping yourself every time you commit the undesired behavior).

©iStock.com/neildev

A. Before you begin your reward or punishment program, measure the behavior for at least three days. Record this information.

B. Begin your intervention. For one week, keep track of how many times the target behavior occurs. Make use of your reward or punishment every time you repeat the behavior. Record this information daily.

A. Return to baseline. After a week of intervention, stop rewarding or punishing yourself and record the occurrence of the behavior for another three days. Does it return to the preintervention level or stay changed?

IF YOU WANT TO GO FURTHER . . .

Large-Scale Epidemiology: The Opposite Approach

I don't want to give you whiplash by suddenly changing directions, but think with me for a moment about designs that are the opposite of single-subject designs. While studies of a single participant can be very informative, research examining large groups of individuals and identifying patterns are also quite valuable. Epidemiology is the scientific study of patterns, causes, and consequences of health conditions and diseases among particular populations. The populations are usually people, but could be other things (such as another species). This type of research may be especially important for questions in public health policy, identifying best practices in treating a disorder, and identifying sources of disease or factors that may be protective. Depending on the research question at hand, these populations may be defined by geography, race, gender, occupation, or some other characteristic.

Epidemiology can provide unique statistics about the health of populations. For example, researchers can calculate the *incidence rate* of a disease, which is the number of new cases of a disease in a population within a given period of time. This statistic provides information about the risk of contracting or developing a disease and can help researchers understand the etiology of a disease (causes, factors that lead to an illness) and what populations are particularly at risk. Epidemiologists also study the *prevalence* or *morbidity* of a disease or health condition, the total number of cases of a disease (rather than just new cases) in a defined population within a given period of time. This statistic provides information about how widespread the health condition is within a population. For example, look at the Centers for Disease Control and Prevention statistics on the spread of the Ebola virus as of 2014 and find the statistics for incidence and prevalence (http://www .cdc.gov/mmwr/preview/mmwrhtml/mm6339a4.htm {suggested search term *morbidity ebola*}). These researchers also report the *mortality* rate of the disorder (number of people who die from the disorder). Find this statistic at http://www .md-health.com/Ebola-Death-Rate.html {suggested search term *mortality ebola*}.

Suppose your job is to decide whether a particular new test to diagnose a disorder should be implemented on a wide-scale basis. You would likely want to

		Actual Diagnosis		
		Sick	Not Sick	
Test Diagnosis	Sick	**A** (correct)	**B** (test was wrong— false positive)	Total sick based on test (A + B)
	Not Sick	**C** (test was wrong—false negative)	**D** (correct)	Total not sick based on test (C + D)
		Total actually sick (A + C)	Total actually not sick (B + D)	Total # tested (A + B + C + D)

know information about the test's accuracy, such as how often the test correctly diagnoses the disorder among those who actually have it (*sensitivity*), how likely it is to rule out the disorder in people who really aren't sick (*specificity*), as well as how likely it is to give a misdiagnosis. You have two pieces of information for each person: diagnosis based on the new test (sick or not sick) and actual diagnosis (sick or not sick).

In this illustration, cell A is the sensitivity of the test, cell D is the specificity of the test, B is false positives, and C is false negatives.

Let's say you have the following numbers (I'm going to use relatively small numbers here to make it easier to understand):

		Actual Diagnosis		
		Sick	Not Sick	
Test Diagnosis	Sick	18	4	22
	Not Sick	22	210	232
		40	214	254

To calculate percentages, simply multiply the result of your division by 100.

Sensitivity = A/(A+C) = 18/40 = 45% (not very impressive)

Specificity = D/(B+D) = 210/214 = 98% (super)

% False negative = C/(A+C) = 22/40 = 55%

% False positive = B/(B+D) = 4/214 = 2%

Prevalence of the disorder is the number of actual positives out of the entire sample (in this example, 40/254 = .157, or ~16%).

So these numbers suggest the test does a good job of ruling out people who are not sick, but not so good a job at identifying those who actually are sick. Although you can look up "SpIns" (threshold to rule in specificity) and "SnOuts" (threshold to rule out sensitivity), the actual decision of whether to use a test must weigh both, as well as consider the consequences of misdiagnosis and what alternatives are available.

TRY IT YOURSELF

Assume you collected the following data on a new test for lung cancer*:

		Actual Diagnosis		
		Sick	Not Sick	
Test Diagnosis	Sick	80	4,990	5,070
	Not Sick	20	94,910	94,930
		100	99,900	100,000

Calculate the measures of accuracy of this new test and the prevalence of lung cancer. You can check your work with the key below.

In addition to the hypothetical numbers in this example, assume a mortality rate of 5%. Write about your findings on the prevalence and morbidity of lung cancer, and the sensitivity and specificity of this new test for lung cancer. Remember these numbers are made up, so don't draw any conclusions from them about cancer in the "real world."

Epidemiological studies are useful in identifying how illnesses develop, spread, and persist. Such research can have direct applications within public health and health-care policy that can improve the lives of large populations. An advantage of this research is that findings are highly generalizable, and patterns that emerge are more representative of the defined population than

©iStock.com/Courtney Keating

many other research strategies. A disadvantage is that most epidemiological study designs are correlational in nature; the findings can demonstrate associations between variables but cannot confirm cause-and-effect relations. Epidemiological studies can also be very expensive and time consuming, and working with such large sample sizes may require specialized statistical software or analyses capable of handling large data sets.

* Your instructor may want to reframe this illustration to one that is appropriate for your discipline.

Answer Key:

		Actual Diagnosis		
		Sick	Not Sick	
Test Diagnosis	Sick	80	4,990	5,070
	Not Sick	20	94,910	94,930
		100	99,900	100,000

Sensitivity = A/(A+C) = 80/100 = 80%

Specificity = D/(B+D) = 94910/99900 = 95%

% False negative = C/(A+C) = 20/100 = 20%

% False positive = B/(B+D) = 4990/99900 = 5%

Prevalence rate = A+C/total sample = 100/100000 = .1%

LAB 7

Surveys

Objective

The purpose of this lab is to familiarize the student researcher with surveys as a tool to collect many types of data. Advanced material describes how to generate survey items and test their reliability.

Your instructor may want you to do the lab on correlations and/or the one on descriptive and inferential statistics prior to this lab. If not, you can save the data and analyze it after you have covered these labs.

Target Article

Hamrick, H., Cohen, S., & Rodriguez, M. S. (2002). Being popular can be healthy or unhealthy: Stress, social network diversity, and incidence of upper respiratory infection. *Health Psychology, 21*(3), 294–298.

People who have lots of social contacts are exposed to more germs than are people who don't have as many social contacts. Does that suggest that they will be more likely to get sick? These authors measured social network diversity and stressful life events in college students, then interviewed their participants weekly for 12 weeks, recording how many upper respiratory infections they contracted during that time. They found that the answer to whether or not the popular people got sick more often was "it depends." They did become sick more often if they had a high stress score, but not if they reported low stress. In other words, it seemed that stress weakened their resistance to germs, making them more likely to succumb to the germs to which they were exposed.

©iStock.com/aabejon

Surveys are widely used tools to collect data that can be analyzed in various ways or can be used to help understand the characteristics of a population. Surveys can collect both quantitative and qualitative data. Quantitative data is information that can be counted or expressed numerically; this information can be statistically analyzed and represented by graphs, histograms, charts, and tables. Qualitative data is information that is not numerical in nature. These data can provide rich and in-depth information about a population or a certain topic that cannot be gathered from numerical values. This lab will lead you to develop a survey that will generate quantitative data. Your instructor may direct you to design a survey that will collect qualitative data. Before you make a decision about using a survey, think about your hypothesis or research question and what type of data are most suitable to address the specific prediction. Decide whether a survey is the best way to get the data you want to explore the research area or to effectively test the hypothesis.

TYPES OF SURVEY QUESTIONS

Questions on surveys can take several forms. They can be open-ended or closed-ended. Open-ended questions typically provide rich qualitative information; the researcher does not limit the kind of response participants can provide. An example of an open-ended question might be,

"What concerns (if any) do you have about the amount of alcohol you drink?"

Open-ended questions are good for getting answers unique to each participant. However, you then will have to develop some way to convert that information to numbers if you wish to do some type of quantitative analysis. If your goal is qualitative data, you'll still have to take the responses and code them in some way. Closed-ended questions limit participants' responses but often provide information that can be easily converted into numerical form and analyzed. These are examples of closed-ended survey items:

Do you smoke currently? ___ yes   ___ no

When you do well on a test, is it because (check one)

___A. you are smart in that subject?

___B. you worked hard studying for the test?

___C. the teacher likes you?

___D. you were lucky that day?

___E. other reason

When you go to your first class of the day, how sleepy are you usually? Circle the number that best describes you.

____1____2____3____4____5____6____7____8____9____
Very sleepy   Neither sleepy   Not at all
                                  nor alert   sleepy

When you create a survey (or choose one from the literature), there are several issues to keep in mind.

1. Wording of the items

   Give careful thought to the wording of your survey items. Write questions that

   - are written clearly at an appropriate level of difficulty
   - ask only one question per item (e.g., you would not want to ask "Do you litter and are you kind to animals?" all in one item)
   - ask the same question from different perspectives (e.g., "I believe sleep is important for my health" and "I don't think sleep plays a role in my health")
   - offer clear alternatives (answers that don't overlap) and a full range of responses

   Take a moment and think about the difficulties with the following item:

   I am sleepy during the day sometimes (like the guy who plays the younger son on that TV show on Monday nights) and have difficulty with schoolwork because I'm not a diurnal person.

    a. Always true for me

    b. Usually true for me

    c. Sometimes true for me

2. Wording of the instructions

    Your instructions should be clear and straightforward without biasing responses. Be specific. The participant is doing you a favor, so communicate your respect for and appreciation of their answers. Why is the second set of instructions better?

> Psychologists have become interested in the study of health-related behavior because everybody knows you'd have to be an idiot to ignore your health. Answer the following questions.

OR

> Over the last several years, psychologists have become more active in the study of health-related behavior. One important task in this area of research is to collect accurate information on the frequency of healthy behaviors. Therefore, we would appreciate your answering the following questions about healthy behaviors as honestly and accurately as possible. We will not report individual responses, just the behaviors of people in general. We are interested in how frequently you have participated in each activity listed below *in the past month.* Thank you for your participation.

3. Reliability and validity

    Although this concept is being introduced in the context of surveys, it is applicable to any measure. When you measure something, you want to know that the instrument you are using is measuring the construct or behavior accurately and consistently. Let's think about several types of reliability and validity:

Table 7.1 Psychometric Properties: Validity and Reliability

Validity	Reliability
Content—Does it measure what it says it measures?	**Inter-rater**—Will everyone score the data the same way?

(Continued)

Table 7.1 (Continued)

Concurrent—Does it measure the same thing as do other known instruments? **Criterion**—Does it accurately predict an outcome it claims to measure?	**Test-retest**—Will it measure the same thing in the same people each time it is used? **Internal consistency**—Do all the items measure the same thing?

Let's try an example of finding and including this information in a report. *When you describe a study in your Method section, you should include this information if it is known.* Let's continue with the theme of stress and health. Take a look at the article on the validation of the *Perceived Stress Scale* (PSS).

Cohen, S., Kamarck, T., & Mermelstein, R. (1983). A global measure of perceived stress. *Journal of Health and Social Behavior, 24,* 386–396.

The authors needed some objective way to determine whether this was a good way to measure stress. By "good" I mean did it measure stress and not something else (validity) and did it measure stress consistently (reliability); in other words, they needed to demonstrate the psychometric qualities of the instrument. If the instrument is not reliable and valid, then any score it produces may not mean much.

Reliability. Look on p. 390 of the article, third paragraph down on the left (begins with "Coefficient alpha reliability…"). The authors had tried out their new instrument on three different samples. Cronbach's alpha is a measure of how well the items "hang together." In other words, it measures the internal consistency ("split-half reliability"). In this paper, it ranged from .84 to .86. In general, you want an alpha level that is higher than .6 or .7. The alpha levels reported here are good. We also want to know that the measure is similar over time. Further in the same paragraph, you see that test-retest reliability was .85 across a two-day time period and .55 across a 6-week period. Inter-rater reliability could be compared by having several different people score the test and correlating the scores they produced.

Validity. Concurrent validity was established by comparing the score produced by the PSS to an already-established measure of stress (a measure of how many stressful events had been experienced and how stressful the events were perceived to have been; perceived stress should be higher if one has had more stressful experiences). Table 1 shows that the two were moderately correlated, indicating concurrent validity. Predictive validity was tested by correlating PSS scores with symptoms of depression (higher stress should correlate with greater depression). The correlations were fairly high ($rs = .65$ to .76), and did a better job of predicting depression than did a measure of number or severity of stressful life events.

By reporting an instrument's reliability and validity, you are showing your reader that you chose an appropriate instrument to measure your variable of interest, and the scores produced by that instrument are believable. *This is important information, so be sure to include it!*

©iStock.com/amanalang

Survey Distribution

Once you settle on the survey items and instructions, you have to think about how you will disseminate the survey. Should it be done anonymously online or in person? Will you recruit by telephone, mail, approaching people in a public place, or social media? Think in each case about the nature of the survey, the likely participation rate, whether you will be likely to get a representative sample, and, let's not forget, cost and time. Will the data collection method influence how willing people will be to give accurate answers? For example, if you are asking people about sensitive issues, they may be more willing to answer truthfully in an anonymous online format than in person.

TRY IT YOURSELF

How Do You Report Reliability and Validity?

Let's say you used the PSS to collect data on stress and the measure of general health created from the Medical Outcomes Study (MOS). You can find the reliability and validity of this measure at http://www.jstor.org/stable/pdf/3765494.pdf {suggested search term *The MOS Short-Form General Health Survey: Reliability and Validity in a Patient Population*; *Stewart et al. 1988*}. Write the Materials subsection of the Method in which you describe the two instruments. You can use the information above to report the psychometric properties of the PSS, and the article by Anita L. Stewart, Ron D. Hays, and John E. Ware (1988) to describe the MOS health survey. Try this on your own after looking at the example below. Your wording may be different, but you should cover the same points. Remember to include for each instrument

1. The name of the measure and cite the authors

2. Description of what it measures and how it is scored. What do high scores mean?

3. Whether it is appropriate for the population you tested

4. The psychometric properties

WRITING THE METHOD

Materials

Perceived stress was measured using the *Perceived Stress Scale* (PSS; Cohen, Kamarck, & Mermelstein, 1983). This survey indicates the extent to which an individual feels stressed as a result of life events. The survey has acceptable reliability (Chronbach's α from .84-.86; test-retest reliability $r = .85$ across two days, $r = .55$ across six weeks) and validity (concurrent validity with perceived impact of life events $r \geq .24$; predictive validity of depressive symptomatology $r \geq .65$). The PSS includes 14 items that are scored from 0 (never) to 4 (very often). After reverse coding of positively worded items, responses are summed. Higher scores indicate greater perceived stress. It was validated within two samples of college students and one sample of adults in a smoking cessation program.

The Medical Outcomes Study Short-form General Health Survey (MOS-GH; Stewart, Hays, & Ware, 1988) includes 20 items that measure physical functioning, role functioning, social functioning, mental health, perceived health, and pain. Participants in the validation study included a large ($N = 11,186$) group of adults ages 18 to 103. Response options on the items range from 3 to 6. Responses are scored so that higher numbers indicate better health, then summed. Internal consistency within each scale was good ($\geq .81$), and the measure successfully discriminated between healthy and clinical samples. Correlations with demographic characteristics were in predicted directions (e.g., higher education and higher income were positively correlated with better health).

Canned Data

Assume you collected the following data. In addition, you asked for qualitative data on sources of stress. Create an SPSS data file using these data. High stress scores indicate *greater perceived stress* and high health scores indicate *better health*. Bear in mind, I made up these numbers, so actual scores generated by these instruments may look different. Analyze the following data:

Stress	Health
12.00	77.00
21.00	19.00
49.00	12.00
5.00	64.00
12.00	38.00
43.00	19.00
34.00	19.00
4.00	90.00
3.00	70.00
16.00	12.00
8.00	25.00
34.00	57.00
13.00	10.00
34.00	19.00
8.00	32.00
34.00	17.00
18.00	38.00
8.00	45.00
13.00	38.00
12.00	45.00

SOURCE: Based on data from: https://en.wikipedia.org/wiki/Positive_and_negative_predictive_values

Analyses

Eyeball the data. You're going to see this expression used a lot in this lab manual. Examining descriptive information allows you to eyeball the data to ensure the range, mean, and standard deviation values are reasonable.

1. Click ANALYZE, DESCRIPTIVE STATISTICS;

2. then highlight each variable and click the arrow to move it into the *Variable* box;

3. then click OK.

Descriptive Statistics

	N	Minimum	Maximum	Mean	Std. Deviation
PSS	20	3.00	49.00	19.0500	13.85821
MOS_GH	20	10.00	90.00	37.3000	23.62002
Valid *N* (listwise)	20				

You see that you have the sample size, the minimum and maximum scores reported by your participants, the mean score of each variable, and the standard deviation of that score (i.e., the extent to which, on average, the scores differ from the mean). Eyeball the data to make sure the data make sense (a way to catch data entry errors).

You may need to go through the lab on correlations before analyzing these data. Do you expect to get a positive or negative correlation? [Negative; high stress should associate with low health.]

1. *Analyze*

2. *Correlate, bivariate*

3. Put the two variables into the Variables box

4. *Ok*

Is the correlation positive or negative? [negative] Is it statistically significant? [yes] Does it make sense? [yes—although you are free to disagree] What does the negative correlation indicate about the relation between perceived

Correlations

		PSS	MOS_GH
PSS	Pearson Correlation	1	-.558*
	Sig. (2-tailed)		.010
	N	20	20
MOS_GH	Pearson Correlation	-.558*	1
	Sig. (2-tailed)	.010	
	N	20	20

*. Correlation is significant at the 0.05 level (2-tailed).

stress and health (remember high scores indicate more stress and better health)? [people with more perceived stress had lower perceived health]

Let's say that you looked through the qualitative data and categorized the different sources of stress mentioned by participants. You found that the categories most frequently listed were pressure due to school demands, worry about finances, and problems in peer relationships.

Results Section

We are going to include the descriptive information in the Results section. You may also choose to put this information in a table and refer your reader there. Begin by indicating the sample size, mean, and standard deviation

---

Results

Twenty participants completed the survey assessing stress and health. Participants responded to stress items indicating how stressed they were feeling ($M = 19.05$, $SD = 13.86$, range 3–49). Participants also reported how healthy they felt ($M = 37.30$, $SD = 23.62$, range 10–90). Correlation analysis of the total perceived stress score with the health variable indicated that greater stress was associated with lower perceived health, $r(20) = -.56$, $p = .01$. Participants reported sources of their stress, and patterns emerged in which schoolwork, financial concerns, and peer relationship problems were the most commonly named causes of stress.

for each variable. Describe the correlation analysis and explain what it means. Lastly, describe any patterns that emerged from the open-ended question. Study this example, then write the Results section without looking at it.

Compare what you wrote to the example given here. Did you include all the important information? Did you italicize letters used to report statistics?

IF YOU WANT TO COLLECT YOUR OWN DATA . . .

Your instructor will let you know if you should carry out this project independently or as part of a small group. Your task is to (1) decide how you will define stress and general health and find surveys that measure these constructs (for now, let's use published instruments), (2) organize data collection, (3) collect data, and (4) write a short lab report on the topic of stress and health that reports the data you collected.

The two constructs can be defined differently depending on what exactly you want to measure. Take a quick look through peer-reviewed articles and decide which measure of stress and health are most important to you. You can use the measures described here or you can choose others reported in the literature.

Your instructor will let you know if you should find and use existing measures of stress and health, or if you should develop your own survey items. If the latter, ask if you should pilot test the items, and whether you should follow the directions in the If You Want to Go Further . . . section of this lab to test the reliability and validity of your items.

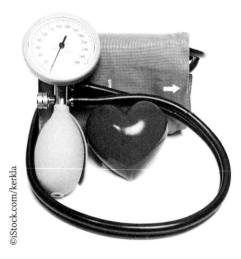

©iStock.com/kerkla

Measuring stress. Stress can be operationalized as physiological measures such as blood pressure, heart rate, galvanic skin response, or respiration rate, or it can be measured in terms of recent stressful life events (such as marriage, death of a loved one), or daily hassles (such as feeling annoyed or frustrated). For example, the PSS is a widely used psychological instrument for measuring the perception of stress, and scores have been associated with other health outcomes such as more colds and greater vulnerability to stress-related depression.

Health. You can operationalize this as the number of visits to health-care providers during the last 12 months (you'll need to specify what you include in the term *health-care pro-vider* for your participants), or you can use a self-report measure cited in the literature such as the MOS-GH. For example, you may ask how many colds a person has had in the last 12 months, how many prescription medicines have been used, or some other indicator of health, and then add up the numbers to produce the health score. If wet lab facilities are available, you could do a test of immunological functioning.

DISTRIBUTING THE SURVEY

When you are satisfied with your choice of instruments, identify whom you wish to include in your study. Decide on a strategy for collecting the data. Remember you are seeking personal information from your participants, so give them the opportunity to read and sign an informed consent form and come up with a way to ensure their anonymity. One way to do this is to have two boxes with slits on top. Participants can put their surveys and consent forms in different boxes. They might want to fold them up first, then shake the box after putting in their information to mix up the contents (making it harder to associate a consent form with that person's survey). Perhaps you can come up with an even better way to keep your participants' responses anonymous or adequately protected.

If this is a group project, you can either collect data from all class members or have group members collect data from people outside the class. If you decide to collect data outside of class, decide how many participants will be recruited by each class member. Each person can use the data collection form below to record the results (or one like it), then bring the results to class and pool them to make one large data set. Enter the data into SPSS, label the variables, then run the appropriate analyses. Instructions on how to do this are in the lab on Descriptive and Inferential Statistics.

One version of a data collection form:

Participant ID	Stress Score	Health Score	Age	Gender	(Other Demographic Information as Needed)
1					
2					
3 (and so on)					

If you are creating your own survey you may need to modify the form to collect data on individual survey items so you can run a reliability analysis. See the If You Want to Go Further . . . section of this lab if you are going to create your own instrument. Here's an example.

Participant ID	Stress Score 1	Stress Score 2	Stress Score 3 . . .	Health Score 1	Health Score 2	Health Score 3 . . .	Age	Gender	(Other Demographic Information as Needed)
1									
2									
3 (and so on)									

INFORMED CONSENT—REALLY, REALLY IMPORTANT!

In most cases, anyone who wants to conduct research should (and often must) first have their research proposal approved by an Institutional Review Board (IRB; refer back to Lab 4 on ethics). The research you are doing for this class, however, is being undertaken for learning purposes rather than research purposes. Is it acceptable to collect data without IRB approval when it is for learning purposes only? Although I don't know the position the IRB at your institution takes, here is how one institution has addressed this question.

http://research.uncc.edu/departments/office-research-compliance-orc/human-subjects/guidelines-research#require%20IRB%20approval {suggested search term *IRB class project*}.

Your instructor will guide you regarding any required approval for data collection. Whether you are required to do so or not, it is always a good idea to obtain an informed consent form. Your participants should be told in advance what you will ask them and know that they can quit whenever they like. Your instructor may want you to use a consent template recommended by your institution, or you can find one from another institution. For example, go to

http://research.uncc.edu/departments/office-research-compliance-orc/
human-subjects/informed-consent {suggested search term *informed consent template*}, scroll to the bottom, and click Consent Template. If you are collecting anonymous data online and your instructor approves, you can use the informed consent statement, which does not require a signature (on the same website look for a link to "online consent") {suggested search term *online consent template*}.

PRODUCING THE ABBREVIATED LAB REPORT

Write an Abstract, along with Introduction, Method, Results, and Discussion sections of a lab report. Include a title page and references. Ask your instructor what types of sources are appropriate for you to use (e.g., textbooks, peer-reviewed articles found on a search engine). An introduction is essentially a literature review, with the purpose and hypothesis for the study described at the end. Set up your literature review to move from a general discussion of the research topic to a more detailed look at the specific topic addressed by this study, then add on a paragraph or two describing the purpose and hypothesis for this study. Describe the participants, materials used (*remember to include reliability and validity!*), procedure, and plan of analysis describing how the data were collected and analyzed. Use headings and subheadings as directed by your instructor.

IF YOU WANT TO GO FURTHER . . .

Let's stick with the theme of stress and health among college students. There are plenty of easily available measures online to measure stress and health, but consider creating your own instruments for this project. Look through the literature to come up with survey items that measure stress, health, or both. Create your measures so that high scores indicate greater stress and more health concerns (i.e., poorer health), respectively.

Developing the Survey

First, review characteristics of good survey items (this is probably described in your textbook). Constructing survey items is a process that requires careful thought and consideration. We could devote an entire course to item construction, but here, we will briefly discuss *validity* and *reliability* of survey items. Validity refers to how

©iStock.com/daneger

well a test measures what it is supposed to measure. Are our survey items really measuring someone's *stress* or are we measuring the personality trait of negative affect? To ensure validity, one should first define the targeted variable (for example, let's define *stress* as "an uncomfortable experience or response to a threat with which we feel we do not have the resources to cope") and design items that pertain to that definition. Validity can be estimated many ways, such as correlating the survey items with related variables.

Survey items should also be reliable. Reliability refers to the degree to which our survey produces stable and consistent results. Let's say you provide your survey to a group of participants (Time 1), and then give them the same survey one month later (Time 2). Participants' scores at Time 1 and Time 2 are highly similar; this means your survey shows good test-retest reliability, and thus shows stable, consistent results. We can also examine internal consistency reliability, which shows the degree to which our individual survey items produce similar results. We will practice examining internal consistency reliability with our canned data. We want our survey items to demonstrate both validity and reliability—why?

Let's say for example that your bathroom scale is off by 8 pounds, but it reads your weight exactly the same each day . . . just 8 pounds off. Your scale is reliable but not valid, and therefore not a good measure of your weight. We can have greater confidence that valid *and* reliable surveys are providing accurate measures of our targeted variables.

Lastly, when constructing survey items, think about the response scale for your survey. Will participants respond to items with a yes or no? Will they pick a number on a scale of frequency from never to always? Choose a response scale and word your items accordingly.

Once you have a number of survey items you think will get the information you want, pilot test them on a few people (similar to those who will be your participants) to identify any problems with the items. Were some of them confusing? Unclear? Did they allow for all possible responses? Ask the pilot testers to comment on each item. Either fix or eliminate poor items.

For these data, we measured stress using three items from the Perceived Stress Scale: (1) In the last month, how often have you been upset because of something that happened unexpectedly? (2) In the last month, how often have you felt that you were unable to control the important things in your life? (3) In the last month, how often have you felt nervous and "stressed"?

   Participants respond to the following scale: 0 (Never), 1 (Almost Never), 2 (Sometimes), 3 (Fairly Often), 4 (Very Often). Higher numbers indicate greater stress. The health measure is number of sickness-related visits to health care providers in the last month and ranged from 0 to 14 (these are hypothetical people, so hypothetically some of them were sick a lot in the last month). Higher numbers, therefore, indicate more instances of sickness, and therefore, worse health. Enter the data as you did before.

Stress1	Stress2	Stress3	Health
1	1	2	4
3	4	4	11
1	2	2	5
2	2	2	5
2	3	2	7
3	3	3	6
4	3	4	10
4	4	4	12
2	1	2	3
4	3	4	14

Let's say you also asked participants the following open-ended question:

   What are causes of stress in your life? _____
   For example, participants might list any of the following:

Sources of Stress
Schoolwork
Money
Family issues
Relationship with my significant other

(Continued)

(Continued)

Sources of Stress
Problems with roommate
Employment
Paying for school
Balancing classes and jobs
Family problems, finances

Analyses

First let's **eyeball the data** (you knew this was coming, didn't you?) by looking at some of the descriptive statistics.

1. Click ANALYZE, DESCRIPTIVE STATISTICS;

2. then highlight each variable and click the arrow to move it into the variable box;

3. then click OK.

Descriptive Statistics

	N	Minimum	Maximum	Mean	Std. Deviation
Stress 1	10	1.00	4.00	2.6000	1.17379
Stress 2	10	1.00	4.00	2.6000	1.07497
Stress 3	10	2.00	4.00	2.9000	.99443
Health	10	3.00	14.00	7.7000	3.77271
Valid N (listwise)	10				

You see that you have the sample size, the minimum and maximum scores reported by your participants, the mean score of each variable, and the standard deviation of that score (i.e., the extent to which, on average, the scores differ from the mean).

Let's interpret the data. The stress score means are 2.6, 2.6, and 2.9. If a score of 2 = Sometimes and a score of 3 = Fairly Often, this means on average, participants responded they are stressed sometimes to fairly often. Our sample of college students reported a fair amount of stress! In fact, the range of responses was either 1–4 or 2–4, meaning no participants reported never experiencing stress. Our standard deviations for the stress items suggest reasonable variation in that scores varied around 1 point above and below the mean. Our health score (remember—the number of doctor's visits over the past month) mean was 7.7, meaning on average our participants visited the doctor nearly 8 times over the past month. The minimum number of visits reported was 3 and the maximum number was 14. The standard deviation was 3.77, meaning scores varied around 4 visits above and below the mean.

Reliability

Now we can examine the internal consistency reliability of our three stress items by using the Cronbach's alpha (α) statistic. To compute this statistic in SPSS,

1. Click ANALYZE, SCALE, RELIABILITY ANALYSIS;
2. then highlight each stress item and click the arrow to move it into the items box;
3. then click OK.

Reliability Statistics

Cronbach's Alpha	N of Items
.926	3

Our Cronbach's alpha (α) is .93. What does this mean? A rule of thumb for internal consistency is

$\alpha \geq 0.9$ Excellent internal consistency reliability

$0.7 \leq \alpha < 0.9$ Good internal consistency reliability

$0.6 \leq \alpha < 0.7$ Acceptable internal consistency reliability

$\alpha < 0.6$ Poor internal consistency reliability

Do our items show reasonable internal consistency reliability? Our estimate of $\alpha = .93$ means our items demonstrated excellent reliability, and we can have more confidence in the accuracy of our measure of stress.

Since our stress items have good reliability, let's combine them by adding them together.

1. Click TRANSFORM, CREATE VARIABLE;

2. Enter a name for the new variable, then in the box to the right, type sum(). Alternatively, you could get an average score by using mean(). Highlight each stress variable, use the right arrow to enter it within the parentheses. Separate each stress variable name with a comma;

3. then click OK.

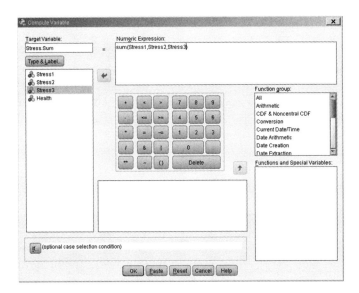

At the end of your variable spreadsheet you should see the new variable you created. In this example, this is the sum of the three stress variables.

Run a correlation analysis between stress and health. Interpret the resulting correlation.

In this example we found that $r(10) = .92$, $p < .01$. Are the two variables significantly correlated? Since this is a positive correlation, it tells you that higher stress scores (more stress) tend to co-occur with more visits to a health care provider.

Correlations

		Health	Stress.Sum
Health	Pearson Correlation	1	.915**
	Sig. (2-tailed)		.000
	N	10	10
Stress. Sum	Pearson Correlation	.915**	1
	Sig. (2-tailed)	.000	
	N	10	10

**. Correlation is significant at the 0.01 level (2-tailed).

Don't stop yet. You can investigate test-retest reliability by giving the survey to the same people at two different times and correlate the scores. Higher correlations indicate greater test-retest reliability.

How about validity? You can give your participants your measure of stress and other published measures of stress. If your survey is measuring the same construct as the other stress measures, then you should get moderate to high correlations between the score on your new survey and scores from the other already-established surveys.

In a pretend Results section, describe how a survey you created demonstrated

- Internal consistency reliability
- Test-retest reliability
- Validity

You're making up data here, so feel free to make your survey have stellar psychometric properties!

LAB 8

Descriptive and Inferential Statistics

Objective

The purpose of this lab is to refresh students' memories on the concepts of descriptive and inferential statistics, and scales of measurement. Instructions are included to produce descriptive analyses using SPSS. It introduces the concepts of statistical significance, power, and effect size. Additional information is included on effect size.

Target Article

Nathanson, R., & Saywitz, K. J. (2003). The effects of the courtroom context on children's memory and anxiety. *Journal of Psychiatry and Law, 31*(1), 67–98.

C hildren's memory seems to be sensitive to context; they remember better in familiar, more comfortable settings. This study measured the memory and anxiety level (operationalized as heart rate) of 8- to 10-year-old children in two different settings: a mock courtroom and a small, private room. Children interviewed in the courtroom had greater heart-rate variability, indicating stress, and poorer recall than children interviewed in the smaller room.

DESCRIPTIVE VERSUS INFERENTIAL STATISTICS

©iStock.com/abalcazar

We're going to look at two categories of statistical information for a set of data—descriptive and inferential. Descriptive statistics—no surprise here—describe the characteristics of a set of data. We're going to look at a measure of central tendency (the mean or the "middleness" of a set of scores) and dispersion from the mean (the extent to which scores differ from the mean). Measures of central tendency include the mean (average), median (middle score), and the mode (most frequently occurring score). Measures of dispersion include the range (lowest and highest scores) and standard deviation (extent to which, on average, scores differ from the mean). A large (relative to the mean) standard deviation indicates the scores are more widely spread out, whereas a small standard deviation tells you the scores are similar to the mean. For example, consider two sets of scores: 5, 6, 7, 14 and 7, 8, 8, 9. Both sets of scores have a mean (average) of 8, but the standard deviation for the first set is 4.08 and the standard deviation for the second set is .82. Can you see that the larger standard deviation described a set of scores with greater spread?

Inferential statistics allow us to infer something about the relation between groups or variables. They are used to determine whether group means or counts are significantly different, or whether variables are significantly related to each other. If you use the word *significant* about data, you should have some type of inferential statistics to support your claim.

SCALES OF MEASUREMENT

First, let's think about the nature of data. There are at least four types of measures: nominal, ordinal, interval, and ratio (I use the French word *noir*, the combination of the first letter of each scale, to help me remember their order). They range from categorical to continuous scores.

Nominal (categorical) data simply identify groups, and the value of the number doesn't indicate that one group is greater than or less than the others, just different. For example, you may indicate males as 0 and females as 1, or writers from states north of the Mason–Dixon line as 1 and those south as 2.

Ordinal data do indicate value (2 may be more than 1), such as people diagnosed with diabetes (for now let's indicate this as group 2) versus those with insulin resistance but not diabetes (group = 1) versus those not diagnosed with any illness (group = 0). This information doesn't produce equivalent intervals. For example, think of the health of people with type I diabetes. Those diagnosed with the full disorder (e.g., identified in your data as 2) may have more health problems than those with insulin resistance (group = 1), but there may be an even bigger difference in health between those with insulin resistance and those with no disorder (group = 0). Even though 2 > 1 and 1 > 0, the intervals between numbers aren't consistent.

Interval data do indicate value, do have equal intervals, but don't have a true 0. For these data, a score of 0 does not necessarily indicate the complete absence of whatever the scale measures. For example, if you used a scale to measure a particular personality trait, a person might score 0 on that instrument, but that doesn't necessarily mean the complete absence of that particular trait.

Ratio data indicate value, have equal intervals, and a true 0. A measure of 0 indicates the complete absence of whatever is measured. Number of children in a family could be an example of this; 0 children means the absence of children.

Table 8.1 Types of Measures

Type of Measure	Differentiate Groups?	Number Value?	Equal Intervals?	True 0?
Nominal	Yes	No	No	No
Ordinal	Yes	Yes	No	No
Interval	Yes	Yes	Yes	No
Ratio	Yes	Yes	Yes	Yes

So, what difference does it make? Because categorical data use numbers simply to establish categories rather than indicate value, one generally uses nonparametric statistics for analysis of a nominal outcome variable. An example of this is a χ^2 (chi square) analysis or logistic regression, both of which will be introduced later. Ordinal data are somewhat in between; the type of analysis you'd use would depend on things like the nature of the measure, the distribution of the responses, and the nature of the research question. For now, let's just distinguish between categorical data and continuous data, which could take on any value within a given range (e.g., height).

TRY IT YOURSELF

Canned Data

In the canned data set below, we are comparing the number of correct facts recalled by children in two different contexts. Higher numbers indicate greater correct recall. Children's recall was assessed under two different conditions, once in the courtroom and once in a small, informal room. Good design requires that the order in which each child was tested be counterbalanced. That means that some children were tested first in the courtroom followed by the small room, whereas others began in the small room and moved to the courtroom. Notice, however, that each child was tested in both conditions. We could have tested different children in the two settings; in this case we opted to test the same children twice.

FYI

Note that all "canned" data sets in this lab manual were made up by the authors, and did not come from the study described in the target article (or any other published source). Don't assume the findings represent current thinking about a given research question.

Setting up the SPSS Data File

Note that the instructions and illustrations for SPSS are from version 21. Different versions may not look like the illustrations here. *Setting up the SPSS Data File*

1. Open SPSS. You'll see a box that asks, "What would you like to do?"

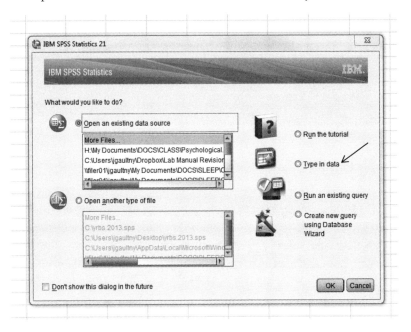

2. Click *Type in Data*

3. and *OK*. Now you have a blank spreadsheet.

4. Let's start by labeling the variables. In the bottom left corner, click the tab that says *Variable View*. Next to the number 1, enter *grade* followed by *courtroom* for 2, then, *small_room* next to the number 3. SPSS accepts variable names that begin with a letter and that have no spaces. You can separate words with a period or an underscore.

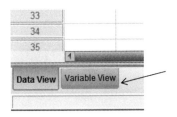

5.

	Name	Label	Values
1	Grade	Grade in school	
2	Courtroom	Children's memory in courtroom setting	
3	Small_room	Children's memory in small-room setting	

6. Just so I'll remember later, I enter a description of each variable under *label*. That way I'll know exactly what I meant by each variable name. It also helps you interpret the output of SPSS as you'll see below. Click the right side of the *Value label* box. Use the dropdown menu to identify 1 as Grade 1, and 4 as Grade 4.

You can ignore the other columns for now.

7. Now click the tab at the bottom that says *Data View*. Type in these numbers:

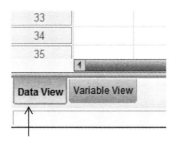

Grade	Courtroom	Small_room
1	15	14
1	12	13
1	9	10
1	3	4
1	6	5
1	12	14

(Continued)

(Continued)

Grade	Courtroom	Small_room
1	10	10
1	8	10
1	4	6
1	17	19
4	6	8
4	8	6
4	2	3
4	9	10
4	14	15
4	21	22
4	5	7
4	3	4
4	8	8
4	9	11

Save your file. In my experience, you can never save your data too often!

1. Save by clicking *File* in the top left corner,

2. then *Save As*.

3. Specify the drive and file name you want, then click *Save*. Thereafter, you can simply click *Save* or the save icon, if you'd like to complete the process more quickly.

Finding Descriptive Statistics

Now we'll use descriptive statistics to get an idea of the characteristics of our data.

1. Click on *Analyze*

2. *Descriptive Statistics*

3. *Descriptives*

4. Move the courtroom and small_room variables into the *Variable* box by highlighting each and clicking the arrow to the right.

5. When they have both been moved, click *OK*. This will produce the following information:

Descriptive Statistics

	N	Minimum	Maximum	Mean	Std. Deviation
children's memory in courtroom setting	20	2.00	21.00	9.0500	4.97864
children's memory in small room setting	20	3.00	22.00	9.9500	5.06250
Valid N (listwise)	20				

The descriptive data above are for the entire sample; it doesn't separate out the two grade groups. See how, instead of the somewhat cryptic variable name, SPSS has provided the label for that variable? This is the information I typed in under the *label* column in variable view. From this table we know the sample size (N), the smallest and largest values for each variable (the range), along with its mean and standard deviation. Recall that the standard deviation is the extent to which, on average, the scores differ from the mean. Large (relative to the mean) standard deviations indicate more spread in the scores; small (relative to the mean) deviations indicate less spread. It is easier to compare two means when their standard deviations are similar.

Let's find out how many children I have in each grade. Follow steps 1 and 2 above, then click *Frequencies*. Move *grade* into the *Variable* box. *OK*.

Grade

		Frequency	*Percent*	Valid Percent	Cumulative Percent
	1	10	50.0	50.0	50.0
Valid	4	10	50.0	50.0	100.0
Total		20	100.0	100.0	

Although it would be easy enough to count how many are in each grade in this small sample, imagine how useful this statistic would be if you had 1,000 participants in your data!

There may be times when you want to run both Descriptives and Frequencies since they give you different information (descriptive vs. count).

Eyeball the data. Examining descriptive information allows you to eyeball the data to ensure the range, mean, and standard deviation values are reasonable. For example, what if the maximum recall value for children in the courtroom setting was 222? This would suggest you either have an outlier value, or you made an error in entering data (more likely). Or, what if your standard deviation for children's memory in the small room setting was .002? This would suggest that everyone in your sample reported nearly the exact same recall in this condition. This may suggest a problem with methodology or an error in data entry that the researcher will need to go back and evaluate before drawing conclusions based on these data. Eyeballing your data throughout the statistical process ensures "checkpoints" for accurate data entry and analyses.

Inferential Statistics

Now, we know that the two settings produced different average recall, but how do we know if they are different enough to say that one setting prompted better (significantly greater) recall? So far we *don't* know, and can't make any statements about whether the differences are significant. In order to do that, we must make use of the other statistical category: inferential statistics. Without inferential statistics, all you have is your subjective opinion. Begin this section by reviewing the tutorial at http://www.wadsworth.com/psychology_d/templates/ student_resources/workshops/stat_workshp/hypth_test/hypth_test_01.html.

We'll get into more details about two-group comparisons in a later lab. For now, just follow these instructions.

1. Click *Analyze*

2. *Compare Means*

3. *Paired-Samples T-Test*

4. Click *both* variables (you may need to use ctrl click to get them both highlighted) *then* the right arrow to move them into the *Paired Variables* box.

5. Click *OK*. Your output will look like this:

T-Test

Paired Samples Statistics

		Mean	N	Std. Deviation	Std. Error Mean
Pair 1	children's recall in courtroom setting	9.0500	20	4.97864	1.11326
	children's recall in small room setting	9.9500	20	5.06250	1.13201

Paired Samples Correlations

		N	Correlation	Sig.
Pair 1	children's recall in courtroom setting & children's recall in small room setting	20	.973	.000

Paired Samples Test

		Paired Differences					t	df	Sig. (2-tailed)
					95% Confidence Interval of the Difference				
		Mean	Std. Deviation	Std. Error Mean	Lower	Upper			
Pair 1	children's recall in courtroom setting - children's recall in small room setting	-.90000	1.16529	.26057	-1.44537	-.35463	-3.454	19	.003

You got a recap of some of the descriptive information, followed by the correlation of our two variables. We'll get to correlations in a later lab.

Eyeball the data. Glance at the descriptive information to make sure you have the same values as before. This ensures you have chosen the correct variables.

The paired samples *t*-test shows that the difference between the two means is significant, $t(19) = -3.45, p = .003$. How do I know the difference is significant? Look in the last cell that is labeled *Sig. (2-tailed)*. If this value is less than .05, then I can say the difference between the means is significant. We now know that the difference is significant, but in order to know which condition was associated with greater recall, we'll have to look back at the descriptive statistics to see which mean was higher. When you report this information, you'll include both the descriptive and inferential statistics.

Statistical Significance

Inferential statistics allow you to speculate about what is true in a population based on data generated by a sample. Although we can look at whichever statistic we are using, at what point is the difference/change/association/ prediction big enough to be statistically meaningful? That's a tricky question, because the answer is "It depends." When you run inferential statistics in SPSS, the output will give you a significance level as well as the value of the statistic (in the example above look under the column labeled *Sig. 2-tailed*). Traditionally, science has accepted a cut-off level of significance of $p < .05$. When p is $< .05$ you can declare the statistic to be "significant."

$$!! \frown !!$$
$$-.07-.06-\mathbf{.05}-.04-.03-$$

What is so special about .05? What does $p < .05$ tell us? It means that you are taking less than a 5% chance of making a type I error (see next section). This has generally come to be considered a reasonable compromise between risk for type I and type II error. There's nothing statistically magical about .05; it doesn't guarantee your decision will be correct. Once you make the call of significant or not, there are two possibilities; either you were correct (your sample accurately reflected the population) or you were wrong (sample was misleading). Of course, you usually can't measure everyone in a population, so you might never really know if you were right or not. If you are wrong, you made one of two types of error called type I and type II error.

When Good Statistics Go Bad

You may remember from a statistics course that an experimental analysis starts with a null hypothesis (there will be no change, no difference, no association . . . nothing here to see, folks . . .). You then propose an experimental hypothesis (there *will* be a change, difference, association, etc.). When you use inferential statistics, you are actually testing whether you can *support the null hypothesis* rather than *testing the experimental hypothesis* (the reason has to do with conditional logic).

Type I error occurs when there really *is no difference in the population* (null hypothesis is correct) but, based on your sample, you decide to declare the population means are probably different. In that case, you'd be wrong because you went with the experimental hypothesis when, in fact, the null hypothesis was correct. For example, assume that in reality there's not a gender difference in memory ability, but because the value for a particular sample reached statistical significance, I decided that such a difference existed. I made a type I error.

Type II error occurs when there really *is a difference* in the population (null hypothesis is not correct) but, based on the sample, you decide to declare there is not a difference. In that case, you'd be wrong because you voted in favor of the null hypothesis. For example, in reality, older children remember longer strings of random numbers than do younger children, but because my statistic did not reach statistical significance, I decided that no such age difference existed. I made a type II error.

Think of a seesaw with type I error sitting on one end and type II error sitting on the other end. If you *decrease* your chance of making a type I error (by insisting on a smaller level of significance, like $p < .001$ rather than $p < .05$), you *increase* your chance of making a type II error. If you try to minimize your chance of type II error (by accepting a value for p greater than .05), chance of type I error goes up. As a rule of thumb, you should be more concerned about making a type I error, but that is not a hard rule. It may depend on the consequences of your decision.

Figure 8.1 Type I and Type II Errors and Level of Significance

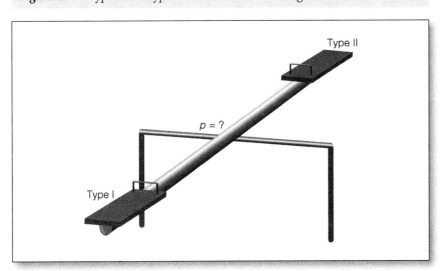

SOURCE: publicdomainvectors.org

Power

You may have come across studies that have examined the same topic, in which one study found that the independent variable (IV) made a significant difference while the other study found no effect of the IV. The results are contradictory. Why is this? One reason may be that the study that found no effect didn't have enough participants or used a weaker design. Large samples and within subjects designs (we'll define this in a later lab) have greater statistical "power." Power refers to the probability of correctly rejecting the null hypothesis. In other words, it is the probability that you were right when you decided, based on your sample, that the IV did produce a significant difference in the population.

So . . . what difference does power make to you? You want to give your experimental hypothesis a good chance of being supported, so you maximize the possibility that your statistical finding is significant. One way is to use a larger sample size. There are formulas and tables that can tell you how many participants you'll need to achieve a given power level—I'll leave the details for your statistics class. When you have a choice, go for a larger rather than a smaller sample size. Another way to increase power is to use a research design that minimizes the potential for error. More on this later.

Effect Size

Some statisticians think that, rather than basing your decision on the *p* value (since this is very influenced by sample size), you should look at the effect size instead. We know that a *p* value provides you information about the statistical significance of an effect, and that a larger sample size increases the likelihood of detecting significance. But what is an effect size, exactly? An effect size is a quantitative (i.e., a numerical value) measure of the strength of a phenomenon of interest. We can choose different types of analyses (such as group mean comparisons or correlations) to provide answers to different types of questions, and thus provide different measures of effect size. For example, in the lab exercise above, our *p* value tells us that our groups significantly differ, but by how much do they differ? An effect size tells us the strength or size of the effect. For a two-group comparison, one can use group means and standard deviations in a statistical formula to calculate an effect size called Cohen's *d*, and the strength of this value can be roughly categorized as a small, medium, or large effect size. Different statistical tests call for different ways of indicating effect size. While we won't go into detail here (see the additional material below for greater discussion and practice on this topic), be aware that it's important to report both p values and effect sizes in your research; this provides information on both the statistical significance of your results, as well as the strength or magnitude of the effect.

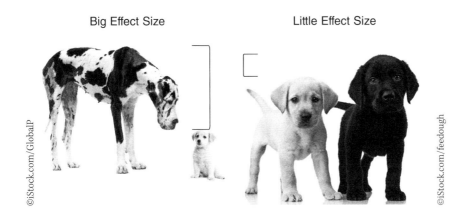

Big Effect Size   Little Effect Size

©iStock.com/GlobalP

©iStock.com/feedough

CLOSURE

Reviewing what you've learned, answer the following questions:

1. Why do researchers use inferential statistics? Why can't you look at two means, see that they are different, and decide that the difference is significant?

2. What do you know about the difference between two means when p is less than .05?

3. Why do most scientists use $p < .05$ (instead of some other value) as the criterion to determine significance?

4. How does the p value relate to type I and type II error?

5. What is statistical power?

6. What is an effect size?

The answers to these questions are given at the end of the lab, but try to answer them on your own.

IF YOU WANT TO GO FURTHER . . .

More About Effect Size

Increasingly large effect sizes . . .

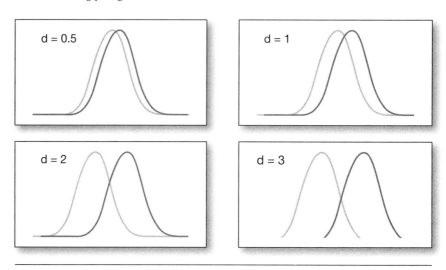

SOURCE: © Skbkekas / Wikimedia

There is a movement within health care to integrate care of both mental and physical health. Traditionally, physical and mental disorders have been treated in isolation from each other, reflecting a tendency to think of mind and body as separable (blame it on Descartes, a 17th century philosopher). More and more, however, we are coming to understand—or at least respect—mind–body interactions. What you think or your mental state might be able to heal or hurt you. Also, physical illness or disorder can have mental consequences. Dr. Ronald Levant, president of the APA at the time of this writing, called for more integration of health care,[1] in which one treats the whole person rather than just the body or the mind. In this scenario, physicians and psychologists would work together to treat patients. Psychological interventions would be used along with traditional (and perhaps nontraditional) health-care approaches to treat illness and injury. For example, relaxation techniques have been used to counteract the deleterious effects of stress hormones in conditions such as hypertension, depression, and insomnia.[2]

[1]http://www.apa.org/monitor/may05/pc.html

[2]http://www.apa.org/monitor/may05/physician.html

Is there a distinction between *statistically significant* differences and the *size* of the differences? In other words, is the significance level produced by an analysis a good measure to use to decide if something has real-world importance? Is a significance level of .001 necessarily better than a level of .04? In this lab, you will learn about the rationale for reporting effect sizes.

©iStock.com/kieferpix

Here's an article from the literature of mind–body health you could use to see an example of how an effect size is reported and interpreted. Note two things in the article cited below. First, notice how writing was used to manage physical pain in women with fibromyalgia. Second, notice how the authors put the significant group differences in perspective by including estimates of effect size.

Broderick, J. E., Junghaenel, D. U., & Schwartz, J. E. (2005). Written emotional expression produces health benefits in fibromyalgia patients. *Psychosomatic Medicine, 67*(2), 326–334. doi:10.1097/01.psy.0000156933.04566.bd

Writing about traumatic experiences has been successfully used in the past to improve health outcomes associated with several disorders such as rheumatoid arthritis, asthma, and breast cancer. The study cited here was intended to determine whether writing could improve psychological and physical well-being among women with fibromyalgia, a disorder associated with chronic pain and fatigue. Ninety-two women were randomly assigned to one of three groups—a "trauma-writing" group, a control-writing group, or a group that received standard treatment. Trauma writing refers to an emotional recounting of personal traumatic experiences. The control-writing group wrote about day-to-day activities. Psychological well-being, pain, and fatigue were assessed at four points in time: prior to receiving treatment, posttreatment, four months later, and 10 months later. Significant reductions in pain (effect size = .49), fatigue (effect size = .62), and improved psychological well-being (effect size = .47) were found at the four-month follow-up visit, but not at the 10-month follow-up. Trauma writing produced at least short-term gains in both psychological and physical outcomes.

For more information on fibromyalgia, see the following websites:

http://www.niams.nih.gov/Health_Info/Fibromyalgia/

http://www.mayoclinic.org/diseases-conditions/fibromyalgia/basics/definition/con-20019243?_ga=1.124954575.436922376.1414513651

Consideration of effect size is increasingly regarded as important by editors and reviewers. Whether or not you find group differences or relationships to be significant is partially driven by sample size. Let's say I want to know if delaying the start of high school until 9:00 a.m. (allowing adolescents to sleep longer in the morning) would improve academic performance. Perhaps I compared before and after academic performance at schools across the country that switched from a 7:00 a.m. start time to 9:00 a.m. If my sample is large enough, even very small differences between the scores would be significant, but how can I tell if the difference is big enough to be meaningful? Sometimes the results of studies are used as the basis of social changes or policies that affect many lives. You might not want to draw a conclusion about, for example, the effects of a particular early intervention program on IQ on the basis of a statistically significant but very tiny group difference. If the early intervention program raised IQ scores by ½ point, is that a big enough improvement to justify spending millions of dollars and years of time on this program? One way to evaluate this is to include a measure of effect size in our analysis. Effect size is an estimate of the magnitude of differences between means in terms of standard deviations or proportions of variance explained.

In the target article, effect size was calculated using two methods, a *d* score as well as a more conservative estimate. The estimates of effect size indicated that not only did trauma writing produce a statistically significant change, the change was large, making it more likely that it produced a meaningful change. If you were deciding whether to make this part of the standard treatment of fibromyalgia, then you would have a good basis for including it.

TYPES OF EFFECT SIZE STATISTICS

There are several different measures of effect size, such as the *r*-Family, and various members of the *d*-Family. To compare the relative merits of these measures is not our goal (a type of analysis that will be covered in a later lab). Instead, let's think about a few types of effect size measures you may come across.

For example, with a correlation, you can square the *r* for an estimate of effect size. Let's say you ran a correlation and found that $r = -.685$. Square the *r* and you have $r^2 = .47$. For correlations, a rule of thumb is .10 is small, .3 is moderate, and .5 is large. On a *t*-test, SPSS provides you with confidence intervals for the mean difference between the two variables or groups. The confidence interval tells you the probability that the difference between the two population means falls between two values. For example, let's say your sample means are 102.57 for the control group and 130 for the experimental group. The group means differ from each other by 27.43. Remember $p < .05$ means less than a 5% chance of a type 1 error; therefore there is $> 95\%$ chance of being correct. If the 95% confidence interval is 23.23 and 31.63, we know that there is a 95% probability that the actual difference between the population means lies somewhere between 23.23 and 31.63.

You may wish to learn to calculate Cohen's d from SPSS output since it is a widely reported measure of effect size for a two-group design.

$$d = \frac{\text{mean for group 1} - \text{mean for group 2}}{\text{square root of [(squared standard deviation for group 1 +}}$$
$$\text{squared standard deviation for group 2)/2]}$$

Let's say you have found a significant difference between the means of two groups having the following values:

	Mean	Standard Deviation
Group 1	10.9	2.36
Group 2	9.8	2.82

$$d = \frac{10.9 - 9.8}{\text{square root of } [2.36^2 + 2.82^2/2]}$$

$$d = \frac{1.1}{\text{square root of } [5.57 + 7.95/2]}$$

$$d = \frac{1.1}{\text{square root of } [6.76]}$$

$$d = \frac{1.1}{2.6} = .42$$

Calculate the effect size for the following values:

Group Statistics

	group	N	Mean	Std. Deviation	Std. Error Mean
ontask	meds	10	186.0000	32.27658	10.20675
	no meds	10	159.7000	32.02447	10.12703

$d =$ _____ (see the answer key at the end of the chapter to check your work)

HOW BIG IS BIG ENOUGH?

So, is an effect size of .489 high? Low? Midway? This would generally be considered a moderate to high effect size. A somewhat arbitrary but widely used rule of thumb for Cohen's d is that .2 is small, .5 is moderate, and .8 is large. Effect sizes in social sciences tend to be low, depending on the nature of the dependent variable (DV). Anything above 0 may be worth talking about, although don't put too much weight on values under .05, whereas a value of .10 may be noteworthy. Look back at the effect sizes reported in the Broderick et al. (2005) article. Did trauma writing have a small effect or a medium-to-large effect?

TO SUMMARIZE

Just because something is statistically significant doesn't necessarily mean it has practical significance. The effect size is a step in deciding how important the difference is, but in the end the effect size has to be interpreted using professional knowledge, judgment, and logic. Just because an effect size is small does not necessarily mean that the finding is worthless. There are no hard and fast rules. A small effect size in a large population may make a difference for many people. For example, an immunization that prevents a disease in a small percentage of people may nonetheless improve health in thousands of people. According to Kathleen McCartney and Robert Rosenthal (2000, p. 175), "There are no easy conventions for determining practical importance. Just as children are best understood in context, so are effect sizes." This is one of those times when your computer can't tell you how to interpret your data.

McCartney, K., & Rosenthal, R. (2000). Effect size, practical importance, and social policy for children. *Child Development, 71,* 173–180. doi:10.1111/1467-8624.00131

Apply What You've Learned

Now that you've been introduced to the concept of effect size, look for another article that reports effect size. One suggestion from a journal likely to be widely available is . . .

Kalman, D., Lee, A., Chan, E., Miller, D. R., Spiro, A., III, Ren, X. S., & Kazis, L. E. (2004). Alcohol dependence, other psychiatric disorders, and health-related quality of life: A replication study in a large random sample of enrollees in the Veterans Health Administration. *American Journal of Drug and Alcohol Abuse, 30*(2), 473–486. doi:10.1081/ADA-120037389

. . . but try to find an article from a journal within your discipline. Go to an academic search engine and type in *effect size and* _____. Fill in the blank with the topic of your project or any other topic that interests you. For example, my research area is sleep, so I typed in *effect size and sleep* and found multiple entries. You will need to choose an article from a source available in your library or available full text on line. Alternatively, your instructor may direct you to a specific article to use.

Read the article, then briefly describe the purpose and findings of the research, including the effect size (pick one if there are many).

Which statistic was used to estimate effect size?

What did the effect size tell you about the results?

Be the Consultant

Let's pretend you are a highly regarded researcher in the area of family studies or public policy. You have been asked to address a policy-making body on the advisability of implementing an intervention program in which unemployed parents are provided with parenting classes in hopes that this program will raise the school-readiness scores of their preschool children. In general, the results of studies of this program have produced statistically significant results, showing improved school-readiness scores. You did a meta-analysis of many studies on the topic and found an average effect size of .25. What

advice would you tell the policy makers about implementing this program on a wide-spread basis? Explain your recommendation. Remember, you have to use your best judgment on a conclusion—there aren't hard and fast rules.
What would you have advised (and why) had the effect size been .03?

REVIEWING WHAT YOU'VE LEARNED: ANSWER KEY

1. Why do researchers use inferential statistics? Why can't you look at two means, see that they are different, and decide that the difference is significant?

   The researcher (who can't help but be biased to some extent) doesn't get to make a subjective call on whether data from the sample were strong enough to make a decision about a population. Inferential statistics are a way to objectively make the decision of whether a null hypothesis is supported or not.

2. What do you know about the difference between two means when p is less than .05?

   The chance of making a type I error is < 5% (or you could say that the finding falls within the 95th percentile confidence intervals).

3. Why do most scientists use $p < .05$ (instead of some other value) as the criterion to determine significance?

   A p value of .05 is used because of convention, the need to make a conservative decision, and concern about avoiding a type I error.

4. How does the p value relate to type I and type II error?

   As chances of making one type of error goes up, the other goes down. A higher p value ($p < .10$, for example) will decrease chance of type II error but increase the chance of a type I error. Likewise, you can decrease chances of making a type I error by accepting a lower p value ($p < .01$, for example), but this will raise the chance of type II error.

5. What is statistical power?

Power refers to the probability of correctly rejecting the null hypothesis.

6. What is an effect size?

An effect size is a quantitative (i.e., a numerical value) measure of the strength of a phenomenon.

Group Statistics

	group	N	Mean	Std. Deviation	Std. Error Mean
ontask	meds	10	186.0000	32.27658	10.20675
	no meds	10	159.7000	32.02447	10.12703

Answer Key

Calculate the effect size for the following values:

$d =$ _____.82_____

LAB 9

Correlational Design

Objective

This lab introduces correlational designs and explores analysis and interpretation of these designs. Additional material is included on statistically controlling covariates and the concept of partial correlations.

Target Article

Cavallo, A., Ris, M. D., & Succop, P. (2003). The night float paradigm to decrease sleep deprivation: Good solution or a new problem? *Ergonomics,46(7),*653–663.doi:10.1080/0014013031000085671

This study examined the impact of a "night float rotation" on the sleep, mood, and performance of medical residents. Night float rotation is a work schedule in which the individual works at night but has no daytime duties (as compared to being on duty for, say, 24 hours at a time). Even though the residents had enough time during the day to sleep, they got fewer hours of sleep than they did while on a typical daytime rotation. Measures of fatigue during the night float rotation were correlated with measures of attention. Greater sleepiness was associated with more errors of attention.

EXPERIMENTAL VERSUS NON-EXPERIMENTAL

The next few labs can be divided into two groups: non-experimental methods and experimental methods. What is the difference between the two? Experimental studies use random assignment to groups and have an independent variable (IV) that is manipulated. Some research questions simply can't be studied using an experimental design, so a non-experimental one is chosen. Correlation designs are usually non-experimental. Regression, two-group, three-group, and factorial designs may be experimental if random assignment to groups is used, but the designs can also be used for quasi-experimental research in which random assignment to groups is not possible. One type of quasi-experimental design is an ex post facto or non-equivalent groups design in which some participant characteristic is used as an IV. In this situation, the design looks like a duck (my analogy here for an experimental design) and quacks like a duck, but isn't actually a duck. For example, if you want to look at gender differences in access to health care, you don't get to randomly assign participants to the male or female group; they come to you already in one group or the other. In that case, the data collection and analysis are the same as an experimental design. The difference comes in your interpretation of the findings. When you can't use random assignment to groups, your findings are shakier. You have not demonstrated cause and effect and need to proceed cautiously in your conclusions.

©iStock.com/geotrac

In this lab, we'll look at non-experimental correlational designs. This is appropriate to use when your hypothesis predicts an association between variables (the rank orders of the scores vary in some systematic way relative to each other). Do high scores on one variable tend to co-occur with high or low scores on another variable? There is no IV or DV—just two variables to compare. A correlation is reported as r and can vary from -1.00 to 1.00. The closer to 0, the less relationship there is between the two variables. The closer to -1 or 1, the stronger the correlation.

A positive correlation means that high scores on one variable go with high scores on the other variable . . .

. . . and a negative correlation means that high scores on one variable are associated with low scores on the other variable.

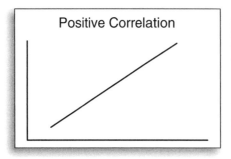

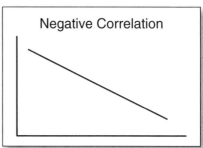

TRY IT YOURSELF

Do Sleepier People Have More Accidents at Work?

Impaired attention could cause more accidents and errors when working. For this lab, we're going to examine the relation (or association) between average hours of sleep and number of accidents on the job. We're going to compare the rank-ordering of these two variables. We won't be comparing group means. We want to know if the rank ordering varies in a systematic way. We are predicting that people who get the most sleep tend to have the fewest accidents. To do this, we will measure two variables—amount of sleep and number of accidents—for each participant and then correlate the variables.

©iStock.com/RTimages

You will set up a data file, run and interpret a correlation analysis, and write a short Results section for the analysis.

First of all, let's review the use of correlation designs and the correlation statistic. Read the tutorial at http://www.wadsworth.com/psychology_d/templates/student_resources/workshops/stat_workshp/correlation/correlation_01.html. Now go to http://www.stat.berkeley.edu/~stark/Java/Html/Correlation.htm to review what scatter plots for positive and negative, strong and weak correlations look like. Click the regression line button to see the linear association of two variables. At the top of the figure, play around with correlations close to 0 (e.g., .08) and ones that are larger (e.g., .80). Try positive and negative correlations.

Canned Data

Entering and Analyzing the Data

Enter and save the following data into SPSS. The variable labeled *Avg_slp* is the average hours slept at night and *Accidents* indicates the number of accidents over the previous 12 months. Higher numbers indicate more sleep and more accidents, respectively.

Avg_slp	Accidents
7.00	2.00
6.00	4.00
4.00	3.00
7.00	3.00
4.00	6.00
5.00	6.00
4.00	7.00
9.00	2.00
9.00	4.00
8.00	3.00
7.00	4.00
4.00	5.00
6.00	3.00
9.00	1.00
8.00	2.00
5.00	5.00
6.00	4.00
8.00	5.00
5.00	6.00
7.00	6.00

Eyeball the data. Run descriptive and frequency analyses for your variables then check to make sure everything looks the way you expected it. When you are sure your data are accurate, proceed.

Run the correlational analysis.

1. Click *Analyze*

2. *Correlate*

3. *Bivariate*

4. Highlight the names of the two variables and click the arrow to the right to move them into the *Variable* box.

5. Now click *OK*.

Your output should look like this:

Correlations

		AVG_SLP	ACCIDENT
AVG_SLP	Pearson Correlation	1	-.634**
	Sig. (2-tailed)	.	.003
	N	20	20
ACCIDENT	Pearson Correlation	-.634**	1
	Sig. (2-tailed)	.003	.
	N	20	20

**. Correlation is significant at the 0.01 level (2-tailed).

Notice that we are using the Pearson correlation. This is used when both variables are interval or ratio scale measures. There are other measures that can be used when one or both variables use another scale.

The correlation between hours slept and number of accidents is −.634, the sample size was 20, and the significance level is .003. Is this a significant correlation? ____ The fact that it is negative means that people who get more sleep have _____ (more or fewer) accidents. _____ Does this support our prediction? ____ [yes, fewer, yes]

If you'd like to see a scatterplot of the data, go to Graphs, Legacy, Scatterplot*. Put average sleep on the *x*-axis and number of accidents on the *y*-axis.

* The wording may be slightly different depending on the version of SPSS being used.

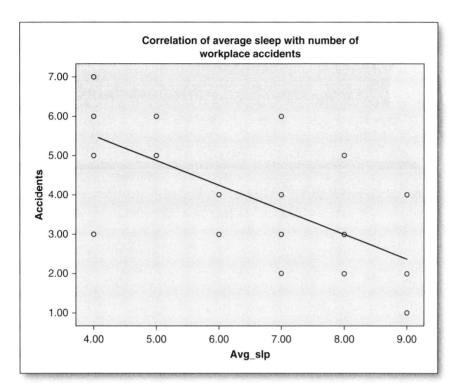

I've added the diagonal line so you can visualize the correlation.

Reporting the Results

Now we're going to write a very short Results section about these data. Since this may be your first try at a Results section, I'll give you an example. I'm going to round the value of the correlation.

Results

The average hours slept by participants were correlated with the number of accidents they had reported during the previous 12 months. The two variables were significantly correlated, $r(20) = -.634$, $p = .003$, indicating that participants who averaged more hours of sleep at night tended to have fewer accidents.

Notice several things here. You told the reader what statistic was used, what the variables were, and that they were significantly correlated, then you backed that up by reporting the statistics. The *r* and *p* are both lower case and italicized, and the sample size is indicated after the *r*. Finally, you helped the reader understand what the significant statistic meant.

What can we conclude based on these data? We can claim only that less sleep is associated with a higher accident rate. We don't know if lack of sleep *caused* the accident, if being accident-prone *caused* less sleep, or if they are really not connected with each other, but rather there is some other factor causing both of them. We can't speculate on cause based on these data.

Now . . . close this lab manual, look at the SPSS output, and write a short Results section. When you are done, compare what you wrote to the example above. Did you include all the relevant information? Did you report the statistics using proper format? Did you explain the correlation to the reader? Make corrections if needed. I'm not worried about plagiarism here; it's OK if your corrected writing is similar to what is modeled here. DO TRY to write this on your own, however; the day is coming when you will be expected to know how to do this without a model.

IF YOU WANT TO COLLECT YOUR OWN DATA . . .

If you'd like to analyze data generated by your class, you could collect data on the association of sleep duration and academic performance. You can use the chart below to keep track of how much time participants slept the night before an exam (perhaps all those in your class who are willing to contribute data can serve as participants). The two variables correlated will be number of hours slept and grade on the exam. What would you predict about a correlation between these two variables? Let's say you hypothesize that people who report more sleep the night before an exam will have a higher grade on the exam. Bear in mind that staying up at night to cram for a test is not a productive study strategy for at least two reasons. We know that distributed practice (smaller study sessions over several study periods) produces better recall than does massed practice (one intensive study session), and sleep deprivation may decrease your ability to do things like encode and consolidate new material, recall, pay attention, solve problems, organize your thoughts, and so on. Alternatively, it is possible that people who tend to skimp on sleep use poor study practices in general!

Hours slept the night before the exam: _____

Grade in exam: _____

Now you need to include your data with that of your other classmates. Pass around a spreadsheet and have everyone (anonymously) fill in their numbers or data they collected from others. Enter these data into an SPSS file and analyze as described above.

	Hours slept	Grade
Person 1	_____	_____
Person 2	_____	_____
Person 3	_____	_____

. . . and so on.

Notice that we aren't trying to demonstrate that one variable caused the other. We're just comparing rank order to see if two things co-occur in a discernible pattern.

Closure

Correlations do

1. compare the nature of association between two variables, indicating whether or not there is a relation.

2. indicate whether the relationship is strong, weak, or non-existent, and whether the factors measured vary in the same direction (positive correlations) or opposite directions (negative correlations).

Correlations do not

1. compare group means.

2. have an IV or DV.

3. indicate cause and effect. Variable A *may* have caused variable B, but it is just as possible that variable B caused variable A, or that there is some other variable, C, out there that is causing both A and B. We can't tell on the basis of the correlation.

IF YOU WANT TO GO FURTHER...

Partial Correlations

As stated above, we know that a correlation between variables A and B does not necessarily equal causation, and it is possible that a variable C may in fact be causing both A and B. What can you do with your statistical analysis when you know some extraneous variable may be responsible for a correlation between A and B? You can control those extraneous variables statistically by measuring them and entering them into your analysis as covariates. For the moment, we'll talk about covariates in correlation since that is the analysis du jour. Before we go further, let's note that it is better to control extraneous variables using design rather than statistics, but sometimes statistical control is your best option.

Pretend you found a significant correlation between ice cream consumption and murder rates—does this mean eating ice cream is related somehow to committing murder? Absolutely not. There could be a confounding variable, *hot temperature*, that is associated with both variables. Higher temperatures are associated with more ice cream eating (yum!) and more aggressive behaviors leading to homicides (not cool). If I correlated ice cream consumption and murder rates, I might get a significant correlation. However, this would be misleading, because ice cream and murder are not directly related. Instead, both are a byproduct of hot weather. If a partial correlation was analyzed controlling for temperature, the significant association between ice cream and murder rates would likely disappear.

Let's say I am interested in examining the relationship between sleep quality and body mass index (BMI)—I first want to know if a relationship exists before I jumpstart a research project looking at poor sleep quality as a risk factor for obesity. Research has repeatedly shown associations between lower sleep quality and greater BMI (Cappuccio et. al., 2008); however, studies have also shown that depression is related to both higher BMI (e.g., Johnston, Johnson, McLeod, & Johnston, 2004) and worse sleep quality (e.g., Alvaro, Roberts, & Harris, 2013). How then can we know if sleep quality and BMI have a *unique* association, *above and beyond* shared relations with depression? In other words, we want to know if sleep and BMI are correlated even when we control for depression.

This is a common scenario in scientific studies, where researchers want to *control covariates*. A covariate is a third (or more) variable that can

©iStock.com/cheische

affect the relationship between two other variables of interest—let's call this our variable C. If we can separate out the **covariance** (how much the variables vary in a corresponding manner) of variable C from variables A and B, we can leave behind only the covariance of variables A and B. This can tell us if there is still a relationship left behind between variables A and B once we've controlled or accounted for variable C. See the figure below; if we can completely remove the association with depression, we are left with the *partial correlation* between sleep and BMI.

Figure 9.1   Partial Correlations

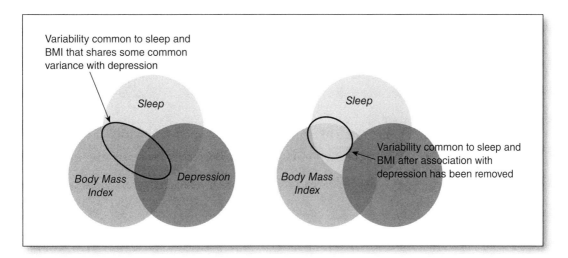

We can test our hypothesis that sleep and BMI are associated even after completely controlling for depression by calculating a partial correlation using SPSS. Let's pretend we've measured self-reported quality of sleep per night, BMI using the standard formula (which can range from > 15 to < 40 kg/m²), and depression (on a scale of 0–30). Higher scores indicate better sleep quality, greater BMI, and more depressive symptoms. Enter and save the data below in SPSS.

Sleep	BMI	Depress
10	17	9
8	18	8

(Continued)

(Continued)

Sleep	BMI	Depress
7	26	13
9	21	9
9	19	8
8	25	5
6	33	17
5	34	22
11	16	4
7	24	12
10	18.5	8
5	35	14
7	26.6	15
6	32	14
9	20	7
5	40	21
8	17.5	11
9	22	10
7	16.5	13
10	18	9

As always, **eyeball the data.**

Once the data are entered, run descriptive and frequency analyses for your variables, then check to make sure everything looks the way you expected it. When you are sure your data are accurate, proceed.

Let's first run the correlational analysis (do you remember how?) to see if all three variables are significantly correlated with each other. Review instructions from earlier in the lab for running a bivariate correlation, but this time choose all three variables. The bivariate correlation (that includes no covariates) is also called the *zero-order* correlation.

Your output should look like this:

Correlations

		Sleep	BMI	Depress
Sleep	Pearson Correlation	1	-.864**	-.856**
	Sig. (2-tailed)		.000	.000
	N	20	20	20
BMI	Pearson Correlation	-.864**	1	.802**
	Sig. (2-tailed)	.000		.000
	N	20	20	20
Depress	Pearson Correlation	-.856**	.802**	1
	Sig. (2-tailed)	.000	.000	
	N	20	20	20

**. Correlation is significant at the 0.01 level (2-tailed).

Are the correlations significant? Yes—we see sleep quality is strongly correlated with both BMI [$r(20) = -.86$, $p < .001$] and depression [$r(20) = -.86$, $p < .001$], and depression and BMI are also strongly correlated [$r(20) = .80$, $p < .001$]. Now what happens if we control for depression (i.e., take away any covariation it has with the two variables of interest) using a partial correlation?

Run the partial correlational analysis.

1. Click *Analyze*

2. *Correlate*

3. *Partial*

4. Highlight the names of the two variables of interest (Sleep quality and BMI) and click the arrow to the top right to move them into the *Variables* box.

5. Highlight the name of the variable we want to control for (Depression) and click the arrow to the bottom right to move it to the *Controlling for:* box.

6. Now click *OK*.

Your output should look like this:

Correlations

Control Variables			Sleep	BMI
Depress	Sleep	Correlation	1.000	-.574
		Significance (2-tailed)	.	.010
		df	0	17
	BMI	Correlation	-.574	1.000
		Significance (2-tailed)	.010	.
		df	17	0

Think about the following questions (no peeking at the answers until you've given them a shot!):

1. Is the partial correlation still significant?

2. What does this information tell you about the relationship between sleep quality and BMI?

3. If the partial correlation had <u>not</u> been significant, what could we conclude?

ANSWERS

1. Is the partial correlation still significant?

Yes.

2. What does this information tell you about the relationship between sleep quality and BMI?

Sleep quality and BMI are related above and beyond associations with depression, meaning the relationship is not solely due to the statistical influence of depression. While the partial correlation does not imply cause and effect, it provides evidence that a relationship may exist that is not due to a confounding effect of a third variable (or at least not the covariate we measured).

3. If the partial correlation had *not* been significant, what could we conclude?

That the zero-order (bivariate) correlation between sleep quality and BMI was due to associations with depression rather than a unique association. See the visual below to aid in understanding—we can see that the only "association" between sleep quality and BMI would be due to overlapping associations with depression. Pretty neat!

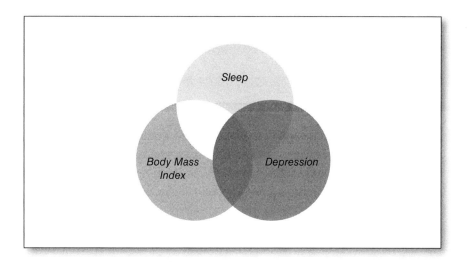

REFERENCES

Alvaro, P. K., Roberts, R. M., & Harris, J. K. (2013). A systematic review assessing bidirectionality between sleep disturbances, anxiety, and depression. *Sleep, 36*(7), 1059–1068. Retrieved from http://www.ncbi.nlm.nih.gov/pmc/articles/PMC3669059/pdf/aasm.36.7.1059.pdf

Cappuccio, F. P., Taggart, F. M., Kandala, N. B., Currie, A., Peile, E., Stranges, S., & Miller, M. A. (2008). Meta-analysis of short sleep duration and obesity in children and adults. *Sleep, 31*(5), 619–626. Retrieved from http://www.ncbi.nlm.nih.gov/pmc/articles/PMC2398753/pdf/aasm.31.5.619.pdf

Johnston, E., Johnson, S., McLeod, P., & Johnston, M. (2004). The relation of body mass index to depressive symptoms. *Canadian Journal of Public Health, 95*(3), 179–183. Retrieved from http://journal.cpha.ca/index.php/cjph/article/viewFile/489/489

LAB 10

Regression Analysis

Objective

In this lab, we discuss the use of predictor and outcome variables in regression analysis. You will conduct and interpret a regression analysis. Additional material introduces hierarchical regression.

©iStock.com/graphic-bee

Target Article

Shane, J. M. (2010). Organizational stressors and police performance. *Journal of Criminal Justice*, *38*, 807–818. doi:10.1016/j.jcrimjus.2010.05.008 Available at http://www.sciencedirect.com/science/article/pii/S0047235210001200

How stressful is it to work as a police officer? Does the stress come from the nature of their work responsibilities, or is it due more to organizational variables (such as interacting with a manager, co-workers, bureaucracy, etc.)? Authors of this article used multiple regression (among other statistical techniques; this summary refers only to the section describing Table 6) to examine whether organizational issues predicted police performance. They controlled for demographic variables such as age, education, and number of children, for example. After controlling for demographic variables, organizational issues accounted for almost 45% of the variability in officer performance. Lower performance ratings were predicted by difficulties in relationships with co-workers and several variables regarding the police organization. The study found that police organization was a greater stressor than police operations.

A STEP UP

In the last lab, we considered quantitative research questions that can be tested using a correlation design. We were able to ask whether two things co-occurred or were associated in some way. Now we're going to take this a step further by doing a regression analysis. A regression analysis can look at how well one or more predictor variables explain variability in some outcome variable.

Correlation analysis included just two variables of interest. A regression analysis with just one predictor tells you much the same information as does a correlation but adds an error term. Regression analysis lets you look at the association between an outcome variable and one or more predictors *as a group or individually*.

Table 10.1   Comparison of Correlation and Regression

Correlation	Regression
No assumption about directionality	Assumes a direction (predictor→outcome), but only the experimental design can actually test that (the statistic is not a "magic bullet" that determines cause and effect), so continue to be cautious how you interpret your results.
No IV or DV	Outcome = DV, Predictor(s) = IV(s)
Looks at association of two variables	Examines relationship between one DV and one or more IVs (multiple predictors)
Provides limited information	Provides more information than correlation

There are several types of research questions that can be examined via regression. As you interpret these, remember that whether or not something is statistically significant will vary depending on sample size and effect size.

1. I can use existing data to predict future data. For example, how many bags will be checked for a particular flight (outcome) if the cost per bag (predictor) is

$5? Using these data, we see that 85 bags are checked when the cost is $0, 75 when the cost is $2, and so on. We want to know how many bags to expect if the cost per bag is $5. A regression analysis uses the following form:

Bags checked (Y)	Cost per bag (X)			
85	0			
75	2			
35	10			
??	5			
Y	=	a (constant)	+	b(X)
# bags checked	=	# bags when cost = $0	+	b(cost/bag)

Model		Unstandardized Coefficients		95.0% Confidence Interval for B	
		B	Std. Error	Lower Bound	Upper Bound
1	(Constant)	85.000	.000	85.000	85.000
	Cars_deployed	-5.000	.000	-5.000	-5.000

The regression equation will solve for *a* (the constant; the value of *Y* when all predictors are 0) and *b* (the unstandardized coefficient), allowing for the possibility of error. We can plug numbers into the formula and predict the answer. We will ignore the error term for now.

Let's say the regression analysis tells us that *b* is -5 and the constant is 85. *Y* is the outcome we want to predict: the number of bags that would be checked if the charge is *X* ($5 per bag). Using that information, we predict that 60 bags will be checked if the charge is $5 per bag.

$$Y = 85 + -5(X) \text{ and } X = 5, \text{ so} \dots$$

$$Y = 85 + -5(5) = 85 + (-25) = 60$$

Let's try a different question. How many checked bags would you expect if the cost per bag was $15? Plug in the new value to the equation.

$$Y = 85 + -5(15) = 85 + (-75) = 10$$

2. I can use regression to test how effectively a *group* of predictor variables explain variability in the outcome. Remember that any group of scores has some variability (extent to which the scores differ from the mean). I can ask how much of that variability can be explained by a *set* of predictors. For example, maybe I wonder whether police officers' job evaluation score is adequately predicted by education level and years on the job. If the regression analysis shows that these two predictors do a pretty good job of predicting job evaluation scores, then I know I can predict more-or-less accurately a police officer's future job evaluation score (assuming I have reliable and valid measures of each variable). If those two predictors alone aren't very informative, then I know I'll need to find other variables that are better predictors. I can answer this question by looking at the R^2 generated by the regression analysis.

Model Summary

Model	R	R Square	Adjusted R Square	Std. Error of the Estimate
1	.843[a]	.710	.690	3.96740

a. Predictors: (Constant), Yrs.Job, Educa.level

The R^2 statistic usually runs from 0 to 1; the closer it is to 1, the more variability has been explained by the predictors. We can interpret these numbers as percentages; if we find $R^2 = .71$, we can interpret this as the predictors (as a group, if there is more than one predictor) accounting for 71% of the variability in the outcome. If I calculated a regression using education level and years on the job to predict evaluation scores and found that $R^2 = .03$ (3% of the variability), then I would conclude these two predictors didn't do a good job of explaining variability in test scores. I can determine if the value of R^2 is statistically significant by looking at the F and p values in a separate table automatically provided by SPSS that uses an ANOVA to test the significance of the overall model.

ANOVA[a]

Model		Sum of Squares	df	Mean Square	F	Sig.
1	Regression	1268.050	2	634.025	35.288	.000[b]
	Residual	188.883	12	15.740		
	Total	1456.933	14			

a. Dependent Variable: Job.eval.score

b. Predictors: (Constant), Yrs.Job, Educa.level

3. I can use regression to determine if one predictor does a better job than another one. Again, let's ask whether education or years on the job will better predict job evaluation score. This question can be answered using the standardized coefficients. By "standardized," I mean that the coefficients have been converted to a common metric, and can therefore be compared. This information is under a column labeled beta (β). Beta ranges from 0–1, and can be interpreted like a correlation statistic. In this example let's say the beta value is .54 for education and .26 for years on the job. This tells us that education may be a stronger predictor.

Coefficients[a]

Model		Unstandardized Coefficients		Standardized Coefficients	t	Sig.
		B	Std. Error	Beta		
1	(Constant)	7.820	1.261		6.200	.000
	education	.397	.108	.537	-3.670	.001
	Years on job	.447	.249	.263	1.797	.082

4. Finally, I can use regression to determine how much influence the individual predictors have on the outcome. Continuing with the scenario described above, I can look at the unstandardized coefficients (in the column headed by *b* or *B*). These numbers reflect the metric used by the predictors, so it wouldn't make sense to compare these to each other. Each coefficient assumes that the other coefficient(s) is the same for everybody (the other predictors are "controlled for"—they act like covariates). If the coefficient for educational level is .397, this tells us that for every one unit increase in the predictor (in this case,

every additional year of education) the outcome (job evaluation score) went up ~.40 points after controlling for years on the job. Is this predictor statistically significant? I can answer that by looking at the *t*-test and resulting *p* value for each predictor on the right side of the box (education is statistically significant in this sample).

PRACTICE AND REVIEW

Take a look at this output from a regression analysis. We continue to consider whether educational level and years on the job predict a job evaluation score. The numbers in brackets relate to the four points above.

To predict a future evaluation score by educational level and years on the job, I can plug in educational level (X_1) and years on the job (X_2) into this equation generated by the regression analysis of existing data:

Predicted evaluation score $= 46.27 + 2.77(X_1) + 8.53(X_2)$ (the numbers in the equation came from the regression analysis below, in the coefficients table).

Let's try it for an educational level of 3.00, and 8 years on the job (in other words, a projected job evaluation score next year for someone who has currently worked seven years).

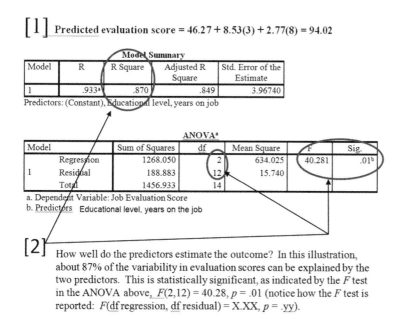

[1] Predicted evaluation score $= 46.27 + 8.53(3) + 2.77(8) = 94.02$

Model Summary

Model	R	R Square	Adjusted R Square	Std. Error of the Estimate
1	.933ª	.870	.849	3.96740

Predictors: (Constant), Educational level, years on job

ANOVAª

Model		Sum of Squares	df	Mean Square	F	Sig.
1	Regression	1268.050	2	634.025	40.281	.01ᵇ
	Residual	188.883	12	15.740		
	Total	1456.933	14			

a. Dependent Variable: Job Evaluation Score
b. Predictors Educational level, years on the job

[2] How well do the predictors estimate the outcome? In this illustration, about 87% of the variability in evaluation scores can be explained by the two predictors. This is statistically significant, as indicated by the *F* test in the ANOVA above, $F(2,12) = 40.28$, $p = .01$ (notice how the *F* test is reported: $F(df \text{ regression, } df \text{ residual}) = X.XX, p = .yy$).

[1]

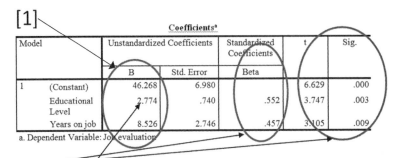

Coefficients[a]

Model		Unstandardized Coefficients		Standardized Coefficients	t	Sig.
		B	Std. Error	Beta		
1	(Constant)	46.268	6.980		6.629	.000
	Educational Level	2.774	.740	.552	3.747	.003
	Years on job	8.526	2.746	.457	3.105	.009

a. Dependent Variable: Job evaluation

[3] Is educational level or years on the job the better predictor? Using the standardized coefficients (beta) above, I see that educational level is a slightly stronger predictor. However, both predictors are statistically significant. Note that no beta is given for the constant.

[4] What impact does educational level have on job evaluation? The unstandardized coefficient in the table above tells us that for every one unit increase in the predictor (in this case, for every additional education level), the outcome (job evaluation score) goes up by 2.77 points.

TRY IT YOURSELF

Your turn!

In today's lab, we'll consider whether income and education predict job satisfaction among police officers. In this illustration, job satisfaction is the outcome variable, and income and education are predictors. Another way to say this is "job satisfaction regressed on income and education."

©iStock.com/hanya78

Canned Data

1. Enter and save the data provided below. The data below should be set up as three separate variables. The words "predictors" and "outcome" will not be part of the variable name; they are just there to help you understand the role of the variables.

Predictors		Outcome
Annual Income (in thousands)	Educational Attainment (in years)	Job Satisfaction
35.00	9.00	3.00
12.00	10.00	1.00
22.00	10.00	4.00
37.00	11.00	3.00
42.00	13.00	4.00
37.00	12.00	4.00
25.00	14.00	6.00
48.00	12.00	2.00
24.00	10.00	2.00
37.00	12.00	3.00
50.00	16.00	6.00
76.00	16.00	6.00
50.00	14.00	4.00
55.00	14.00	4.00
39.00	16.00	2.00
43.00	12.00	3.00
77.00	12.00	4.00
60.00	14.00	5.00
49.00	18.00	6.00
49.00	14.00	5.00
56.00	14.00	5.00
43.00	12.00	2.00

2. After all data are entered into SPSS, generate descriptive statistics (means and standard deviations for each variable).

   a. At the top of the screen, click on *Analyze, Descriptive Statistics, Descriptives.*

   b. Move all three variables into the *Variables* column on the right side of the screen.

   c. Click *OK*

   d. Do the same for *Descriptive Statistics, Frequency*

3. **Eyeball the data.** Do the means and frequencies look like they should? Given the data you entered, does anything stick out as odd? If so, go back and check your data for errors.

4. Copy and paste descriptive data results into a Word document.

5. After pasting data, perform multiple regression analysis on data.

   a. Click on *Analyze, Regression, Linear.*

   b. Move the dependent variable (job satisfaction) into the *Dependent* block at the top of the screen.

   c. Move the two independent (predictor) variables into the *Independent* block in the middle of the screen.

   d. Click *Statistics* and *Confidence intervals* (this is a way to look at effect size).

   e. Click *Continue, OK.*

6. Copy and paste regression results into the Word document.

Your regression output should look like this:

Model Summary

Model	R	R Square	Adjusted R Square	Std. Error of the Estimate
1	.680[a]	.463	.406	1.15601

ANOVA[a]

Model		Sum of Squares	df	Mean Square	F	Sig.
1	Regression	21.882	2	10.941	8.187	.003[b]
	Residual	25.391	19	1.336		
	Total	47.273	21			

a. Dependent Variable: Job Satisfaction

b. Predictors: (Constant), Education, Ann.Incom.K

Coefficients[a]

Model	Unstandardized Coefficients		Standardized Coefficients	t	Sig.	95.0% Confidence Interval for B	
	B	Std. Error	Beta			Lower Bound	Upper Bound
1 (Constant)	-1.701	1.444		-1.178	.253	-4.724	1.322
Ann.Incom.K	.018	.019	.193	.976	.341	-.021	.057
Education	.364	.129	.558	2.815	.011	.093	.635

a. Dependent Variable: JobSatisfaction

7. Report your results.

Now that you have your output, how will you communicate these findings to your reader? In the Results section, phrase your answer in terms of your research questions or hypothesis. Tell the reader what kind of analysis you did, the order in which you entered variables and why you chose that order (if applicable), followed by the relevant data. Refer the reader to Table 10.2 (shown below) with the regression data. Interpret the findings for your reader.

Table 10.2 Analysis of Quality of Life Regressed on Age, Gender, Relationship Satisfaction, and Job Risk Level

Block 1	$R^2 \Delta = .49$, $F(3,33) = 10.45$, $p<.01$					
Constant	5.71	8.54	—	.67	−11.66	23.08
Age	−.07	.12	−.07	−.57	−.31	.18
Gender	−.04	.82	−.01	−.05	−1.72	1.64
Rel. Satisfaction	1.91	.36	.69	5.39*	1.19	1.63
Block 2	$R^2 \Delta = .25$, $F(1,32) = 30.39$, $p<.01$					
Constant	8.48	6.23	——	1.36	−4.20	21.17
Age	−.06	.09	−.06	−.68	−.24	.12
Gender	.30	.60	.05	.51	−.92	1.53
Rel. Satisfaction	1.38	.28	.50	5.00*	.82	1.94
Risk Level	−.22	.04	−.54	−5.51*	−.29	−.14

NOTE: * $p < .05$; SE = standard error; CI = confidence interval; Rel. Satisfaction = relationship satisfaction

Results

A regression analysis tested whether the model including annual income and education as predictors of job satisfaction was a good fit for the existing data, whether one predictor was stronger than the other, and the extent to which education predicted job satisfaction. See Table 1 for the regression data. The model explained 46% of the variability in job satisfaction, $R^2 = .46$, $F(2,19) = 8.19$, $p = .003$. Only level of education was a significant predictor, with each additional year of education predicting an increase of just over one third of a point (.36) in job satisfaction.

Include a table (this goes on a separate page placed after the references; for purposes of this lab, put it on a separate page at the end of your assignment) with the following information. IMPORTANT: Notice the table had to be typed out—you can't copy and paste the output from SPSS. Use horizontal but not vertical lines to organize the information.

	B	SE	Beta	t	95%	CI
Constant	−1.70	1.44	—	−1.18	−4.72	1.32
Annual Income	.02	.02	.19	.98	−.02	.06
Education	.36*	.13	.56*	2.82*	.09	.64

NOTE: * p < .05; SE = standard error; CI = confidence interval

If you like, you can use the Greek letter β instead of the word *Beta*. Remember this column lists the standardized coefficients, whereas *b* (or *B)* is unstandardized.

Collect Your Own Data

How stressed out are people in your state? What factors might predict a state's rank order for stress? Instead of collecting data directly from people, in this lab we'll collect archived data. Go to http://www.movoto.com/blog/opinions/stressed-states-maps/. Click on each state to see its stress rank and several variables that may contribute to that stress level. For each state, enter into a data file at least two predictors (for example, I tried unemployment rate and length of commute) and the rank number. Lower stress rank numbers mean greater stress (e.g., 1 = most stressful state). Run a regression analysis to see (1) how well the predictors you chose predicted rank order (how much variability in ranking was explained by your predictors as a group), and (2) which predictors explained significant amounts of variability in the outcome. What else can you learn from your regression analysis? Look at the four points above.

Alternatively, you could ask everyone in the class who is willing to participate to report their overall GPA, how many hours they spent studying for their most recent test, and their SAT score. Make GPA the outcome and hours studying and SAT score the predictors. You can make the data anonymous.

SUMMING UP

Whether you collected your own data or analyzed the canned data, answer the following questions using the outcome for the canned data (predictors of job satisfaction shown earlier).

Questions

1. Why do researchers use regression analysis? What can they learn from it?

2. Using the analysis from the data above, how well does this model predict job satisfaction? In other words, how much variability in job satisfaction is explained by these predictors (hint: R^2)?

3. Is the overall model tested here significant (hint: look for the ANOVA)? Report the statistic using correct APA format (hint: look back at the sample results section above. The ANOVA produces an F score).

4. Are both of the predictors significant? How can you tell? Which predictor is the greater contributor (remember to use standardized coefficients for this question)?

5. For every one unit increase in years of schooling, how much does job satisfaction go up (assuming income is unchanged)?

6. Assume a new hire made $80,000/year (this would be entered in the data as '80' since the variable is thousands/year) and had 13 years of school. Use the values you obtained from this analysis to predict their job satisfaction score. Remember the equation you'll use is Y = constant + unstandardized coefficient$_{\text{annual income}}$ (annual income) + coefficient$_{\text{education}}$(education). [In other words, predicted literacy score = $-1.70 + .02(X_1) + .36(X_2)$.] We'll ignore the error term for now.

You can check your work below after you have answered the questions independently.

Answers

1. Why do researchers use regression analysis?

   It allows more predictors and provides more information than a correlational analysis.

2. Using the analysis from the data above, how well does this model predict job satisfaction? In other words, how much variability in job satisfaction is explained by these predictors (hint: R^2)?

   The model explains 46% of the variability in job satisfaction scores.

3. Is the <u>overall</u> model tested here significant (hint: look for the ANOVA)? Report the statistic using correct APA format.

   Yes: $F(2,19) = 8.19, p = .003$

4. Are both of the predictors significant? How can you tell?

   No, only education is significant. The t-test for the coefficient is significant.

   Which predictor is the greater contributor (remember to use standardized values for this question)?

   Education (.56 > .19)

5. For every one unit increase in years of schooling, how much does job satisfaction go up (assuming income is held constant)?

   .36 points (~ one third of a point)

6. Assume a new hire made $80,000/year and had 13 years of school. Predict their job satisfaction score.

$$\text{Predicted literacy score} = \text{constant} + .02(X_1) + .36(X_2)$$

$$= -1.70 + .02(80) + .36(13)$$

$$= 4.58$$

IF YOU WANT TO GO FURTHER . . .

Hierarchical Regression

The use of hierarchical regression modeling allows the researcher to get information about how much additional variability is explained by one or more new variables, over and above other variables that are important, but not necessarily of primary interest. You can do this by adding blocks of variables as predictors. For example, in an adaptation of the target article, let's say you want to predict police officers' quality of life, using the personal characteristics of age, gender, relationship (with romantic partner or spouse) satisfaction, and job risk level as predictors. Specifically, you want to know if the risk level of the job predicts variability in quality of life after controlling for personal characteristics. Enter the following data in a file. Assume 1 = male, and for all other variables, higher numbers indicate more of the construct measured.

Age	Gender	Rel.Sat.	RiskLevel	QOL
61.00	1.00	4.00	4.00	10.00
66.00	2.00	3.00	4.00	9.00
68.00	1.00	1.00	4.00	8.00
68.00	1.00	1.00	6.00	7.00
72.00	2.00	1.00	8.00	6.00
68.00	1.00	1.00	11.00	5.00
70.00	1.00	1.00	12.00	4.00
60.00	2.00	1.00	14.00	3.00

(Continued)

(Continued)

Age	Gender	Rel.Sat.	RiskLevel	QOL
68.00	2.00	1.00	15.00	2.00
65.00	2.00	1.00	25.00	1.00
71.00	1.00	5.00	7.00	14.00
73.00	2.00	2.00	25.00	2.00
65.00	1.00	2.00	23.00	2.25
73.00	2.00	2.00	20.00	2.50
66.00	1.00	2.00	17.00	2.75
71.00	1.00	2.00	15.00	3.00
70.00	2.00	1.80	16.00	2.40
69.00	1.00	1.60	19.00	1.80
64.00	2.00	1.40	21.00	1.20
69.00	1.00	1.20	24.00	.60
67.00	1.00	1.00	25.00	.00
67.00	2.00	.00	25.00	1.00
70.00	1.00	2.00	9.00	4.50
69.00	1.00	4.00	2.00	8.00
72.00	1.00	1.00	13.00	5.00
73.00	2.00	.67	10.00	5.00
67.00	2.00	.33	5.00	5.00
62.00	2.00	.00	3.00	5.00
67.00	2.00	2.00	13.00	5.00
66.00	1.00	.00	25.00	.00
69.00	2.00	.00	25.00	.00
69.00	1.00	.00	18.00	.00
70.00	2.00	.00	25.00	.00
71.00	1.00	.00	25.00	2.00
71.00	2.00	1.00	22.00	1.00
70.00	1.00	1.00	7.00	1.00
75.00	1.00	1.00	1.00	1.00

It's a good idea to check your data for accuracy by running descriptives and correlations and eyeball the data to make sure everything makes sense and appears to be entered correctly. Do all the means and correlations look reasonable? Is your sample size what you expected? Are correlations in the expected direction? If not, that doesn't necessarily mean your data are incorrect, but it is a good idea to double check your data.

You can test the hypothesis by creating a regression analysis with two blocks. Click *Analyze, Regression, Linear*. Set up quality life as the dependent variable and enter age, gender, and relationship status as predictors. Then click *Next* and put risk level into the predictor block. You can have multiple predictors in each block. Click *Statistics, R^2 Change, Descriptives*, and *Confidence Intervals*.

Interpret the output and report your findings. Remember these are pretend-data, so don't draw any real-life conclusions from them. Let's say this is your output (I have left out the correlations and descriptive data to save room). Elements reported below are highlighted.

Model Summary

Model	R	R Square	Adjusted R Square	Std. Error of the Estimate	Change Statistics				
					R Square Change	F Change	df1	df2	Sig. F Change
1	.698a	.487	.441	2.42076	.487	10.451	3	33	.000
2	.858b	.737	.704	1.76062	.250	30.386	1	32	.000

a Predictors: (Constant), Relationship Satisfaction, Age, Gender

b Predictors: (Constant), Relationship Satisfaction, Age, Gender, Risk Level of Job

ANOVA[a]

Model		Sum of Squares	df	Mean Square	F	Sig.
1	Regression	183.732	3	61.244	10.451	.000[b]
	Residual	193.382	33	5.860		
	Total	377.114	36			
2	Regression	277.921	4	69.480	22.415	.000[c]
	Residual	99.193	32	3.100		
	Total	377.114	36			

a. Dependent Variable: Quality of Life

b. Predictors: (Constant), Relationship Satisfaction, Age, Gender

c. Predictors: (Constant), Relationship Satisfaction, Age, Gender, Risk Level of Job

Coefficients

Model	Unstandardized					95% Confidence Intervals	
	B	Std. Error	Beta	t	Sig.	Lower Bound	Upper Bound
1 (Constant)	5.714	8.537		.669	.508	-11.655	23.084
Age	-.069	.121	-.071	-.569	.573	-.314	.177
Gender	-.044	.825	-.007	-.053	.958	-1.722	1.635
Relationship Satisfaction	1.912	.355	.690	5.388	.000	1.190	2.634
2 (Constant)	8.485	6.230		1.362	.183	-4.204	21.174
Age	-.060	.088	-.062	-.683	.499	-.239	.119
Gender	.305	.603	.048	.506	.616	-.923	1.534
Relationship Satisfaction	1.378	.276	.498	5.001	.000	.817	1.940
Risk Level of Job	-.215	.039	-.543	-5.512	.000	-.294	-.135

a Dependent Variable: Quality of Life

There are several pieces of information here.

1. Overall, how well do these variables account for variability in officers' quality of life? In this question, we are interested in model 2 because the question is about *all* the predictors. To answer this, look at the model summary, and report that $R^2 = .74$, and that *given this sample size*, the variability explained by the model is statistically significant, $F(4,32) = 22.42, p < .01.$* This F score is found in the ANOVA.

2. Are personal characteristics significant predictors? This refers to model 1. Look at the R^2 change (sometimes reported as $R^2\Delta$) for model 1. Here .49 (49%) of explained variability is compared to 0%. The F test of the change is statistically significant, so you can report yes.

3. Say I want to know how much relationship satisfaction alone (controlling for other personal characteristics, but <u>not</u> risk level) accounts for variability in quality of life. Look at the unstandardized coefficient for Relationship Satisfaction in model 1. For each unit of increase in relationship satisfaction, quality of life scores increase by 1.91 points. The t-test for this predictor is significant.

4. Does the level of risk associated with the job account for significantly more variability than the personal characteristics? Now we're referring to model 2. Again, find $R^2\Delta$ for model 2 and look at the F test for that

---

*SPSS gives significance levels out to three decimal places. If the p value is very small, it appears that p is .000. However, the chance of making a type 1 error is never actually 0, so rather than report "$p = .00$" say that $p < .001$ (or .01, or .05—all are correct).

amount of change. The answer is that risk level accounts for a significant, additional 25% of the variability in quality of life. Again, the change score F is significant.

Report R^2 change ($R^2 \Delta$), F-test for $R^2 \Delta$, $B(b)$, standard error, β, and confidence intervals in a table. Do this for both models 1 and 2, and indicate which coefficients are statistically significant. An example of the correlated table is on page 145, but try it on your own after you look over my example.

I left off the significance level of t to save room and communicated significance with an asterisk. Notice I gave the reader all the information needed to interpret the table in a note, including how significance is indicated and what abbreviations mean. Some researchers prefer to report the R^2 instead of the value of the R^2 change for each block. In this case, R^2 would be .49* for block 1 (all predictors except risk level) and .74* for block 2 (all predictors as a group). Look at the confidence intervals. Notice that the effects that are significant do NOT include 0 within the confidence intervals.

If you are or your instructor has available data, try to run a hierarchical regression on your own.

LAB 11

Two-Group Designs

Objective

This lab introduces the two-group comparison. The simplest experimental design compares two-group means or counts. The two groups can be between subjects (different people/animals/cells/eras—whatever is being compared) or within subjects (same units, natural units, matched units); this determines which *t*-test is used to compare means. Additional material describes the use of chi squared analysis to compare two-group counts.

Target Articles

©iStock.com/VLADGRIN

Craik, F. I., & Lockhart, R. S. (1972). Levels of processing: A framework for memory research. *Journal of Verbal Learning and Verbal Behavior, 11*(6), 671–684.

Craik, F. I., & Tulving, E. (1975). Depth of processing and the retention of words in episodic memory. *Journal of Experimental Psychology: General, 104*(3), 268–294.

I n 1972, Fergus I. M. Craik and Robert S. Lockhart proposed a theory of memory called "levels of processing" (also called depth of processing). This suggested that not all long-term memories are created equally; some have been deeply encoded, making them more durable and easier to recall, whereas others were encoded shallowly, and are therefore less likely to endure or be retrieved. Depth of encoding refers to the amount of meaningfulness used when encoding a memory and the extent to which the input is elaborated (connected to other memories). If you studied a list of words by thinking of a specific example of each word, then you are forced to think about the meaning of the word as well as relating it to your existing memories, and it is therefore encoded more deeply. On the other hand, if you study a list of words focusing on whether each word contains any letters with curved lines, then the words are encoded shallowly because you don't necessarily access the meaning of the word or relate it to any other memories.

THE TWO-GROUP DESIGN

The simplest possible experimental design is to compare two groups. In this situation, there is one independent variable (IV) that has two levels. Comparisons could be before or after some stimulus (e.g., measure acceptance of diversity before and after a training program), experimental versus control group (e.g., an experimental group that views a distressing picture versus a control group that views a neutral picture), comparison of different levels of some IV (e.g., 10 mg of a new drug versus 5 mg), or ex post facto (in which a participant characteristic is used as the IV, e.g., gender differences). Of course, it is only truly an experiment when you can randomly assign people to groups.

For the moment, let me illustrate using people as the units to be analyzed. The two groups may be between-subjects (different people in each group) or within-subjects. Within-subjects means that one of three situations is true about the groups: they are repeated measures (same people measured twice), natural pairs (such as twins), or matched pairs. Matched pairs are different people who have been matched for one or more potential extraneous variables. For example, since I know that hyperactivity scores are different based on age and gender, I could make sure that for every 8-year-old boy in the experimental group there is an 8-year-old boy in the control group.

This table summarizes some of the information about two group designs. Ps in this case refers to "participants." Within-subject comparisons give you a statistical advantage because you have diminished some of the possibility of error by making your groups similar or the same; therefore, you can use a *t*-test that assumes less error in its calculations. Between-subjects designs, which include different people in each group, must be assumed to contain a certain amount of error, so these are analyzed using a *t*-test that assumes more error.

Table 11.1 The Two-Group Design

Between-(Independent) Subject Comparison	Within-(Paired;Correlated) Subject Comparison
• Different individuals	• Matched pairs • Repeated measures • Natural pairs
Advantages: • Easier to get Ps (don't need to match) • Random assignment • Asks less commitment from Ps	Advantages: • Greater experimental control • Reduced experimental error • Greater statistical power
Disadvantages: • Less statistical power	Disadvantages: • May not be practical or possible to obtain appropriate pairs or matches • May not be able to "reuse" Ps
Test: Independent-samples *t*-test	Test: Dependent (paired)-samples *t*-test

Between-groups and within-groups analyses are ALIKE in that they produce the same means and standard deviations. They are DIFFERENT in that they may require a different number of participants to create groups of a particular size. For example, if you decided you needed 20 people in each group (the number of participants needed is determined by a power analysis), then if you use a between-groups design you will need to recruit 40 participants. If you are using a repeated-measures design, you need only 20 (since you will measure the same thing in each person twice). They also differ in how much error must be taken into account and in how the data set is organized. More about that in a minute.

Your choice of which type of two-group design to use will depend on your research question, the nature of the participants, methods, and statistical and practical considerations.

TRY IT YOURSELF

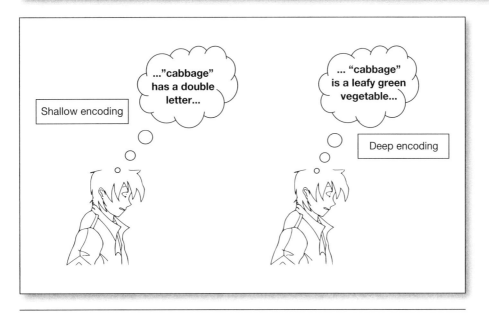

SOURCE: http://www.clker.com/clipart-29794.html

In today's lab, the same data will be analyzed in two different scenarios—once as if it had been a between-subjects design and once as if it had been a repeated-measures design. Bear in mind that in reality, you'll use one design or the other. For learning purposes, we're going to have to *pretend* that data were collected (1) from different people, then *pretend* the data were collected (2) using a repeated measures (same people measured repeatedly) design. Analyzing the same data using two different designs will help you see how different designs can produce different statistical outcomes.

Canned Data

Note that there are several products that will be generated by this lab; one is the output from the analyses described below, the other is a practice lab report that will be written in sections. For this lab, do just the literature review. You can add practice Method, Results, and Discussion sections as each is covered in future labs.

1. Analyze the canned data in two ways—once as a within-subjects design and once as a between-subjects design. Notice that the data must be entered differently for each design. Label the output of these different analyses as *between-subjects* and *within-subjects* design.

2. Using good APA style, write the introduction section to this lab. Close your sources when you write! If your work is copied or closely paraphrased, it will not be accepted. Since the topic is levels of processing, your introduction should summarize the general findings about memory processed at different levels. End the introduction by explaining the purpose and hypothesis for the current study. Our purpose was to further refine an understanding of the role of levels of processing in memory by comparing superficial (shallow; focused on spelling rather than meaning) encoding to deep (meaning-based) encoding. We hypothesized that words encoded deeply (based on their meaning) would be better recalled than words encoded at a more shallow level.

Background

1. For more information on levels of processing, see http://en.wikipedia .org/wiki/Levels-of-processing_effect. You can also use a search engine such as PsycINFO or JSTOR to look for additional articles on this.

2. Now review independent versus repeated-measures designs in your textbook or at http://www.wadsworth.com/psychology_d/templates/student_ resources/workshops/stat_workshp/ttest_betwn/ttest_betwn_01.html.

Analyses

Within-Subjects Design. First, let's analyze your data as a repeated-measures design (also called within-subjects), in which the same people were tested in both conditions (using different lists of words). I'll illustrate data entry and analysis using canned data, but if you decide to collect your own data, you can follow the instructions below to analyze it.

To set up a data file for a repeated measures design you'll need one column for each level of the independent variable. In this case we have two levels, the double-letter condition (participants decide if each presented word contains double letters or not) and the concrete versus abstract condition (participants decide if each presented word represents a concrete or abstract concept).

Double-Letter	Concrete
12.00	12.00
9.00	8.00
13.00	14.00
7.00	11.00
9.00	10.00
14.00	14.00
5.00	7.00
8.00	10.00
5.00	7.00
10.00	11.00
11.00	12.00
13.00	14.00
12.00	8.00
13.00	10.00
6.00	12.00
10.00	10.00
7.00	9.00
13.00	14.00
10.00	14.00
9.00	11.00

Because we have the same people in both groups, we can use the paired-samples *t*-test.

1. Click *Analyze*

2. *Compare means*

3. *Paired-samples T-test*

4. Highlight both variables then move them into the *Paired Variables* box, then click *OK*.

Your output should look like this (with different numbers, of course, if you used your own data):

T-Test

Paired-Samples Statistics

		Mean	N	Std. Deviation	Std. Error Mean
Pair 1	doub_let	9.8000	20	2.82097	.63079
	concrete	10.9000	20	2.35975	.52766

Paired-Samples Correlations

		N	Correlation	Sig.
Pair 1	doub_let & concrete	20	.637	.003

Paired-Samples Test

	Paired Differences					t	df	Sig. (2-tailed)
	Mean	Std. Deviation	Std. Error Mean	95% Confidence Interval of the Difference Lower	Upper			
Pair 1 doub_let - concrete	-1.10000	2.24546	.50210	-2.15091	-.04909	-2.191	19	.041

Is the difference in recall in the two conditions significant? Make sure you can locate the descriptive information, the values for *t*, *p*, and degrees of freedom. Whether the statistic is negative or not is not necessarily reported. That depends on which mean was subtracted from the other (e.g., $5 - 3 = 2$ but $3 - 5 = -2$). I'm going to report the absolute value of the *t*-test. Here's one way to report this information.

Results

Data from the 20 participants were analyzed using a paired-samples *t*-test. Recall in the concrete condition ($M = 10.0$, $SD = 2.36$) was significantly higher than recall in the double letter condition ($M = 9.8$, $SD = 2.82$), $t(19) = 2.19$, $p = .04$. As predicted, deeper encoding produced greater recall.

Changing the scenario...

Between-Subjects Design. Now let's pretend that we collected this data using a between-subjects design. In this scenario, 20 people were assigned to the double-letter condition and 20 *different* people were assigned to the concrete condition. Now how many participants do you have? _____ [40] Since we have different people in the two conditions, we must now use the independent-samples *t*-test. To set up a data file for this design, you will need one column for the independent variable and one for the dependent variable. Since each participant was tested under only one condition, the first column is used here to identify each participant's group; let's use 1 to indicate the double-letter condition and 2 to indicate the concrete condition. A few days from now, you may not remember which condition was identified as 1 and which one as 2. Identify the meaning of those numbers by using the *Values* column of the *Variable View*. In *Variable View*, on the same line as the word *condition*,

1. click the box under *Values* then click the small gray box that pops up in the right of that area.

2. Enter the value of 1 and the label *double letter*, then click *Add*.

3. Follow the same steps to identify 2 as *concrete*, then click *OK.* You can set up the recall column quickly by cutting and pasting the data from the within-subjects file.

4. Save the new file under a new name.

Condition	Recall
1	12.00
1	9.00
1	13.00
1	7.00
1	9.00
1	14.00
1	5.00
1	8.00
1	5.00
1	10.00

(Continued)

(Continued)

Condition	Recall
1	11.00
1	13.00
1	12.00
1	13.00
1	6.00
1	10.00
1	7.00
1	13.00
1	10.00
1	9.00
2	12.00
2	8.00
2	14.00
2	11.00
2	10.00
2	14.00
2	7.00
2	10.00
2	7.00
2	11.00
2	12.00
2	14.00
2	8.00
2	10.00
2	12.00
2	10.00
2	9.00
2	14.00
2	14.00
2	11.00

Because we are assuming there are different people in each group, we need to use an independent-samples *t*-test.

1. Click *Analyze*

2. *Compare Means*

3. *Independent-Samples T-Test*

4. Move recall into the *Test Variable* box, and condition into the *Grouping Variable* box.

5. Click *Define Groups*

6. Enter a 1 for group 1 (our designation for the double-letter condition) and 2 for group 2 (our designation for the concrete condition).

7. Click *Continue* and *OK*.

Your output should look like this (again, the numbers will be different if you used your own data):

T-Test

Group Statistics

	condition	N	Mean	Std. Deviation	Std. Error Mean
recall	1.00	20	9.8000	2.82097	.63079
	2.00	20	10.9000	2.35975	.52766

Independent Samples Test

		Levene's Test for Equality of Variances		t-test for Equality of Means							
									95% Confidence Interval of the Difference	
		F	Sig.	t	df	Sig. (2-tailed)	Mean Difference	Std. Error Difference	Lower	Upper
recall	Equal variances assumed	.836	.366	-1.338	38	.189	-1.10000	.82238	-2.76483	.56483
	Equal variances not assumed			-1.338	36.850	.189	-1.10000	.82238	-2.76654	.56654

What's different about the outcome using this design? The descriptives are the same, but the values for *t, p,* and degrees of freedom have changed. This time the difference using the canned data is *not* significant. Why is that the case?

(The between-subjects design is assumed to include more error. Increasing the amount of error lowered the value of *t*.)

Write the results of this analysis. Here is an example:

Results

Data from the 40 participants were analyzed using an independent-samples t-test. Recall in the concrete condition ($M = 10.0$, $SD = 2.36$) was not significantly different from recall in the double-letter condition ($M = 9.8$, $SD = 2.82$), $t(38) = 1.34$, $p = .19$. Contrary to the hypothesis, deeper encoding did not produce greater recall.

IF YOU WANT TO COLLECT YOUR OWN DATA . . .

Be the Participant

Let's begin by serving as your own participants. Someone will serve as the experimenter. The experimenter will read the instructions below. You will record your own data then compile it into one large data set. To assign participants to either group 1 or 2, flip a coin for each person (or draw a card, or throw a die—something random). Tell Group 1 to analyze each word as it is given for whether or not it has double letters (yes or no for each word) and Group 2 to decide if each word is concrete or not (yes/no for each word). Don't let the participants know this is a memory task until after the words have been given.

Script

I am going to read a list of words to you. I want you to analyze the words by following the instructions assigned to your group. Use the *yes* and *no* columns on the next page to keep your tally. I will then tell you how to score the data.

Read the list of words at a rate of about one per two seconds. Use a stopwatch or a watch with a second hand to help you keep a steady pace.

	Word List
horse	
cabbage	
elephant	
gold	
trout	
rabbit	
uncle	
knee	
duck	
memory	
brain	
picnic	
grill	
earlobe	

After presenting the words, do a distracter task (such as counting backward by 3s, starting with 369, or reciting the words to your school's alma mater—anything that prevents thinking about the words) for about 30 seconds then ask participants to write down all the words from that list they recall.

Let participants give themselves a point for each word correctly recalled. Write that number in the box next to the tally box. You can pass around a data sheet and ask each person to enter their group number and correct recall. Alternatively, you can have each person turn in their data anonymously then you can compile their responses into one data file.

Enter and analyze the data using the instructions above. Here is a data collection form you could use. Participants could write the words they recall on the right side of the page.

LEVELS OF PROCESSING DATA

Group #____ (1 = Double-letter, 2 = Concrete)

Word #	Yes	No
1		
2		
3		
4		
5		
6		
7		
8		
9		
10		
11		
12		
13		
14		

Here are several points for you to think about:

What was the purpose of this study? We wanted to test the Levels of Processing prediction that words more deeply encoded will be better recalled. We operationalized deep encoding as deciding whether each word was concrete or abstract. Shallow processing was operationalized as deciding whether each word contained a double letter or not.

What did we hypothesize? Words processed for meaning (deeper processing) would be better recalled than those processed for spelling (shallow processing)—Double letter < Concrete

Why were you asked to think about something else (counting backward by 3s) before you recalled the words? This is called a buffer-clearing task. When you have been attending to something, traces of it remain in your short-term memory for about 20 to 30 seconds. I wanted to get your mind off the words long enough for the words to decay from short-term memory. In other words, I wanted to know what you encoded in long-term memory and not what was still active in short-term memory.

Flexible Design

The two-group design can also be used to analyze data that don't qualify as a "true" experiment because assignment to groups wasn't random. For instance, if I had wanted to compare recall in males and females, I couldn't randomly assign participants to the male or female group. When this happens, you are using some characteristic of your participants as your IV, and this is called an ex post facto design. Despite the fact that it would not be a true experiment, I could still use the two-group design and the same types of analyses described above to compare the group means.

IF YOU WANT TO GO FURTHER . . .

But wait—that's not all! What if I'm comparing counts instead of means?

Sometimes, you may want to compare the counts from two groups instead of means. In other words, you are using nominal data instead of ordinal, interval, or ratio data. We'll try a chi-squared (χ^2) analysis below.

Chi-Squared Analysis

Using a *t*-test or ANOVA is well and good when comparing group means, but what if you want to compare counts (how many participants were in each cell)? In this case you are using nominal data. Let me give you an example. Let's say you wonder whether children in either kindergarten or first grade will be more likely to pick up a handgun (definitely one that is <u>not</u> loaded—I'd have a police officer or some weapon expert on the scene when I collected data, just to be safe) when they find it among toys. Let's say the children had been told to never touch a gun. Who will be most likely to pick up the gun—kindergartners or first graders? In this case, you just want a count. You can analyze the data using a chi (rhymes with pie and starts with a 'k' sound)-squared (χ^2) analysis. BTW, I got the fancy χ by using the "insert, symbol" feature of the word processing program. The underlying theory of this study is that older children have better developed inhibitory control. Based on that theory, we hypothesize that first graders will be less likely to pick up the gun.

Suppose this is what you find:

Grade: 1 = kindergarten, 2 = first grade

Gun: 1 = picked up gun, 2 = did not pick up gun

Note that I could have used 0 and 1 instead of 1 and 2 to indicate groups because the numeric value is irrelevant in this example. We are assuming that first grade is more than kindergarten, but the numbers used to make the distinction are not meaningful. Whether or not the child picked up the gun is categorical data, and therefore the numbers serve only to distinguish the two groups. To help you remember what the numbers mean, use the *Values* column in *Variable View* to identify what each number means.

Grade	*Gun*
1.00	2.00
1.00	2.00
1.00	2.00
1.00	2.00
1.00	2.00
1.00	2.00
1.00	2.00
1.00	2.00
1.00	2.00
1.00	2.00
1.00	1.00
1.00	1.00
1.00	1.00
1.00	1.00
1.00	1.00
1.00	1.00

Grade	Gun
1.00	1.00
1.00	1.00
1.00	1.00
1.00	1.00
2.00	2.00
2.00	2.00
2.00	2.00
2.00	2.00
2.00	2.00
2.00	2.00
2.00	2.00
2.00	2.00
2.00	2.00
2.00	2.00
2.00	2.00
2.00	2.00
2.00	2.00
2.00	2.00
2.00	2.00
2.00	2.00
2.00	2.00
2.00	1.00
2.00	1.00
2.00	1.00

Enter these data into a data file and save.

1. Click *Analyze*

2. *Descriptives*

3. *Crosstabs.* Enter *Grade* in the row box and *Gun* in the column box.

4. Click *Statistics*

5. *Chi Square*

6. *Continue*

7. *OK*

Your data should be similar to this:

Just by looking at the table, we can see that kindergarten children are just as likely to pick up the gun as not, whereas first graders are less likely to pick it up. Just because the data appear to support that conclusion is not enough; we have to back it up with some type of statistic.

Grade * Gun Cross-tabulation

Count

		Gun		Total
		picked up gun	did not pick up gun	
Grade	kindergarten	10	10	20
	first grade	3	17	20
Total		13	27	40

Chi-Square Tests

	Value	Df	Asymp. Sig. (2-sided)	Exact Sig. (2-sided)	Exact Sig. (1-sided)
Pearson Chi-Square	5.584[a]	1	.018		
Continuity Correction[b]	4.103	1	.043		
Likelihood Ratio	5.812	1	.016		
Fisher's Exact Test				.041	.020
Linear-by-Linear Association	5.444	1	.020		
N of Valid Cases	40				

a. 0 cells (0.0%) have expected count less than 5. The minimum expected count is 6.50.

b. Computed only for a 2 x 2 table

The Pearson χ^2 compares the number of children in each cell against what might be expected if neither variable influenced the outcome. In this case, the chi squared is significant, and has 1 degree of freedom.

You would report the chi squared like this:

$$\chi^2(1, N = 40) = 5.58, \ p = .018 \text{ (or you can round to .02)}$$

Write the Results. As usual, report the descriptive information (or refer to it in a table), make a claim, and support it with a statistic.

Results

A chi-squared analysis examined counts in each grade x outcome cell (see Table 1). Children in kindergarten were just as likely to pick up the gun as not, whereas first graders were less likely to pick it up, $\chi^2(1, N = 40) = 5.58$, $p = .02$. These data supported the hypothesis that fewer first graders would pick up the gun.

Table 11.2   Grade x Outcome (Picking Up the Gun) Counts for 20 Kindergarten and 20 First-Grade Children

	Picked Up Gun	Did Not Pick Up Gun
Kindergarten	10	10
First Grade	17	3

mmaher@uncc.edu

LAB 12

Multiple-Groups Designs

Objective

This lab introduces a design with one independent variable (IV) that includes three or more levels (experimental conditions). The analysis of variance (ANOVA) is introduced as a control for family-wise error, followed by post hoc testing. Additional information introduces coding categorical variables for regression, logistic regression, and interpreting odds ratios (ORs).

©iStock.com/Victor_Brave

Target Article

Campbell, C. G., Kuehn, S. M., Richards, P. M., Ventureyra, E., & Hutchinson, J. S. (2004). Medical and cognitive outcome in children with traumatic brain injury. *Canadian Journal of Neurological Science, 31*(2), 213–219.

Traumatic brain injury (TBI) can result from a concussion or closed head injury. A mild injury may produce a brief change in consciousness, whereas a severe injury can result in a period of unconsciousness of 30 minutes or more. The injury may be associated with amnesia, impaired cognitive functioning, and may produce long-term disabilities or death. The article by Campbell et al. (2004) followed children ages 1 to 18 who had a moderate or severe head injury, measuring their cognitive and memory performance at three points in time: baseline (less than 4 months since the injury), early in the recovery process (5 to 15 months post injury), and during a follow-up period (16 to 38 months after injury). IQ scores moved from "low average" at baseline to average later in recovery, but a higher proportion of the scores remained more than 1.5 standard deviations below the mean relative to noninjured groups. Children who experienced a more severe coma were more likely to have lower IQ and verbal memory scores.

For more information on traumatic brain injury from the Centers for Disease Control and Prevention, go to http://www.cdc.gov/healthcommunication/toolstemplates/entertainmented/tips/braininjury.html or search for a reliable source on the topic "traumatic brain injury."

GOING BEYOND THE TWO-GROUP DESIGN

Start by going through the tutorial at http://www.wadsworth.com/psychology_d/templates/student_resources/workshops/stat_workshp/one_anova/one_anova_01.html {suggested search term *tutorial ANOVA*}

In this lab, we'll look at designs that have just one IV with three or more levels. This is a step up from the two-group designs already covered. In this situation, you need to compare three or more group means (for now, let's call them groups A, B, and C). You *could* do this by running three *t*-tests comparing (1) A to B, (2), B to C, and (3) A to C. The problem with doing that has to do with the chance of making a type 1 error.

Quick review: When you test group differences, you are making a decision about what is true in the population based on the data generated by your sample. This is why you want your sample to be representative of the population. Now, in reality, you will seldom know what is true about an entire population because you can't get data from everyone in the population. You have to make the best decision

©iStock.com/ George Clerk

you can based on the data available to you. Any time you use inferential statistics to decide if groups are significantly different, there are three possible outcomes:

1. Correct decision: You might be right—the conclusion (significant or not) you made based on your sample matches what is true for the population.

2. Type 1 error: You might err by deciding your statistic is significant, but, in reality, if you could test everyone in the population, your result would have been not significant.

3. Type 2 error: You might incorrectly say your data are not statistically significant, but, in reality, if you could test everyone in the population, your result would have been significant.

A p value less than .05 means we are taking a less than 5% chance of making a type 1 error. When you run multiple statistical tests of the same data, you increase the possibility that some of the tests will be significant by chance ("family-wise" error), leading you to say something is significant when it really isn't (a type 1 error).

That brings us to the multiple group designs. If you have three means to compare, you must run three tests of pairs. If you had four means, you'd have to run six (A vs. B, B vs. C, C vs. D, A vs. C, A vs. D, B vs. D). As the number of comparisons increases, so does the chance of making a type 1 error. To keep this as simple as possible, let's limit our conversation for now to one IV with three levels.

In order to minimize the chance of type 1 error, we have to run a preliminary test in which all three tests of pairs of means are compared simultaneously while keeping family-wise error less than .05. The test we're using today is the **Analysis of Variance** (ANOVA). It can be used when your design has three or more groups to compare.

The ANOVA acts like a gatekeeper—if the ANOVA is significant, that means that somewhere in all the possible comparisons of means, there is at least one pair that is significantly different when family-wise error is kept less than .05. We don't know how many pairs are different or which pairs are different, but the ANOVA has given us permission to look. A significant ANOVA (it produces an F-score) involving three or more means must be followed by some type of post hoc procedure in which pairs of means are compared. There are many different types of post hoc tests you could use, but since you're familiar with t-tests, we'll stick with that for now.

What happens if the ANOVA is not significant?

Nothing. That is a stop sign, indicating that you have no reason to look any further. Family-wise error was > .05, so there is no need to do post hoc tests.

Before we go further, let's clarify some terminology. So far we've talked about between-subject and within-subject designs. Those terms apply here, too. In a three-group design, you might have different people in the three groups (between-subjects) or you might have used a within-subjects design in which you tested the same people in three different conditions (repeated measures), tested naturally occurring triads, or matched groups.

Now, however, we're adding some new and potentially confusing terms. Let this circle illustrate the total variability (extent to which scores differ from the mean) in dependent variable (DV) scores. The job of the ANOVA is to look at all the variability in scores and divide it into two sources: variability due to the IV and variability due to error.

Variability due to the IV is sometimes called *between-group*, and variability due to error called *within-group*. So . . .

The word *subjects* indicates a design.

Between-subjects

Within-subjects

The word *groups* refers to sources of variability.

Between-groups

Within-groups

The ANOVA separates out between-group variability and within-group variability.

Figure 12.1   The ANOVA Pie

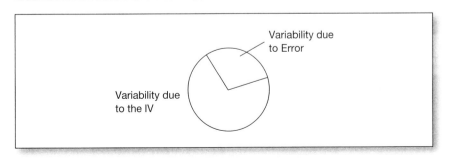

©iStock.com/ PhotoHamster

TRY IT YOURSELF

Canned Data

Analyze the hypothetical data below. Do two separate analyses, once as a between-subjects design and once as a within-subjects (repeated-measures) design. Label the analyses on your output. Remember, in real life, you would choose one design or the other; you wouldn't do both. Analyzing the same data differently for each design illustrates how the design can influence the outcome.

There is one IV (time after injury) with three levels: baseline (within 1 month of injury), early recovery (4 months post-injury), and follow-up (> 6 months postinjury). Because you will analyze these data in two different ways, you will need to set up two different data files; however, you can cut and paste the numbers to make this easy. You are going to examine whether children's IQ scores change from immediately after receiving a traumatic brain injury, to 4 months later and > 6 months later.

Between-Subjects Design

First analyze the data as if it involved three groups of different individuals: one group that has a very recent TBI, one group that is recovering (4 months since injury), and another group that has recovered from the injury and is being seen in follow-up (> 6 months since injury). Since this is a between-subject design, you'll need one column to identify the IV (group membership; 1 = baseline, 2 = recovery, 3 = follow-up) and a column for the DV (IQ scores). Enter the data, labeling the variables and identify the values for groups 1, 2, and 3.

Time_aftr_tbi	IQ
1.00	86.00
1.00	95.00
1.00	90.00
1.00	88.00
1.00	87.00
1.00	65.00
1.00	67.00

1.00	70.00
1.00	71.00
1.00	84.00
2.00	91.00
2.00	100.00
2.00	95.00
2.00	89.00
2.00	93.00
2.00	85.00
2.00	87.00
2.00	82.00
2.00	88.00
2.00	96.00
3.00	101.00
3.00	102.00
3.00	99.00
3.00	92.00
3.00	104.00
3.00	88.00
3.00	95.00
3.00	93.00
3.00	99.00
3.00	105.00

Once your data have been entered, save the file.

Since you have more than two groups, you can't initially analyze the data using a series of *t*-tests because of problems with family-wise error. Note that in this situation, you could also use the quickie version of an ANOVA (called *one-way ANOVA* in SPSS; *one-way* just means one IV). Your instructor will let you know if you should learn to run this version of the ANOVA. In this example, however, we're going to choose the more flexible univariate ANOVA. When there is only one IV, the one-way ANOVA and the univariate ANOVA will end up at the same conclusion.

SPSS instructions

1. *Analyze*

2. *Compare Means*

3. *General* (not *Generalized*) *Linear Model*

4. *Univariate Analysis*

5. Move the IQ score to the *Dependent Variable* box and *aftr_tbi* to the *Fixed Factor* box.

6. *Options*

7. *Descriptive, Estimate of Effect Size* (it is always a good idea to get a measure of effect size)

8. *Continue*

9. *OK*

By now you know what the first step will be . . . **eyeball the data!** Exactly, eyeball your descriptive data! Save yourself time and frustration later by identifying anomalies or errors early.

Descriptives

Full IQ score

	N	Mean	Std. Deviation	Std. Error	95% Confidence Interval for Mean		Minimum	Maximum
					Lower Bound	Upper Bound		
baseline	10	80.3000	10.87352	3.43851	72.5216	88.0784	65.00	95.00
recovery	10	90.6000	5.48128	1.73333	86.6789	94.5211	82.00	100.00
followup	10	97.8000	5.59365	1.76887	93.7985	101.8015	88.00	105.00
Total	30	89.5667	10.44421	1.90684	85.6667	93.4666	65.00	105.00

Tests of Between-Subjects Effects

Dependent Variable: IQ

Source	Type III Sum of Squares	df	Mean Square	F	Sig.	Partial Eta Squared
Corrected Model	1547.267[a]	2	773.633	12.925	.000	.489
Intercept	240665.633	1	240665.633	4020.774	.000	.993
Time_aftr_tbi	1547.267	2	773.633	12.925	.000	.489
Error	1616.100	27	59.856			
Total	243829.000	30				
Corrected Total	3163.367	29				

a. R Squared = .489 (Adjusted R Squared = .451)

What did you find? Was the *F*-test significant? Notice that *F* scores are reported with two values for degrees of freedom (*df*): the *df* associated with the effect you are reporting and the *df* for the error term. This would be reported using the following format: $F(2,27) = 12.92, p < 001$.

Note the placement of the degrees of freedom, the value of the *F*-test, and the *p* value. Which letter(s) should be italicized? _____ (*F* and *p*; any letter reporting a statistic) Which is capitalized?_____ (*F*)

Since the *F* is significant you know that there is <u>at least</u> one significant difference among all possible pairs of means, but you don't know specifically which means are significantly different. To find that out, you must do some sort of post hoc ("after this") test. One option would be to do a series of three independent *t*-tests. Another option is to use one of the post hoc tests provided by SPSS such as the Tukey HSD. Ask your instructor which you should use. For now, go ahead and run the three *t*-tests. There are different people in each group, so use the independent samples *t*-test. Refer back to instructions in the lab on Two-Group Designs if needed. You will need to define the groups as 1 vs. 2, 2 vs. 3, and 1 vs. 3. Which pairs are significantly different? _____

_____ (all three pairs are significantly different)

Check your work.

1 vs. 2: $t(18) = 2.68, p = .02$

1 vs. 3: $t(18) = 4.53, p < .001$

2 vs. 3: $t(18) = 2.91, p = .01$

Within-Subjects Design

Now, let's pretend that instead of comparing IQ scores for three *different* groups of children, you followed the *same* children and measured each child's IQ at three different times after the TBI occurred. Quick review: the between-subjects design in this illustration is *cross-sectional*, while the repeated measures design is *longitudinal*. We'll use the same data, but this time we don't need a separate column to indicate group membership. Why not? (everybody is in each group or condition)

Since everyone has three IQ scores, we'll need three columns of data, one for each level of the IV (i.e., time since injury). You can use the data you've already typed by deleting the

©iStock.com/aleksei-veprev

"aftr_tbi" column, then cutting and pasting the recovery and follow-up scores into new columns. Label the columns. Save the data under a new file name.

Baseline	Recovery	Follow-up
86.00	91.00	101.00
95.00	100.00	102.00
90.00	95.00	99.00
88.00	89.00	92.00
87.00	93.00	104.00
65.00	85.00	88.00
67.00	87.00	95.00
70.00	82.00	93.00
71.00	88.00	99.00
84.00	96.00	105.00

Because you are measuring something in the same people "repeatedly," you'll need to use a repeated-measures ANOVA rather than the univariate.

1. Click *Analyze*

2. *General Linear Model*

3. *Repeated Measures*

4. Now you are asked for a within-subject factor name. This is the IV—the time after the TBI when IQ was measured. Name the within-subject factor *testtime*, indicate it has three levels, then

5. Click *Add*

6. *Define*

7. Highlight the three levels of the IV and move them into the *Within-Subjects Variables* box. Ignore the other boxes for now.

8. Click *Options*

9. *Descriptive Statistics, Estimate of Effect Size*

10. *Continue*

11. *OK*

Eyeball the descriptives. They should be the same as the ones you ran earlier.

Your source table should look like this:

Tests of Within-Subjects Effects

Measure: MEASURE_1

Source		Type III Sum of Squares	df	Mean Square	F	Sig.	Partial Eta Squared
time	Sphericity Assumed	1547.267	2	773.633	34.237	.000	.792
	Greenhouse-Geisser	1547.267	1.263	1225.115	34.237	.000	.792
	Huynh-Feldt	1547.267	1.374	1126.224	34.237	.000	.792
	Lower-bound	1547.267	1.000	1547.267	34.237	.000	.792
Error(time)	Sphericity Assumed	406.733	18	22.596			
	Greenhouse-Geisser	406.733	11.367	35.783			
	Huynh-Feldt	406.733	12.365	32.895			
	Lower-bound	406.733	9.000	45.193			

Is the IV significant? ____ (yes) Report the F-score. _____[$F(2,18) =$ 34.24, $p < .001$] Why can't I say $p = .000$? _____ (the value is never really 0, just smaller than .001) Is there a large effect size? [yes; partial eta squared = .79]

Why is the F-score so much larger this time? Hint: Compare the *Mean Square Within Group* in the univariate ANOVA to the *Mean Square Error* in this ANOVA. Both of these terms refer to an estimate of error. The larger the error, the larger the denominator used to calculate the F, and therefore the smaller the value of F. Using the within-subjects design ruled out some potential error right off the bat, so the repeated measures ANOVA calculates a smaller amount of variability due to error, resulting in a higher F value.

You still don't know which pairs of means are significantly different so you'll need to run post hoc tests. This time do a series of three paired-samples t-tests. Why use paired tests instead of independent tests? (The means you want to compare were produced by the same people, so the paired-samples test is the appropriate one.) Again, compare group 1 to group 2, 1 to 3, and 2 to 3. Refer back to the previous lab if you need a reminder how to run the t-test.

What did you find? Report the means, standard deviations, and t and p values for each pair. Get means and standard deviations from the descriptives you included with the ANOVA.

Test times compared   Statistics

Baseline vs. recovery   Baseline $M =$_____ , $SD =$_____ , $t($___$) =$_____ ,
$p =$_____

Recovery vs. follow-up   Baseline $M =$_____ , $SD =$_____ , $t($___$) =$_____ ,
$p <$_____

Baseline vs. follow-up   Baseline $M =$_____ , $SD =$_____ , $t($___$) =$_____ ,
$p <$_____

You can compare your output to the numbers included in the Results section below.

Results

Choose the results of one of the designs used today (between-subjects or within-subjects) and write a brief results section. Remember to tell the reader how you analyzed the data, state the findings (including means and standard deviations), and back it up with appropriate statistics. Report on the ANOVA first, then report any post hoc tests. When you are done, compare your results section to the sample below. Did you include all the important components? Did you report the statistics accurately, using good APA style?

The following example of a results section is specific to the <u>repeated-measures</u> design.

Results

A repeated-measures ANOVA tested for differences in IQ scores at the three test times after the injury. This produced a significant main effect of test time, $F(2,18) = 34.24$, $p < .001$, partial eta squared = .79. Post hoc paired t-tests indicated that IQ scores increased from baseline ($M = 80.30$, $SD = 10.87$) to recovery ($M = 90.60$, $SD = 5.48$), $t(9) = 4.72$, $p = .001$ and from recovery to follow-up ($M = 97.80$, $SD = 5.59$), $t(9) = 6.05$, $p < .001$. The change from baseline to follow-up was also significant, $t(9) = 6.44$, $p < .001$.

Still Flexible

As was true for the two-group design, the three-group design can be used to analyze data that compare three group means even if it was not possible to randomly assign participants to the three groups. For example, if you had wanted to compare IQ among three groups of 10-year-old children—one group that had never had a brain injury, a group that had a brain injury prior to the age of 2, and a group whose brain injury occurred after the age of 2—you couldn't decide who went in each group. They came to you already in one of those groups. You may recall that this design is called *ex post facto*. In this case we aren't doing a true experiment, but we're still doing a three-group comparison and would analyze the data in the same way. Because it wouldn't be a true experiment, you'd have to be very cautious as to how you interpreted your findings.

That's Not All You Can Do

Let's add one more refinement to this analysis. In the lab on correlations, you were introduced to the idea of controlling variables by entering them as covariates. That works with ANOVAs, too. Let's say we're interested in the same question as above—IQ score change across time after a TBI—but we want to rule out, or control for, any effect of individual socioeconomic status (SES). We know from the literature review that SES predicts IQ. We have a measure of SES for each individual, and we want to know about changes in IQ that AREN'T affected by differences in SES. In other words, we want to control for SES by making it a covariate. A covariate is a variable other than an IV that might influence the outcome. It might just be an extraneous variable, or it might be something of interest to us. Covariates can be added to most analyses (ANOVAS, correlations, regressions, etc.). When possible, it is better to control for extraneous variables in the design phase of research rather than retrospectively using a statistic. However, if you can't control an extraneous variable in the design, you can control it by measuring it and entering it in your analysis as a covariate.

SES	Baseline	Recovery	Follow-up
1	86.00	91.00	101.00
5	95.00	100.00	102.00
1	90.00	95.00	99.00
4	88.00	89.00	92.00
2	87.00	93.00	104.00
3	65.00	85.00	88.00
4	67.00	87.00	95.00
5	70.00	82.00	93.00
3	71.00	88.00	99.00
2	84.00	96.00	105.00

I'll illustrate here using the within-subject data from above. We'll need to add an additional variable, SES. Let's say I have a measure of parental SES that ranges from 1 (low education, low income) to 5 (high education, high income).

Run the repeated measures ANOVA as you did above, but this time you will add a covariate, making this an Analysis of Covariance (ANCOVA). When you get to the screen on which you define the variables that comprise the within-subject factor, move SES into the covariate box. SPSS will treat it like a between-subject variable. As you can see in the source tables,

Source		Type III Sum of Squares	df	Mean Square	F	Sig.
time	Sphericity Assumed	250.876	2	125.438	5.026	.020
	Greenhouse-Geisser	250.876	1.240	202.397	5.026	.043
	Huynh-Feldt	250.876	1.538	163.155	5.026	.032
	Lower-bound	250.876	1.000	250.876	5.026	.055
time * SES	Sphericity Assumed	7.433	2	3.717	.149	.863
	Greenhouse-Geisser	7.433	1.240	5.997	.149	.761
	Huynh-Feldt	7.433	1.538	4.834	.149	.809
	Lower-bound	7.433	1.000	7.433	.149	.710
Error(time)	Sphericity Assumed	399.300	16	24.956		
	Greenhouse-Geisser	399.300	9.916	40.267		
	Huynh-Feldt	399.300	12.301	32.460		
	Lower-bound	399.300	8.000	49.913		

Source	Type III Sum of Squares	df	Mean Square	F	Sig.
Intercept	48316.074	1	48316.074	360.786	.000
SES	138.017	1	138.017	1.031	.340
Error	1071.350	8	133.919		

As you can see in the source tables we still have a significant main effect of change over time, $F(2,16) = 5.03$, $p = .02$. It turns out that SES wasn't a significant predictor of IQ scores in this sample, $F(1,8) = 1.03$, $p = .34$, which is why adding it to the model didn't have much effect on the outcome.

IF YOU WANT TO COLLECT YOUR OWN DATA . . .

If your instructor would like you to collect your own data, it probably will not be practical for you to track down and test people who have experienced a traumatic brain injury (the topic of the canned data), nor have most of you been trained to administer, score, and interpret the kinds of tests used by a clinical neuropsychologist. Therefore, I'm going to suggest a simpler but unrelated project that will let you practice using the three-group design. If you have a large class, you can collect data from just yourselves. If you have a small class or would like to include a more representative sample, you can collect information from others. Discuss with your instructor who your participants might be and how they will be recruited.

The Question. Let's see if there's a difference in the daytime sleepiness levels of three groups of people: those who report multiple characteristics of Internet addiction (high), those who report few symptoms (moderate), and those who report little to no symptoms (low). Let's hypothesize that people who show the most symptoms of Internet addiction will have greater daytime sleepiness (perhaps due to spending time on the Internet instead of sleeping, or because exposure to light at night confuses your circadian

system making it hard to fall asleep?). You can do background research on addictions in general and their association with sleep. An article you can use as a reference is

Nalwa, K., & Anand, A. P. (2003). Internet addiction in students: A cause of concern. *CyberPsychology and Behavior, 6*(6), 653–656. doi:10.1089/109493103322725441

The Instrument. Let's measure the number of symptoms of Internet addiction by developing a survey based on the measure found at http://netaddiction .com/internet-addiction-test/ {suggested search term *measure internet addiction*} or another one you locate in the scholarly literature.

These questions can be asked either in the form of an anonymous written or online survey. Informed consent is still important even when collecting anonymous data. See more about this below.

Using the scoring system described at http://netaddiction.com/internet-addiction-test/ or the scoring instructions that go with the instrument you chose, classify participants as low, moderate, or high risk of Internet addiction (we'll identify them as group 1, 2, or 3).

Measure daytime sleepiness by using the Epworth Sleepiness Scale which can be found, among other places, at http://epworthsleepinessscale.com/ {suggested search term *Epworth Sleepiness Scale*}. Use the suggested scoring system and come up with a sleepiness score by totaling the points.

Now, follow the instructions given with the canned data to compare the sleepiness scores of your three groups. Remember, you have different people in each group.

If you write about these data, be sure to cite the authors of the instruments as well as psychometric properties of the instruments such as validity and reliability.

Cautions!

Make sure you come up with a system to guarantee anonymity for your participants. You are asking for sensitive information. Protect their privacy.

Just the experience of answering questions about Internet addiction may raise concern in your participants. Note, however, that you are not proposing to *diagnose* an addiction in anybody. You aren't qualified to address this issue—neither am I—but there may be a counseling center on your campus that can be a resource for students. End the survey by suggesting that if the participant has any concerns about their Internet use or sleep, they can seek assistance at the counseling center (or the student health center or whatever resource is most appropriate).

If you collect data in person, either keep signed consent separate from the data (so no one can associate the data with the name), or since signing the consent form may compromise anonymity, you could read the consent statement to the potential participant and ask if they'd like to continue. If you use an anonymous online survey, you can waive the consent signature and just start the survey with an informed consent statement. State that the participant is indicating their consent by continuing with the survey. Let your instructor guide you on this. In real-life research, the decision of whether to waive the signature would ultimately be decided by the Institutional Review Board (IRB). Here's an example of an online consent statement: http://www.wartburg.edu/harrc/informed-consentexample.pdf {suggested search term *informed consent online*}.

When you enter your data in a database, don't include identifying information. You can assign each participant a study number if you need to know identities temporarily.

PUTTING IT ALL TOGETHER

It's time to integrate all that you've been learning about writing lab reports. You've practiced writing each section individually (except, perhaps, the discussion section), so you are ready to write at least a partial lab report. Refer back to the labs titled *How to Write a Literature Review* and *After the Literature Review: Theory→Hypothesis → Design → Analysis →Results→Interpretation*. APA-style papers are double spaced throughout (even the references) and have a 1-inch margin on all sides. Use the data from the between-subjects *or* the within-subjects design. A complete report should include (1) a title page, (2) an abstract, (3) an introduction, (4) a method section (details, details, details!), (5) a results section, (6) a discussion section, and (7); a reference page, *or* whatever elements are assigned by your instructor.

Any tables or figures will go on separate pages at the end. The paper should be in APA format. In order to do an introduction section, you may need to do a little background reading on the topic, so you will need to find one or more relevant, peer-reviewed articles or a section of a textbook to help you bone up on the subject.

If you use the canned data, you didn't actually carry out the study. Since you didn't actually collect the data you will have to write the Method section *as if* you had done it (i.e., a bit of creative writing!). You can look at the Method section in one of your source articles and use that as a guide. Make sure your procedure matches the design you chose; for example, if you chose a between-subjects design, you should describe different people in each group. If you chose the within-subjects design, you should describe how the same people were tested longitudinally. You may choose to write about children or adults. You may use the reference cited above as well as those listed below if you wish to do so. Other scholarly references you find are fine, too.

Sometimes questions arise on how recent your sources should be. There's not a blanket answer to that. While recent research tells you where the research area is now, sometimes there are good reasons to use older articles. For example, some of your instruments may have been validated many years ago, but you'd still want to cite them. Perhaps you'll want to go back and identify the earliest research in the area so you can show how it became modified over time. Your instructor will have to tell you what's appropriate for your discipline.

Potential references:

Children

Arroyos-Jurado, E., Paulsen, J. S., Ehly, S., & Max, J. E. (2006). Traumatic brain injury in children and adolescents: Academic and intellectual outcomes following injury. *Exceptionality, 14*(3), 125–140. doi:10.1207/s15327035ex1403_2

Ewing-Cobbs, L., Fletcher, J. M., Levin, H. S., Francis, D. J., Davidson, K., & Miner, M. E. (1997). Longitudinal neuropsychological outcome in infants and preschoolers with traumatic brain injury. *Journal of the International Neuropsychological Society, 3*(6), 581–591.

Adults

Mathias, J. L., Bowden, S. C., Bigler, E. D., & Rosenfeld, J. V. (2007). Is performance on the Wechsler Test of Adult Reading affected by traumatic brain injury? *British Journal of Clinical Psychology, 46*(4), 457–466. doi:10.1348/014466507X190197

Senathi-Raja, D. D., Ponsford, J. J., Schönberger, M. M. (2010). Impact of age on long-term cognitive function after traumatic brain injury. *Neuropsychology 24*(3), 336–344. doi:10.1037/a0018239

IF YOU WANT TO GO FURTHER . . .

Categorical IVs and DVs in Regression

Participant categories:

(Lion = 1)

©iStock.com/
compassandcamera

(Tiger = 2)

©iStock.com/DPLight

(Bear = 3)

©iStock.com/Dirk Freder

(Oh my! = 4)

©iStock.com/artychoke98

Let's refresh our memories here. First, remember that a categorical variable is measured on a nominal scale, which means the scores do not represent amounts or degrees of the variable, but rather mutually exclusive groups. For example, let's say I ask participants where they were initially treated after their TBI. I have measured the variable "place of treatment." I code "hospital" as 1, "private practice" as 2, and "clinic" as 3. This does not mean private practice is 1 unit more of a place of treatment than private practice, just that the categories are different.

In this lab, you have learned how to compare three or more group means—that is, you've learned how to compare averages of a dependent variable (we can stick with IQ for the moment) among participants in three or more groups. In some cases, however, you might want more information than is provided by the ANOVA. For example, you might want to know how much variance in the DV is accounted for by each level of the IV (in this illustration, place of initial treatment), or perhaps all the groups as a unit. Using a coding system such as hospital = 1, private practice = 2, and clinic = 3 would not make sense in regression. Remember that in regression (review regression lab) the unstandardized regression coefficient (*b*) tells us how much influence our predictor has on the outcome. We interpret this value as "for every one unit increase in the predictor, there is a ___ change in the outcome." However, it would not make sense to talk about a 1 unit increase in place of treatment. To answer such questions, we need to create coded, categorical independent variables using a procedure called dummy coding that will have the value of 0 or 1.

That's fine for predictors, but how could you use regression to examine a binary outcome? For example, what if the outcome was recovered versus not recovered, or survived versus did not survive? In order to test the contributions of the predictors to these binary outcomes, we need to use a special form of regression called binary logistic regression. If you have a categorical DV with three or more outcomes you can use multinomial logistic regression. Ordinal DVs can be analyzed using ordinal regression. Because the process of setting up and interpreting the analyses are similar, the illustrations here will be just of binary logistic regression.

CODING CATEGORICAL PREDICTOR VARIABLES FOR REGRESSION

Dummy Coding

In dummy coding, we are creating a new *set* of codes that function together to conceptually and statistically represent our originally coded variable. Our codes will be binary, meaning they will consist only of scores 0 or 1. With our new coding system, we will always create <u>one less</u> column of coding than we have categories or groups. In our example of place of initial treatment where we had three categories, we would recode the variable into <u>two</u> new columns of data (3 categories − 1 = 2). We still have a single IV (place of initial treatment) but it has been split into two coded *terms* that together express the IV. This means one category or group will not have a specific code that identifies it; this category or group will be our "reference group" to which all other groups will be compared. Let's walk through this step by step.

1. **Pick your reference group.** The reference group is the one to which all others are compared. It is represented by the item value of 0. This group should be meaningful in some way—typically this group has the largest sample size (the majority of your sample is made up of this group), it is the standard group (such as the control group in an experiment or the "typical" member of your categorical variable), or this group has the most extreme values on your dependent variable. In our place of treatment

example above, we may pick *Hospital* to be our reference group because the majority of our sample was initially treated at a hospital.

Place of Treatment	Dummy Codes	
	Place_private_prac	*Place_clinic*
Hospital (Reference Group)	0	0
Private Practice	1	0
Public Clinic	0	1

2. **Create your coding system.** Next we will create a new column of data for all categories except your chosen reference group. A "0" will represent not being in a group, and a "1" will represent membership in that group. Note—your categories must be mutually exclusive, meaning you cannot be a member of more than 1 group (in our pretend study, all participants were initially treated in just one place). In the table, our new set of codes is titled *Place_private_prac* and *Place_clinic*.

Remember that our originally coded variable was labeled hospital = 1, private practice = 2, and public clinic = 3. All scores of 1 will now be presented by a 0 in the first column and a 0 in the second column. All scores of 2 will now be presented by 1 and 0. All scores of 3 will now be presented by 0 and 1.

Let's practice our dummy coding and run a regression. We'll continue with examining place of initial treatment and IQ. We are interested in knowing (1) if IQ varied by place of initial treatment and (2) how much variance in IQ was predicted by place of initial treatment.

Step 1: Pick your reference group.

Enter and save the data below into SPSS.

Place of Initial Treatment	IQ
1	80
2	110
1	90

1	95
3	70
2	115
1	80
1	100
1	115
3	80
1	75
3	90
1	95
3	75
2	100
3	65
3	75
2	95
2	90
1	85

As always—**eyeball the data!** But wait—is it useful to look at means and standard deviations of a categorical variable? Nope! What you will do is run your typical descriptives for your continuous variable (IQ), but will run frequency statistics to see how many participants are in each place category. Running both should provide the following output:

Descriptive Statistics

	N	Minimum	Maximum	Mean	Std. Deviation
IQ	20	65.00	115.00	89.0000	14.38201
Valid N (listwise)	20				

Place_treat

		Frequency	Percent	Valid Percent	Cumulative Percent
Valid	1.00	9	45.0	45.0	45.0
	2.00	5	25.0	25.0	70.0
	3.00	6	30.0	30.0	100.0
	Total	20	100.0	100.0	

By examining the frequency descriptives of our place of treatment variable, who has the largest *N*? There are 9 participants categorized as hospital, 5 as private practice, and 6 as clinic. If we set our criteria for choosing our reference group as largest *N*, then we now pick hospital as our reference group. From here, we will create our new dummy codes.

First, I'm going to tell you about a familiar but tedious way to do this, then I'll tell you about a less familiar but quicker way to create the codes.

We will first create our columns of *Place_private_prac* and *place_clinic* and set the default value to 0. *NOTE: If we had any missing data that had been labeled as 0 in our* place of treatment *column, this would create errors. Be sure you have no missing data or seek sources for coding missing data in SPSS.*

To create the new columns using the Dropdown Menu,

a. Click on *Transform, Compute Variable*

b. Under *Target Variable*, type Place_private_prac

c. Under *Numeric Expression*, type 0

d. Click *Continue, OK*

Then,

a. Click on *Transform, Compute Variable*

b. Under *Target Variable*, type Place_clinic

c. Under *Numeric Expression*, type 0

d. Click *Continue, OK*

You should now see two new columns of data in your data set. Next,

a. Click on *Transform, Compute Variable*

b. Under *Target Variable*, retype Place_private_prac

   c. Under *Numeric Expression*, type 1

   d. At the bottom left, click *If* . . .

   e. Click *Include If Case Satisfies Condition*

   f. Type in the box: Place_treat = 2

   g. Click *Continue*, *OK*

   h. When box pops up to ask *Change Existing Variable?*, click *OK*.

Then,

   a. Click on *Transform*, *Compute Variable*

   b. Under *Target Variable*, retype Place_clinic

   c. Under *Numeric Expression*, type 1

   d. At the bottom left, click *If* . . .

   e. Click *Include If Case Satisfies Condition*

   f. Type in the box: Place_treat = 3

   g. Click *Continue*, *OK*

   h. When a box pops up to ask *Change Existing Variable?*, click *OK*.

Whew! Want to know a secret? It is much easier to do this using Syntax. Syntax is a way to tell SPSS what to do without using the point-and-click commands.

   a. Click *File, New, Syntax*.

   b. Type (or copy and paste) in the following:

      compute Place_private_prac = 0.

      compute Place_clinic = 0.

      Execute.

       If Place_treat = 2 Place_private_prac = 1.

       If Place_treat = 3 Place_clinic = 1.

      Execute.

c. Highlight all the syntax commands and click the green triangle (*Run Selection*). Viola! Dummy coding made easy. You can also save your Syntax file so you can quickly run this dummy coding again.

Take a look at your data file. You should have two new columns with all 0s and 1s. Save your data. Let's run our regression now, looking to see if place of initial treatment predicts IQ.

a. Click on *Analyze, Regression, Linear*

b. Move the dependent variable (IQ) into the *Dependent* block.

c. Move the independent variables (new items for place of treatment— Place_private_prac, Place_clinic) into the *Independent* block.

d. Click *Statistics* and *Confidence Intervals*

e. Click *Continue, OK*

Your output should look like this:

Model Summary

Model	R	R Square	Adjusted R Square	Std. Error of the Estimate
1	.697[a]	.485	.425	10.90886

a. Predictors: (Constant), Place_Clinic, Place_private_prac

ANOVA[a]

Model		Sum of Squares	df	Mean Square	F	Sig.
1	Regression	1906.944	2	953.472	8.012	.004[b]
	Residual	2023.056	17	119.003		
	Total	3930.000	19			

a. Dependent Variable: IQ

b. Predictors: (Constant), Place_Clinic, Place_private_prac

Coefficients[a]

Model		Unstandardized Coefficients		Standardized Coefficients	t	Sig.	95.0% Confidence Interval for B	
		B	Std. Error	Beta			Lower Bound	Upper Bound
1	(Constant)	90.556	3.636		24.903	.000	82.884	98.227
	Place_Private_prac	11.444	6.085	.354	1.881	.077	-1.393	24.282
	Place_Clinic	-14.722	5.749	-.481	-2.561	.020	-26.853	-2.592

a. Dependent Variable: IQ

Let's interpret these results to answer our questions of (1) whether IQ varied by place of initial treatment and (2) how much variance in IQ was predicted by initial treatment.

If you look at our unstandardized regression coefficients (highlighted above under the B column), we interpret these as we did before, but consider what a 0 now means. We learned that we interpret the constant as the value of Y (here, IQ) when all predictors are set at 0. Using our dummy coding system, when Place_private_prac and Place_clinic are both 0, this represented our Hospital category. Thus, we interpret the constant or intercept as the average IQ of people initially treated at a hospital (90.56, or just under 91). Similarly, we can interpret the other unstandardized coefficients as the average difference in IQ from the constant, therefore the average IQ for those treated at a private practice was 11.44 points above those treated at a hospital (rounding, $91 + 11 = 102$) and the average IQ for those initially treated at a clinic was 14.72 points below (because the coefficient was negative) those treated at a hospital (rounding, $91 - 15 = 76$). If we look at the significance of the t-tests, we can see that the average for those treated at a clinic was significantly different than those treated at a hospital ($p = .02$) but the average for those treated at a private practice was not ($p = .08$). To answer our question, yes—IQs vary by place of treatment; those treated at a clinic produced significantly lower IQ scores than those treated at a hospital.

Next, we look at our R^2 value to determine if place of treatment predicted a significant amount of the variance in IQ scores. We see that it predicted almost half (48%) of the variance in IQ. This is statistically significant, as indicated by the F-test in the ANOVA above, $F(2,17) = 8.01, p < .01$.

And there you have it!

Other Types of Categorical Coding

Dummy coding is the most simplistic coding scheme for categorical variables, but be aware there are other types, such as weighted and unweighted effect coding. See additional sources on the topic of categorical variable coding below.

http://www.ats.ucla.edu/stat/mult_pkg/faq/general/effect.htm {suggested search term *effect coding*}

http://www.upa.pdx.edu/IOA/newsom/da2/ho_coding1.pdf {suggested search term *coding categorical predictors*}

LOGISTIC REGRESSION

So far we have talked about how to handle categorical *independent* variables, but not categorical *dependent* variables. There are many clinical and scientific research questions where we want to predict dichotomous outcomes, such as a pass/fail, sick/healthy, or yes/no variable. We cannot simply run a linear regression with a dichotomous outcome because it violates assumptions regarding the normality of the residuals (a problem we rarely see with continuous outcomes/dependent variables). However, we can use logistic regression. Rather than predicting the actual score of a continuous outcome, logistic regression predicts the *probability* of being a case (e.g., passing an exam) versus not being a case (e.g., not passing an exam). Now, in order to run a logistic regression, the dichotomous variable must be dummy coded, which is easy to do when there are only two categories. One category will be coded as 0 and the other will be coded as 1 all within the same column of data.

Outcome:

"Won a Race at Least Once" = 1   or   *"Never Won a Race"* = 0

©iStock.com/Michael Krinke

©iStock.com/Avesun

TRY IT YOURSELF

Let's stick with our example of IQ post–TBI. We'll assume we are concerned whether a patient's IQ will be below normal after suffering a TBI. We can ask whether hours of cognitive therapy per week can predict the probability of regaining "normal" cognitive functioning (for the moment let's define normal as an IQ score ≥ 90). Therefore, the outcome variable is dichotomous (same thing as a binary variable): We are coding below normal (IQ < 90) as 0 and normal (≥ 90) as 1.

Enter and save the data below into SPSS.

Hours_Therapy	Normal_IQ
2	0
4	1
3	0
4	0
0	0
6	1
9	1
3	0
3	1
5	0
4	1
11	1
2	0
2	1
7	1
5	0
2	0
6	1
1	0
8	1

Eyeball the data! Run descriptives on Hours_Therapy and frequency on Normal_IQ. If all looks good, let's run the logistic regression.

a. Click on *Analyze, Regression, Binary Logistic*

b. Move the dependent variable (Normal_IQ) into the *Dependent* block.

c. Move the independent variable (Hours_Therapy) into the *Covariates* block.

d. *Options, CI for exp(B), Continue*

e. Click *OK*

Your output should look like this (for the sake of space, I'm including just the tables I'll mention below):

Model Summary

Step	-2 Log likelihood	Cox & Snell R Square	Nagelkerke R Square
1	18.586[a]	.367	.489

Variables in the Equation

		B	S.E.	Wald	df	Sig.	Exp(B)	95% C.I. for EXP(B)	
								Lower	Upper
Step 1[a]	Hours_Therapy	.734	.339	4.685	1	.030	2.084	1.072	4.051
	Constant	-2.992	1.418	4.449	1	.035	.050		

a. Variable(s) entered on step 1: Hours_Therapy.

Let's take a look at the box titled *Model Summary*. Logistic regression does not provide true model fit, but generates "pseudo-R^2" values that can be interpreted as approximate variance in the outcome accounted for by the predictor(s). SPSS provides Cox/Snell R Square and Nagelkerke R Square values. There is no consensus on which estimate is superior, but both are commonly used. According to these, hours of therapy explained 37% to 49% of the variance in whether IQ was classified as normal or not.

Now look at the *Variables in the Equation* box. This looks somewhat similar to output from a linear regression. We still interpret values as "__ change in Y (normal IQ) per unit change in X (hours of therapy)." However, the coefficients in logistic regression are called *logits*, or the natural logarithm of the odds of the dependent variable being a case. The logit in the above output is located in the second column labeled *B* (.734). Logits are difficult to interpret, so we often use the odds ratio (OR) value, which is the exponentiated coefficient located in the column labeled *Exp(B)*. The OR describes the odds of being a case (in our illustration, classified as having "normal" IQ). If our output had provided an OR = 1, this would mean there is no greater or less likelihood of being a case (i.e., regaining "normal" IQ) per unit change in therapy. We can therefore eyeball our OR to see if our predictor increases or decreases the likelihood of being a case. If OR > 1, the predictor is associated with increased odds of being a case, but if the OR < 1, the predictor is associated with decreased odds of being a case.

We often transform ORs to percentages for easiest interpretation. Let's take our OR from above of 2.08 (which we can see is statistically significant). If we compute (OR − 1)*100, we can interpret this value as the percentage increase or decrease in odds of being a case per unit change in X. So, OR = 2.08, so (2.08 − 1)*100 = 108. Considering the value is positive, we can interpret this as for every one hour increase in therapy per week, there is a 108% increase in the odds of regaining a "normal" IQ. This confirms our hypothesis that hours of therapy per week predict the likelihood of regaining "normal" IQ.

LAB 13

Factorial Designs

Objective

This lab presents designs that include two or more independent variables (IVs), ANOVAs that produce multiple main effects and interaction effects, completely between-subjects, completely within-subjects, and mixed factorial designs. Appropriate post hoc testing is discussed. Additional material addresses using regression to test interaction effects.

Target Article

©iStock.com/artisticco

Cooper, J., Bennett, E. A., & Sukel, H. L. (1996). Complex scientific testimony: How do jurors make decisions? *Law and Human Behavior, 20,* 379–394. doi: 10.1007/BF01498976

P retend for a moment you have been accused of a crime. Your defense rests on whether the jury believes your expert witness or not. Do you want your expert witness to be Dr. X, who is world famous on the topic, or Dr. Y, who is not so famous? The answer is, it depends. In this study, mock jurors were randomly assigned to one of four conditions, created by a 2 (high expertise vs. less expertise) x 2 (complex presentation vs. simpler presentation) factorial design. Therefore, there were two IVs: level of expertise and presentation style. The legal question was whether a plain-tiff's illness had been caused by exposure to polychlorinated biphenyls (PCBs). Participants, pretending to be jurors, watched a one-hour video of a trial in which a high-expertise witness and a low-expertise witness each presented evidence in one of two ways: complex or more simply. The gist of the testimony was the same in all four conditions. The outcome measure was the extent to which the jurors were persuaded by the testimony. While participants were more impressed by the high-expertise witness, this main effect was modified by a significant interac-tion effect. When the testimony was presented in a complicated manner, the high-expertise witness was more persuasive. When the material was presented in a more straightforward manner, however, the participants were less affected by level of expertise. So if the evidence in your favor is highly technical, you may want to go with Dr. X. If the evidence is easier to under-stand, then Dr. Y (who might have less impressive credentials but charge less) would do just as well.

©iStock.com/ImpaKPro

This table, based on one in the article (Cooper, Bennett, & Sukel, 1996, p. 388), shows the participants' perceived probability that the illness had been caused by the PCB exposure.

Witness Credibility	Testimony Complexity	
	High	Low
High	96	53
Low	49	70

BACKGROUND

In today's lab, we're going to think about designs that have two or more IVs. We're still looking at designs that have a single dependent variable (DV). There are designs out there that allow you to look at multiple DVs in one analysis, but that is beyond the scope of this book.

Cooper et al. (1996) could have tested their hypothesis using two, two-group designs. This would let them determine if witness expertise or presentation style was more persuasive, but they would have missed important information had they taken that approach. They could not get at the interaction of the two IVs, which was the important finding in this study. An interaction effect occurs when the effect of one variable is dependent on the level of the other variable. In this case, the persuasiveness of the witness's expertise depended on how the testimony was presented. A factorial design allows you to consider the effects of two IVs simultaneously.

Factorial notation is a sort of shorthand way of describing a factorial design. It tells you how many IVs there are (two or more) and how many levels each IV has (two or more). You can also calculate from this how many cells, or group means, will be created by the largest interaction. There is one digit for each IV, and the value of the digit tells you the number of levels. If you multiply the numbers in the notation, this tells you how many group means (cells) will be in the largest interaction.

For example, a 2 x 3 factorial design has two IVs. The first IV has two levels and the second has three, and the interaction will produce 6 means. Try this for a few more examples:

	# IVs	# levels each IV	# group means
2 x 2 x 2			
3 x 4			

	# IVs	# levels each IV	# group means
2 x 2 x 2	3	2	8
3 x 4	2	first-3, second-4	12

For the sake of simplicity, we're going to concentrate on designs with just two IVs.

A factorial design is analyzed using an ANOVA. Remember the illustration of the ANOVA from the lab on multiple-groups design? It divided total variability in the DV into that which was associated with the IV and that which was associated with error. Now we're looking at a two way (i.e., two IVs) ANOVA. This divides total variability into two main effects and an interaction effect as well as error. A main effect is variability due to just one IV when the other IVs are ignored (or "collapsed across"). For now let's call the two IVs A and B. Each main effect and interaction effect gets a separate *F*-test.

Figure 13.1   The Factorial ANOVA Pie

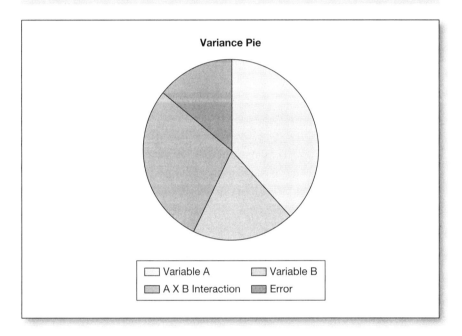

In the target article, expertise of the witness (level of expertise ignoring any differences in how the material was presented) and type of presentation (level of complexity ignoring any differences in level of witness expertise) are the main effects. The interaction effect takes both variables into consideration, allowing you to consider four groups — believability when expertise is high and complexity is high, high expertise and low complexity, low expertise and high complexity, and low expertise and low complexity.

The factorial design can be
- completely between-subjects (all IVs are between-subjects),
- completely within-subjects (all IVs are within-subjects), or
- mixed (at least one between-subjects IV and at least one within-subjects IV).

When we analyze a completely between-subjects ANOVA, we're going to use a univariate ANOVA. To analyze a completely within-subjects or a mixed-factorial design, we'll use a repeated-measures ANOVA.

Now what?

Just as was the case with the multigroup designs, a significant interaction F tells you that somewhere, among all the possible pairings of means, at least one pair is significantly different. You will have to do post hoc testing to find out which pairs are significantly different. A *nonsignificant F* means stop—don't go any further.

How do I know when post hoc testing of a significant effect is needed?

This will depend on how many means are involved in the comparison. Let's think for a moment about a 2 x 3 design. A significant F that involves *three or more means* will need to be followed by post hoc testing. In this illustration, if variable A is significant, then only two means are being compared (A_1 vs. A_2). In that case, there is only one pair of means to compare, so you already know those are the means that are significantly different; therefore you don't need post hoc tests. If variable B is significant, however, it has three levels (B_1, B_2, B_3), and therefore there are three means to compare. In that case, you would need to do post hoc testing to discover which means are significantly different.

What about the interaction effect? In a 2 x 2 design (the simplest factorial design), the interaction involves four means. How many means would be involved in the interaction when using a 2 x 3 design? ___ (6) Therefore, an interaction effect will always include four or more means, and, if significant, will need to be followed by post hoc tests.

Interaction effects trump main effects. Even if main effects A and/or B are significant, a significant interaction modifies our interpretation of the main effect. In that case, we'd say that the significant main effect was modified by a significant interaction effect. Still thinking of a 2 x 3 design, we'd no longer need to do post hoc testing for a significant main effect of B, because we're more interested in the means produced by the significant interaction. Therefore, we would report post hoc tests of just the interaction effect.

TRY IT YOURSELF

Canned Data

Assignment

Begin by reading http://www.wadsworth.com/psychology_d/templates/ student_resources/workshops/stat_workshp/two_anova/two_anova_01.html.

Today, you will think about canned data from a 2 x 2 factorial design. You will analyze the same data in three different ways: once as if it were a completely between-subjects design, once as if it were a completely within-subjects design, and once as if it were a mixed-factorial design.

Practice writing the Results section for the *mixed-factorial design*. This may be a lot wordier than the others we've practiced because factorial designs are more complex and require more explanation. Report the type of ANOVA and report the findings in the following order:

1. ANOVA

    a. main effects

    b. interaction effect

2. Post hoc tests (if needed).

Enter the means and standard deviations in a table, then refer the reader to the table. MAKE SURE you understand the table goes on a separate page AFTER the references (not in the body of the paper). Either follow your instructor's directions to create a table or look at APA-style tables in the lab on Tables and Figures. DO NOT copy and paste an output box from SPSS to create a Results table; type out a new table that follows the formatting rules.

Let's assume that we're going to look at whether witness attractiveness or type of clothing might sway jurors' perception of the witness believability. In other words, will more attractive witnesses be more believable? How about sloppy clothing versus business clothing? Will there be an interaction between attractiveness and type of attire? Remember I'm making these data up, so don't view these findings as accurate. We'll say that participants (who are playing the role of jurors) viewed pictures of the same person (hypothetical witness). The pictures had been modified to (1) an appearance that pilot testing indicated was perceived to be attractive and (2) another version that had been judged to be unattractive. In addition, there were two versions of each attractiveness level: one in which the person was wearing sloppy clothing and one in which the person was wearing business clothing.

Therefore, there were two IVs, each having two levels. How would you write this using factorial notation? _____ (2 x 2) The outcome variable was a measure of believability.

Completely Between-Subjects Factorial Design

First, let's imagine doing this task as a completely between-subjects 2 x 2 factorial design. This means there are different participants (the people who are judging believability) in each of the four cells. Participants were randomly assigned to one of four conditions in which they viewed a set of pictures of hypothetical witnesses who were

1. attractive with sloppy clothing

2. attractive with business clothing

3. unattractive with sloppy clothing

4. unattractive in business clothing

©iStock.com/Justin Horrocks

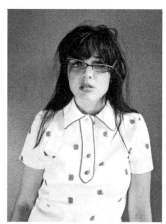
©iStock.com/ImagesbyTrista

Set up your data file. In the column for the first variable, you'll enter either 1 for attractive or 2 for unattractive. For the second variable, we'll let 1 = business clothing and 2 = sloppy clothing. The third column is the outcome measure. Higher numbers indicate greater believability.

Attractiveness	Clothing	Believability
1.00	1.00	240.00
1.00	1.00	231.00
1.00	1.00	188.00
1.00	1.00	197.00
1.00	1.00	155.00
1.00	1.00	242.00
1.00	1.00	215.00

1.00	1.00	190.00
1.00	1.00	179.00
1.00	1.00	167.00
1.00	2.00	196.00
1.00	2.00	162.00
1.00	2.00	142.00
1.00	2.00	140.00
1.00	2.00	160.00
1.00	2.00	204.00
1.00	2.00	173.00
1.00	2.00	179.00
1.00	2.00	175.00
1.00	2.00	134.00
2.00	1.00	221.00
2.00	1.00	207.00
2.00	1.00	187.00
2.00	1.00	173.00
2.00	1.00	129.00
2.00	1.00	223.00
2.00	1.00	209.00
2.00	1.00	189.00
2.00	1.00	165.00
2.00	1.00	141.00
2.00	2.00	198.00
2.00	2.00	164.00
2.00	2.00	144.00
2.00	2.00	142.00
2.00	2.00	128.00
2.00	2.00	206.00

(Continued)

(Continued)

2.00	2.00	175.00
2.00	2.00	181.00
2.00	2.00	177.00
2.00	2.00	108.00

Remember to label your variables and indicate the meaning of the assigned values.

Because both IVs are between-subjects, we'll use the univariate ANOVA to analyze these data.

1. Click *Analyze*

2. *General Linear Model*

3. *Univariate*

4. Move the two IVs into the *Fixed Factors* box and the DV into the Dependent Variable box.

5. Go to *Options*, and click the box to the left of *Descriptives* and *Estimate of Effect Size*.

6. *Continue*

7. *OK*

Save your data. Always start by **eyeballing** the descriptive data. Does everything make sense?

Univariate Analysis of Variance

Between-Subjects Factors

		Value Label	N
Attractiveness	1.00	attractive	20
	2.00	unattractive	20
Clothing	1.00	business	20
	2.00	sloppy	20

This box lets you make sure you set up the analysis correctly.

Descriptive Statistics

Dependent Variable: Believability

Attractiveness	Clothing	Mean	Std. Deviation	N
attractive	Business	200.4000	30.47112	10
	Sloppy	166.5000	23.49586	10
	Total	183.4500	31.68176	20
unattractive	Business	184.4000	32.37351	10
	Sloppy	162.3000	31.24473	10
	Total	173.3500	32.97571	20
Total	Business	192.4000	31.67998	20
	Sloppy	164.4000	26.99201	20
	Total	178.4000	32.32511	40

You'll need this descriptive information to eyeball the data and when you interpret your results.

Tests of Between-Subjects Effects

Dependent Variable: Believability

Source	Type III Sum of Squares	df	Mean Square	F	Sig.	Partial Eta Squared
Corrected Model	9208.200ª	3	3069.400	3.503	.025	.226
Intercept	1273062.400	1	1273062.400	1452.9 27	.000	.976
Attractiveness	1020.100	1	1020.100	1.164	.288	.031
Clothing	7840.000	1	7840.000	8.948	.005	.199
Attractiveness * Clothing	348.100	1	348.100	.397	.532	.011
Error	31543.400	36	876.206			
Total	1313814.000	40				
Corrected Total	40751.600	39				

a. R Squared = .226 (Adjusted R Squared = .161)

Notice that this analysis gives you an *F*-value for each main effect (each variable by itself, not taking into consideration the other variable), as well as an *F*-value for the interaction effect of Attractiveness x Clothing. You will now examine each main effect and the interaction effect to determine if any is significant, and indicate this below. Refer back to the multigroup lab for the format to use when reporting *F* scores [e.g., $F(1,36) = 1.16, p = .29$]. Notice which parts are italicized. Be sure you understand where each number is found in the source table.

You don't have to write down your answers to the short-answer questions embedded in this lab but make sure you can answer them and understand the answer. Ask for help if needed.

Is the main effect of attractiveness significant? Make sure you are looking under the Sig. column. _____ (no) Report the F-value and significance level. _____ [$F(1,36) = 1.16, p = .29$]

Is the main effect of clothing significant? _____ (yes) Report the F-value and significance level. _____ [$F(1,36) = 8.95, p = .01$]

Is the attractiveness x clothing interaction effect significant? ___ (no) Report the F-value and significance level. _____ [$F(1,36) = .40, p = .53$]

Remember that a significant F means that somewhere among all the pairs of means involved in that effect, there is at least one significant difference. If there are only two means in an effect, then you don't need to do any post hoc testing. As we indicated earlier, when there are three or more means involved in a significant effect, some type of post hoc test is needed. Are post hoc tests needed to further test the significant main effect of clothing? _____ (no) Why? _____ (Hint: How many means are being compared by the clothing main effect?) (only two means)

Keep in mind that a nonsignificant F-test means stop. Are post hoc tests needed for the interaction? _____ (no) Why? _____ (not significant)

So, using this design we conclude that business attire was perceived as more believable, but attractiveness didn't make a difference. The interaction of the two IVs was not significant.

Mixed-Factorial Design

Next, let's treat the data as if they had been produced using a mixed-factorial design. In a mixed-factorial design there is at least one between-subjects IV and at least one within-subjects IV. Remember, one enters data differently for between- and within-subjects variables. In this case, let's assume that clothing was the between-subjects variable (different people viewed sloppy vs. business attire), and attractiveness was the within-subjects variable (same people tested twice, once viewing an attractive witness, once viewing an unattractive witness). We're pretending here, anyway, so we may as well pretend that the participants would not realize they were seeing the same person in stimuli depicting attractive versus unattractive.

We need one column to indicate the clothing condition and two columns to indicate the believability of the attractive and unattractive stimuli. Again, let 1 = business clothing and 2 = sloppy clothing. You can use cut and paste to rearrange numbers from the between-subjects data to the new configuration below. Save each data file under a different filename.

Clothing	Believability_attractive	Believability_unattractive
1.00	240.00	221.00
1.00	231.00	207.00
1.00	188.00	187.00
1.00	197.00	173.00
1.00	155.00	129.00
1.00	242.00	223.00
1.00	215.00	209.00
1.00	190.00	189.00
1.00	179.00	165.00
1.00	167.00	141.00
2.00	196.00	198.00
2.00	162.00	164.00
2.00	142.00	144.00
2.00	140.00	142.00
2.00	160.00	128.00
2.00	204.00	206.00
2.00	173.00	175.00
2.00	179.00	181.00
2.00	175.00	177.00
2.00	134.00	108.00

How many participants did we have for the completely between-subjects design? _____ (40) How many do we have for the mixed-factorial design? _____ (20) Why do we have fewer participants this time? _____ _____ (repeated measures on attractiveness variable)

Eyeballing the data: When running analyses, always look at your results and ask whether they make sense in light of what you've already learned about your data. If something seems out of line, go back and double check data entry, whether you used the appropriate statistic, and whether the analysis was set up correctly.

Since we now have a repeated-measure variable, we'll need to use the Repeated-Measures ANOVA.

1. Click *Analyze*

2. *General Linear Model*

3. *Repeated Measures*

4. Attractiveness is the repeated-measures variable, so make the within-subject factor name Attractiveness, indicate it has two levels, then click

5. *Add*

6. *Define*

7. Highlight the two believability variable names and move them using the right arrow into the *Within-subjects variable* box.

8. Move Clothing to the *Between-subjects factor* box

9. Click *Options*

10. *Descriptive Statistics, Estimate Effect Size*

11. *Continue*

12. *OK*

The output will contain more information than we're going to use just now, so I'll reproduce here only the information we'll use.

Check to make sure you set up the design the way you intended to do.

Between-Subjects Factors

		Value Label	N
Clothing	1.00	Business	10
	2.00	Sloppy	10

Descriptive Statistics

	Clothing	Mean	Std. Deviation	N
Believability_attractive	business	200.4000	30.47112	10
	sloppy	166.5000	23.49586	10
	Total	183.4500	31.68176	20
Believability_unattractive	business	184.4000	32.37351	10
	sloppy	162.3000	31.24473	10
	Total	173.3500	32.97571	20

Eyeball your data! Does everything make sense?

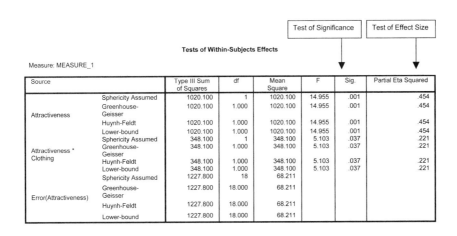

Tests of Within-Subjects Effects

Measure: MEASURE_1

Source		Type III Sum of Squares	df	Mean Square	F	Sig.	Partial Eta Squared
Attractiveness	Sphericity Assumed	1020.100	1	1020.100	14.955	.001	.454
	Greenhouse-Geisser	1020.100	1.000	1020.100	14.955	.001	.454
	Huynh-Feldt	1020.100	1.000	1020.100	14.955	.001	.454
	Lower-bound	1020.100	1.000	1020.100	14.955	.001	.454
Attractiveness * Clothing	Sphericity Assumed	348.100	1	348.100	5.103	.037	.221
	Greenhouse-Geisser	348.100	1.000	348.100	5.103	.037	.221
	Huynh-Feldt	348.100	1.000	348.100	5.103	.037	.221
	Lower-bound	348.100	1.000	348.100	5.103	.037	.221
Error(Attractiveness)	Sphericity Assumed	1227.800	18	68.211			
	Greenhouse-Geisser	1227.800	18.000	68.211			
	Huynh-Feldt	1227.800	18.000	68.211			
	Lower-bound	1227.800	18.000	68.211			

Now, we get to some new stuff. This box will indicate all *within-subjects main effects* and any *interactions that involve within-subjects IVs*. For our purposes, use the values in line with "sphericity assumed."

The box below reports the *between-subjects main effects, and would also report interaction effects of between-subjects variables* (we don't have any in this example). Notice each box (Within-subjects effects and Between-subjects effects) has its own error term and *df*.

Tests of Between-Subjects Effects

Measure: MEASURE_1

Transformed Variable: Average

Source	Type III Sum of Squares	df	Mean Square	F	Sig.	Partial Eta Squared
Intercept	1273062.400	1	1273062.400	755.886	.000	.977
Clothing	7840.000	1	7840.000	4.655	.045	.205
Error	30315.600	18	1684.200			

Is the main effect of attractiveness significant? _____ (yes) Is the main effect of clothing significant? _____ (yes) Is the attractiveness x clothing interaction effect significant? _____ (yes) Using a different design changed the outcome despite the fact that we used the same data.

Why was the interaction significant this time? Remember that when you use a within-subjects design, you are eliminating some potential error between groups because you have used the same people (or matched groups or natural groups). That translates into greater statistical power, or greater sensitivity to detect small differences between groups. In this case, using a different design changed statistical significance. Compare the values in the partial eta squared column for the between subjects and mixed ANOVAs. You should see larger values when the mixed-factorial design was used.

This time the interaction effect is significant, and it involves four means, so you'll have to do some sort of post hoc tests to find the significantly different means. You can get the means and standard deviations from the Descriptives box above.

Here are the means and standard deviations in table form.

	Attractive	Unattractive
Business Clothes	200.40 (30.47)	184.40 (32.37)
Sloppy Clothes	166.50 (23.50)	162.30 (31.24)

NOTE: Standard deviations are in parentheses.

Remember, this is a mixed-factorial design. Since there are *different* people in each type of clothing group, business versus sloppy comparisons require you to use the independent-samples *t*-test. When you are comparing the effects of person attractiveness (attractive vs. unattractive) separately for each type of clothing, you are comparing the *same* people viewing two different levels of attractiveness. For these comparisons, use the paired-samples *t*-test.

We need to make four comparisons.

Comparison 1: Among participants who saw people in business clothing, did stimulus attractiveness influence believability ratings? This compares 200.40 to 184.40. You want to narrow down your data to just those participants who saw stimuli in business clothing, so from the data screen

1. Click *Data*

2. *Select Cases*

3. *If Condition Is Satisfied*

4. *If*

5. We coded business clothing as 1. Highlight Clothing, move it to the box on the right, then type in = 1.

6. Click *Continue*

7. *OK*

This takes you back to the data screen. You should see the participants who viewed sloppy clothing now have a slash over their subject number, indicating that they won't be included in your next test, and SPSS has created a "filter" variable. When we compare believability of attractive versus unattractive stimuli, we are comparing the same people, so run a paired *t*-test. If you don't recall how to do this, refer back to the lab on two-group designs. You'll be able to compare your findings to the *t*-tests reported on the next page to confirm you ran the tests correctly. Is this comparison significant? _____ (yes) Write out this statistic and level of significance. _____ (see below)

Helpful hint: It is very easy to forget which group is included in a particular test when you have selected a subset of your participants. As soon as I ran this paired-samples *t*-test, I went back up to the title *T-Test* at the top of this output and double clicked it. Alternatively, you can click the icon on the far right side of the top banner that allows you to add new text. Type business clothes in the box so you will remember later which subgroup it represents.

Comparison 2: Now go back to the data screen and

1. Have the computer select for clothing = 2, the people who saw stimuli wearing sloppy clothes. This compares 166.50 to 162.30.

2. Test these with the paired *t*-test.

3. Insert a note to label this test, too. Is it significant? _____ (no) Write it out. _____

Before we go any further, go back to the data screen,

1. Click *Data*

2. *Select Cases*

3. *All Cases*

4. *OK*

Now everyone is included again.

Comparisons 3 and 4: The next two comparisons examine the effects of clothing on believability of attractive stimuli (comparison 3) and unattractive stimuli (comparison 4). These compare 200.40 to 166.50 and 184.40 to 162.30. These two comparisons involve <u>different</u> people in each group so you test them using the _____-samples *t*-test. (independent)

1. Use clothing as the grouping variable (remember to define it).

2. Use Believability_attractive as the test variable.

3. You can run both *t*-tests at one time. Go ahead and move the Believability_unattractive variable name to the test variable box as well. The computer will run a *t*-test for each variable.

Thus far, then, we can conclude, using the mixed-factorial design, that

✓ 200.40 > 184.40, $t(9) = 5.06$, $p = .001$ (Participants who saw a stimulus wearing business clothing rated attractive as more believable than unattractive)

✓ 166.50 = 162.30, $t(9) = 1.01$, $p = .34$ (Participants who saw stimuli wearing sloppy clothing rated attractive equally believable as unattractive)

✓ 200.40 > 166.50, $t(18) = 2.79$. $p = .01$ (When viewing an attractive stimulus, participants who viewed business clothing reported higher believability than those who viewed sloppy clothing)

✓ 184.40 = 162.30, $t(18) = 1.55$, $p = .14$ (When viewing an unattractive stimulus, participants who viewed business clothing reported equal believability as did those who viewed sloppy clothing)

Interpretation of the Mixed-Factorial Design

Interactions can be a challenge to recognize and interpret. Let's try to sort it out.

The Research Questions We tested whether attractiveness influenced believability of a witness (as rated by participants pretending to be jurors), and whether attractiveness would be moderated by (i.e., interact with) type of clothing.

What We Found and What It Indicates Using a mixed-factorial design we found significant main effects of both attractiveness and type of clothing as well as a significant interaction of the two variables. The main effects tell us that participants found an attractive stimulus to be more believable, as was also true of a stimulus wearing business clothing. However, since we have the significant interaction effect, we have to say that those main effects are modified by the significant interaction. In other words, the main effects don't tell the whole story; you can't talk about the role of attractiveness without also talking about type of clothing, and vice versa. Participants rated the attractive stimulus as more believable when wearing business clothes, but attractiveness didn't seem to matter if wearing sloppy clothing. Likewise, testimony may be more believable when the witness is wearing business clothing, but only if the witness is also attractive.

The significant interaction tells us that we can't make a statement about the effects of one variable without taking into consideration the other variable; if you try to answer the question of whether attractiveness or clothing influence believability, the answer has to start with "it depends." You can practice identifying main and interaction effects in the upcoming section, More Practice With Interactions.

Completely Within-Subjects Factorial Design

Let's do one more analysis. This time assume that each participant took part in each of the four possible conditions. This would be a completely within-subjects design. There is no between-subjects independent variable; rather, there are two within-subjects IVs. This time, 10 participants are tested in each of four conditions. The four variables below are

1. Attractiveness

    a. Attractive

    b. Unattractive

2. Clothing

    a. Business

    b. Sloppy

We're down to needing just 10 participants because each person is tested in each condition.

Attractive_ business	Unattractive_ business	Attractive_ sloppy	Unattractive_ sloppy
240.00	221.00	196.00	198.00
231.00	207.00	162.00	164.00
188.00	187.00	142.00	144.00
197.00	173.00	140.00	142.00
155.00	129.00	160.00	128.00
242.00	223.00	204.00	206.00
215.00	209.00	173.00	175.00
190.00	189.00	179.00	181.00
179.00	165.00	175.00	177.00
167.00	141.00	134.00	108.00

Both IVs are within subjects, so we'll again use a repeated-measures ANOVA.

1. Click *Analyze*

2. *General Linear Model*

3. *Repeated Measures*

4. If there is already a within-subject variable name in the first large box, highlight it and click *Remove.*

5. We must now set up two within-subjects variables. The first variable is clothing: the first two columns above are believability when wearing business clothing and the last two are believability when wearing sloppy clothing.

6. So let's make the first variable clothing, indicate it has two levels, then add it to the large box.

7. Now, notice that within each type of clothing, the first column refers to the attractive stimulus and the second to the unattractive stimulus. The second within-subjects variable, therefore, is attractiveness, and it has two levels.

8. Click *Add*

9. *Define*

10. Highlight the four variables and move them to the *Within-subjects variables* box.

11. *Options*

12. *Descriptives, Estimate Effect Size*

13. *Continue*

14. *OK*

Save, **then eyeball your data!** Again, I include here only the information that we'll use.

Descriptive Statistics

	Mean	Std. Deviation	N
Attractive_business	200.4000	30.47112	10
Unattractive_business	184.4000	32.37351	10
Attractive_sloppy	166.5000	23.49586	10
Unattractive_sloppy	162.3000	31.24473	10

Tests of Within-Subjects Effects

Source		Type III Sum of Squares	df	Mean Square	F	Sig.	Partial Eta Squared
Clothing	Sphericity Assumed	7840.000	1	7840.000	18.897	.002	.677
	Greenhouse-Geisser	7840.000	1.000	7840.000	18.897	.002	.677
	Huynh-Feldt	7840.000	1.000	7840.000	18.897	.002	.677
	Lower-bound	7840.000	1.000	7840.000	18.897	.002	.677
Error(Clothing)	Sphericity Assumed	3734.000	9	414.889			
	Greenhouse-Geisser	3734.000	9.000	414.889			
	Huynh-Feldt	3734.000	9.000	414.889			
	Lower-bound	3734.000	9.000	414.889			
Attractiveness	Sphericity Assumed	1020.100	1	1020.100	9.937	.012	.525
	Greenhouse-Geisser	1020.100	1.000	1020.100	9.937	.012	.525
	Huynh-Feldt	1020.100	1.000	1020.100	9.937	.012	.525
	Lower-bound	1020.100	1.000	1020.100	9.937	.012	.525
Error(Attractiveness)	Sphericity Assumed	923.900	9	102.656			
	Greenhouse-Geisser	923.900	9.000	102.656			
	Huynh-Feldt	923.900	9.000	102.656			
	Lower-bound	923.900	9.000	102.656			
Clothing * Attractiveness	Sphericity Assumed	348.100	1	348.100	10.309	.011	.534
	Greenhouse-Geisser	348.100	1.000	348.100	10.309	.011	.534
	Huynh-Feldt	348.100	1.000	348.100	10.309	.011	.534
	Lower-bound	348.100	1.000	348.100	10.309	.011	.534
Error(Clothing*Attractiveness)	Sphericity Assumed	303.900	9	33.767			
	Greenhouse-Geisser	303.900	9.000	33.767			
	Huynh-Feldt	303.900	9.000	33.767			
	Lower-bound	303.900	9.000	33.767			

Notice that each main effect and each interaction has its very own error term. Are the main effects significant? _____ (yes) Is the interaction significant? _____ (yes) Write out the F-term and level of significance for each effect.

Main effect of clothing   _____

Main effect of attractiveness   _____

Interaction effect of clothing x attractiveness   _____

$[F(1,9) = 18.90, p = .002$, partial eta squared $= .68; F(1,9) = 9.94, p = .01$, partial eta squared $= .52; F(1,9) = 10.31, p = .01$, partial eta squared $= .53]$

Notice the size of partial eta squared relative to the two previous analyses.

The results are similar to those of the mixed factorial design, so we won't wade through all the post hoc tests this time. If we did, however, which *t*-tests would you use for *all four* comparisons (remember—the same participants are in all four groups)? _____-samples *t*-tests (paired)

Collecting Your Own Data

Would you like to consider some outcome (believability or something else) in light of whether a person is rated as attractive or unattractive? Check out the Chicago Face Database (http://chicagofaces.org/index.html; be sure you cite the creators: Ma, Correll, & Wittenbrink [2015]). The Chicago Face Database: A free stimulus set of faces and norming data. *Behavior Research Methods*, currently available online at http://www.csun.edu/~dma/Ma,%20Correll,%20&%20 Wittenbrink,%202015.pdf.

There are several research questions you could test using these standardized photographs of faces. For example, you might ask participants to rate each face in terms of how likely they would be to hire the pictured person. You might want to test whether expression (smiling, neutral, or angry) interacts with attractiveness category. In that case, you would use a 3 x 2 factorial design. If you choose to have different participants in each condition, you'll have a complete between-subjects design. If all your participants respond to all six conditions, then you have a completely within-subjects factorial design.

ARE WE THERE YET?

Before We Leave This Lab

Because students sometimes find it challenging to understand the differences in main effects and interaction effects, here is . . .

MORE PRACTICE WITH INTERACTIONS

Remember that when you have to say "it depends" to describe the effect of a variable on some outcome, then you probably have an interaction between two variables. In order to describe the effect of one variable, you have to qualify it by noting the effect of another variable.

Identify each effect below as a main effect or an interaction effect. Remember, interaction effects tell you that the effect of one variable depends on the level of the other variable. Answers are at the end of the lab.

_____ 1. People with higher intelligence tend to have better physical health.

_____ 2. Older children generally use more effective memory strategies than do younger children.

_____ 3. Adults usually show better recall than children, but it depends on the participants' knowledge and the type of memory task. Children who are chess experts remember more chess positions than adults who are chess novices, although adults remember longer strings of unrelated numbers than do children.

_____ 4. Female college students expect the instructor to consider effort when assigning a grade more than do male college students.

_____ 5. Medication improved depression levels, but only when it was combined with therapy.

There are two interaction effects listed above. How did you know they were interactions?

_____

Keep going—we're not quite done yet.

You conduct a 2 x 2 factorial experiment examining the effects of age (young adult, older adult) and health (good health, poor health) on memory. You have a significant main effect of age and a significant interaction of age and health. What does this mean? (the effect of age on memory is moderated by health status)

Identify the two IVs and one DV. Answers are below.

IVs: _____   _____

DV: _____

Let's assume these are your means (higher numbers indicate greater recall):

	Health	
	Poor	*Good*
Younger adult	16.41	18.90
Older adult	11.57	18.62

If the *main effect* of health is significant, will you need to do post hoc tests? _____ If the *interaction effect* of age x health is significant, will you need to do post hoc tests? _____ Assume a *completely between-subjects design* was used. For the health variable, let 1 = poor health and 2 = good health. For the age variable, let 1 = younger and 2 = older. If you need to do the post hoc tests for this interaction, what must you do?

- ✓ Select if health = ___, then do a(n) _____-samples *t*-test comparing _____
- ✓ Select if health = ___, then do a(n) _____-samples *t*-test comparing _____
- ✓ Select if age = ___, then do a(n) _____-samples *t*-test comparing _____
- ✓ Select if age = ___, then do a(n) _____-samples *t*-test comparing _____

Are We There Yet?

And now, at last (drumroll), the instruction part of this lab is done. Congratulations—you're now done with the most difficult and lengthy part of this lab manual!!

IF YOU WANT TO GO FURTHER . . .

More About Testing Interactions Using Regression Analyses

We're going to unite information from two labs now: this one and the one on regression. You can get the same information for the two (or more) IV

©iStock.com/Wavebreakmedia

factorial designs described above by running a regression analysis. Note that these instructions apply to a completely between-subjects factorial design in which each predictor is continuous. An interaction effect in regression is called a moderated effect. For example, in the illustration about witness believability above, we could say that the effect of clothing was moderated by witness attractiveness (or vice versa). One advantage of using regression to test an interaction is flexibility; the ANOVA requires you to use categorical independent variables (e.g., younger vs. older), whereas you can use either categorical or continuous (e.g., the person's actual age) predictor variables in regression.

Let's say the following data are measures of how professionally the witness is dressed, how attractive the person is perceived to be, and some type of measure of believability. We could not use an ANOVA to address this question because the IVs are both continuous variables. Create a data file with the following scores. Higher numbers indicate more of the measured construct.

Professional	Attractiveness	Believability
8.00	7.500	.22
6.00	37.000	.01
8.00	33.500	.80
7.00	18.000	−1.97
11.00	18.000	.84
11.00	33.500	1.40
11.00	1.000	1.97
10.00	23.500	.62
11.00	13.000	.64
10.00	3.500	.31
8.00	39.500	−.18
8.00	23.500	.10

9.00	23.500	.14
6.00	7.500	.36
6.00	26.500	−1.39
8.00	37.000	.40
10.00	23.500	.61
6.00	28.500	−.52
6.00	37.000	.11
6.00	26.500	−1.58
8.00	13.000	−.30
6.00	11.000	−.11
10.00	3.500	.33
6.00	5.000	−.28
10.00	33.500	.80
11.00	18.000	−.24
11.00	39.500	1.24
8.00	30.500	.42
10.00	18.000	.24
9.00	18.000	.40
10.00	10.000	1.02
10.00	2.000	−1.97
7.00	13.000	−.10
6.00	9.000	−.28
9.00	30.500	.34
10.00	33.500	.95
10.00	6.000	.13
8.00	18.000	−.59
6.00	18.000	.15
6.00	28.500	−1.39

You could now run a regression analysis in which professional clothing and attractiveness predict believability. This would let you look at the main effect of professional attire and the main effect of attractiveness, but we need another variable to test the interaction of clothing and attractiveness. To do this, we have to first prepare the main effect variables by centering them. This means we calculate the difference between each person's score and the group mean. The reasons for doing this are (1) that it will lessen the inevitable correlation between the main effect variables with the interaction term, and (2) it will make interpretation of the interaction easier. To do this we need to know the mean for each main effect variable. You can get this by running descriptives.

Descriptive Statistics

	N	Minimum	Maximum	Mean	Std. Deviation
Professional	40	6.00	11.00	8.4250	1.86585
Attractiveness	40	1.000	39.500	20.50000	11.640997
Valid N (listwise)	40				

Now we center the variables.

1. Click *Transform*

2. *Compute Variable*

3. Name the new variable something like *Prof_cen* to distinguish it from the original variable.

4. The numeric expression is Professional—8.425.

5. *OK*

Now follow the same steps to create Attract_cen (Attractiveness—20.5). Create the interaction term.

1. Click *Transform*

2. *Compute Variable*

3. Name the new interaction variable something like *Prof.x.Attract* (the *x* means "by").

4. The numeric expression is Prof_cen * Attract_cen.

5. *OK*

Now we can set up the regression analysis to test both the main effects and the interaction. I'm going to put the interaction term in a second block so I can see how much additional variability (over that explained by the main effects as a group) is explained.

1. *Analyze, Regression, Linear*

2. The dependent variable is Believability.

3. Because we are going to enter an interaction term, we have to use the centered variables for the main effects, so put Prof_cen and Attract_cen into the Independent Variable box.

4. Click Next

5. In the new block, put the interaction term you created.

6. We're going to need several additional statistics. Click *Statistics.*

7. *R Squared Change, Confidence Intervals, Descriptives*

8. *Continue*

9. *OK*

Descriptive Statistics

	Mean	Std. Deviation	N
Believability	-.0073	.85791	40
Prof_cen	.0000	1.86585	40
Attract_cen	.0000	11.64100	40
Prof.x.Attract	-2.3375	21.92684	40

Here are the elements of the output we'll need:

The IV means look different from the original variables because they've been centered; the centered mean should be very close to 0. If it is not, go back to see if you calculated the centered variables correctly.

Model Summary

Model	R	R Square	Adjusted R Square	Std. Error of the Estimate	Change Statistics				
					R Square Change	F Change	df1	df2	Sig. F Change
1	.519[a]	.209	.229	.75313	.269	6.804	2	37	.003
2	.653[b]	.426	.378	.67639	.157	9.871	1	36	.003

a. Predictors: (Constant), Attract_cen, Prof_cen

b. Predictors: (Constant), Attract_cen, Prof_cen, Prof.x.Attract

Remember the job of the following ANOVA is to test whether the predictors as a group do a good job of explaining variability in the outcome.

ANOVA[a]

Model		Sum of Squares	df	Mean Square	F	Sig.
1	Regression	7.718	2	3.859	6.804	.003[b]
	Residual	20.986	37	.567		
	Total	28.705	39			
2	Regression	12.234	3	4.078	8.914	.000[c]
	Residual	16.470	36	.458		
	Total	28.705	39			

a. Dependent Variable: Believability

b. Predictors: (Constant), Attract_cen, Prof_cen

c. Predictors: (Constant), Attract_cen, Prof_cen, Prof.x.Attract

Coefficients[a]

Model		Unstandardized Coefficients		Standardized Coefficients	t	Sig.	95.0% Confidence Interval for B	
		B	Std. Error	Beta			Lower Bound	Upper Bound
1	(Constant)	-.007	.119		-.061	.952	-.249	.234
	Prof_cen	.199	.065	.433	3.063	.004	.067	.331
	Attract_cen	.025	.010	.337	2.381	.023	.004	.046
2	(Constant)	.029	.108		.272	.787	-.189	.247
	Prof_cen	.206	.058	.447	3.518	.001	.087	.324
	Attract_cen	.021	.009	.291	2.274	.029	.002	.041
	Prof.x.Attract	.016	.005	.400	3.142	.003	.006	.026

a. Dependent Variable: Believability

As you can see in Model 2, this analysis produced a significant main effect of attractiveness that was modified by a significant Prof x Attract interaction. Notice (in the model summary box) that the main effect variables together (Model 1) predicted 27% of the variability in strategy use, and the interaction explained an additional 16% (Model 2). Both models explained a significant amount of variability in the outcome measure (see ANOVA), but the model containing the interaction term was better (explained significantly more variability).

Now that we know the interaction was significant, how do we interpret that? In order to interpret an interaction in regression, we need to calculate something called *simple slopes*. If you are going to do a lot of regression analyses you should learn more about calculating simple slopes, but for now we're going to use one of the calculators available online. Go to http://www.jeremydawson. co.uk/slopes.htm {suggested search term *Dawson simple slopes two-way interaction calculator*} and choose "2-way unstandardized." This will open with Excel. You need to fill in the name of the IV (Professional), the moderator (Attractiveness—a "moderated" effect is an interaction effect), the unstandardized coefficients (*b or B*; not β) for main effects and interaction effect (get these from the regression analysis: professional: .206, attractiveness: .021, interaction: .016), the constant (.029), then the means and standard deviations of the <u>centered</u> main effects (get this from the descriptives you ran with the regression: .00, 1.86585, .00, 11.641). You will probably have to change the scale on the *y*-axis. Left click the *y-axis scale*, after it highlights do a right click, choose *format axis* and change the values to -2 (minimum) and 2 (maximum). This should produce the graph below (other than a few cosmetic changes I made).

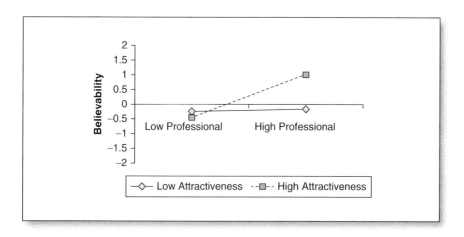

We can see here that attractiveness doesn't seem to matter when people aren't dressed professionally, but of those who were professionally dressed, attractive people were more believable. Likewise, it appears that it makes little difference how unattractive people dress, but for attractive people, more professional attire improves believability.

WHAT HAPPENS WITH CATEGORICAL PREDICTORS?

Categorical variables don't need to be centered. You can skip the centering step and go directly to creating the interaction term.

WHAT HAPPENS WITH REPEATED-MEASURES DATA?

This is a bit more complicated. You can analyze repeated-measures data using multilevel modeling or a mixed model (a combination of fixed and random effects), but this requires multiple steps to set up and is conceptually beyond the scope of this lab manual. In addition, these analyses would require more than two repeated measures.

ANSWERS FOR MORE PRACTICE WITH INTERACTIONS

1. People with higher intelligence tend to have better physical health.
   Higher intelligence > lower intelligence (main effect)

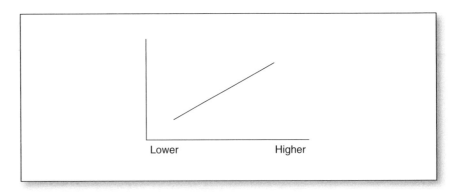

2. Older children generally use more effective memory strategies than do younger children. **Older > younger (main effect)**

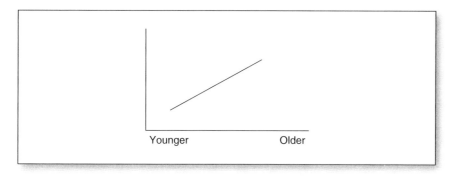

3. Adults usually show better recall than children, but it depends on the participants' knowledge and the type of memory task. Children who are chess experts remember more chess positions than adults who are chess novices, although adults remember longer strings of unrelated numbers than do children.

Do children remember more than adults? It depends on the type of task.

Unrelated strings of numbers: adults (chess novices) > children (chess experts)

Chess positions: children (experts) > adults (novices)

(Interaction)

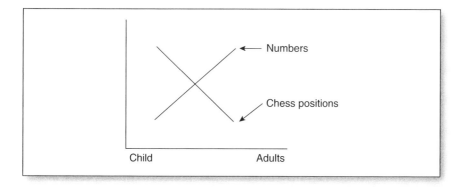

4. Female college students expect the instructor to consider effort when assigning a grade more than do male college students.

Female > Male (main effect)

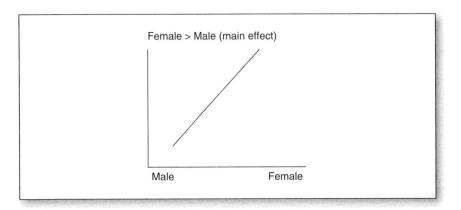

5. Medication improved depression levels, but only when it was combined with therapy.

This is trickier—Does medication improve depression? It depends on whether it is combined with therapy:

With therapy: Medication > no medication

Without therapy: Medication = no medication

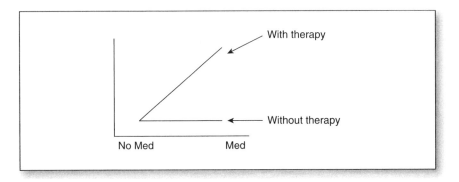

You conduct a 2 x 2 factorial experiment examining the effects of age (young adult, older adult) and health (good health, poor health) on memory. You have a significant main effect of age and a significant interaction of age and health. What does this mean?

The significant main effect of age was modified by a significant age x health interaction. Somewhere in the pairings of four means was at least one pair of means that was significantly different. I can't know how many or which of the pairs are significant until I do post hoc tests.

Identify the two IVs and one DV.

IVs: Age, Health

DV: Memory

Let's assume these are your means (higher numbers indicate greater recall):

	Health	
	Poor	Good
Younger adult	16.41	18.90
Older adult	11.57	18.62

If the *main effect* of health is significant, will you need to do post hoc tests? No—there are only two levels, so it is obvious those are the two means that are significantly different.

If the *interaction effect* of age x health is significant, will you need to do post hoc tests?

Yes

Assume a completely between-subjects design was used. For the health variable, let 1 = poor health and 2 = good health. For the age variable, let 1 = younger and 2 =older. If you need to do the post hoc tests for this interaction, what must you do?

- ✓ Select if health = 1, then do a(n) independent-samples *t*-test comparing young adult to older adult among participants with poor health

- ✓ Select if health = 2, then do a(n) independent-samples *t*-test comparing young adult to older adult among participants with good health

- ✓ Select if age = 1, then do a(n) independent-samples *t*-test comparing good health to poor health among younger adults

- ✓ Select if age = 2, then do a(n) independent-samples *t*-test comparing good health to poor health among older adults

PART III

After Collecting Data

LAB 14

Writing the Discussion Section, Sharing Your Findings Using a Poster or Oral Presentation

Objective

In my experience, the Discussion section of a paper is the hardest for students to write. This is not surprising because this is the part of the paper where you go beyond reporting your results and interpret them. Since you don't yet have a lot of background knowledge on your topic and haven't read the associated literature thoroughly, you may come up blank when trying to interpret what you've found. Years of study will provide you with knowledge about your topic; for now, we'll just concentrate on what sort of information should go in a Discussion section. We'll then talk about sharing your findings via presenting a poster at a conference or in an oral presentation. Additional material is included on the process of publishing in a professional journal.

Target Article

Bartol, S. M., Mellgren, R. L., & Musick, J. A. (2003). Visual acuity of juvenile loggerhead sea turtles (Caretta caretta): A behavioral approach. *International Journal of Comparative Psychology, 16*(2/3), 143–155. Retrieved from https://escholarship.org/uc/item/9vw0g6bt#page-1

©iStock.com/blueringmedia

Have you ever noticed that your vision underwater is different from your vision on land? I am very nearsighted, but (based on anecdotal evidence) can see fairly well underwater. I would be very happy to spend time at the beach in order to obtain additional empirical evidence of this! Sea turtles spend most of their time in the water, but come on land to lay eggs. Like me, they are nearsighted on land. These experimenters used operant conditioning to figure out just how well turtles can see in the water. The turtles were rewarded (raw squid—yum!) when they correctly distinguished between two different visual patterns. Once the turtles were trained, the stimuli were made smaller and smaller until the turtles could no longer tell the difference. The smallest size at which they could distinguish the patterns indicated their acuity.

When writing a Discussion section, bear in mind that your reader, although probably educated, may not be an expert in your particular area. You need to use the Discussion section to make clear to that reader what was found and what it means. Don't assume that your readers will be familiar with your topic.

DISCUSSION SECTION CHECKLIST

✓ **Summarize your findings.** Pull out the important information and organize it for your reader.

✓ **Did your findings support or not support your hypotheses?** You began with specific predictions, research questions, or purposes. Now tell the reader whether the findings are consistent with your hypotheses.

✓ **So what? What does it *mean*, and why should we care?** Even though I already know that one group was significantly different than another (or two variables were positively correlated, or whatever), what does that really mean? Why are your findings important?

✓ **Help the reader see the connections between your findings and those previously reported in the literature.** Remember all those studies you cited in the introduction? How do your findings fit in with this larger picture? Refer back to those studies already cited and explain how your results are consistent with or contradictory to earlier studies. You can also cite work not mentioned in your literature review. Additionally, if you tested a theory-based hypothesis (remember from the lab on theory-based hypotheses?), tie your results back in to the starting theory. Did it support the theory or suggest potential revisions? Did you expand the theory to a new population or topic? Share the significance or implications of your findings in relation to the theoretical framework that informed your study.

✓ **The good, the bad, and the ugly.** Point out explicitly the ways in which your study makes a unique contribution to the literature. Describe other potential explanations for your findings. Could something else (other than what you hypothesized) have caused your findings? Acknowledge the limitations of your study.

✓ **Where do we go from here?** So now what? What do your findings suggest for applications or future research? Can you make any recommendations based on your work? For example, in Zimbardo's prison study cited in an earlier lab, what changes to prison policies based on research findings might the author have suggested? What factors should be considered by future studies?

TRY IT YOURSELF

Assignment 1: Download the target article (.pdf file or hard copy) and use the sticky note feature or a highlighter to identify and label parts of the Discussion section as described below. **Why am I asking you to do a seemingly mindless task?** I realize this seems like a busywork type of assignment that even a fifth grader could do, but in my experience it helps even college students understand how the components of a Discussion section fit together.

1. **Summarize your findings.** Bartol and colleagues do this in the third paragraph on page 151, where they report the visual acuity of juvenile loggerhead turtles. The first two paragraphs set the stage for interpreting the finding. Other authors prefer to begin the Discussion section by summing up their most important findings. Additional findings are mentioned in the bottom paragraph on page 152.

2. **Did your findings support or not support your hypotheses?** This study was more exploratory than experimental. The authors didn't predict what the acuity would be; rather, they simply set out to discover it. Their findings allowed them to draw some conclusions about the turtles' visual acuity.

3. **So what does it *mean*, and why should we care?** The meaning is fairly straightforward in this article; the authors demonstrated new information

about visual acuity in turtles in their natural environment. However, the authors helped the reader see how the results might complement (nope—I'm not talking about telling someone they did a really good job on something!) findings about the structure of turtle brains. Their findings can also be used to understand how turtles use visual information to carry out important turtle work, like finding food, avoiding becoming somebody else's food, defending territory, and so on. It may also have implications for turtle conservation efforts.

4. **Help the reader see the connections between your findings and those previously reported in the literature.** For example, the third paragraph refers to studies that have addressed the same issue using other methodologies. Other studies have examined turtles' visual acuity on land rather than in water. On pages 152 and 153, the authors refer to work examining the acuity of other aquatic species. Notice how the discussion moves from the specific (other turtle studies) to the more general (other species).

5. **The good, the bad, and the ugly.** This is noted in the first two paragraphs of the Discussion. What was good about their methodology? What limitation existed? Another strength is mentioned in the last paragraph.

6. **Where do we go from here?** The authors noted that a future study might test other visual dimensions, such as brightness.

Assignment 2: Now it's your turn. Using the data from one of the labs already completed, discuss with a partner how you could address each of the parts of the discussion listed above for a lab report. Write a Discussion section on the material that is guided by the points listed above.

Communicating Your Findings (Beyond the Written Lab Report)

Research not shared or communicated is research wasted. Let's assume you have formulated your hypothesis, designed your study, collected your data, and now you need to tell the world about it. How do scholars in your discipline do this? For now let's talk just about communicating within the academic community. You can adapt the information if you are communicating to other audiences. We've already covered how to write an APA-style research report, so let's focus here on other forms of communication. Other ways you can share your findings include a poster or an oral presentation at a student or professional conference.

OK, pay attention here—I'm going to tell you something important! Consider getting a *student membership in a professional organization* that is important in your discipline. Your instructor can suggest such organizations. Student memberships are usually inexpensive and it is a good way to begin immersing yourself in the culture of your field. If you decide to go further in your field after graduation, membership demonstrates your commitment to your area. *Attend the conferences of these organizations.* This is an excellent way to learn more about your field. Use the conference to network. Decide before you go who you would like to meet, then find those people at the conference (there are often lists of presenters) and introduce yourself. These contacts may help when you are applying for graduate school or a job.

Another important point—get to know the instructors and researchers in your department. Is there a way for you to *participate in their research*? Do it! You will get a lot of research experience by helping conduct professional research.

CREATING AND PRESENTING A POSTER

When Would I Use a Poster?

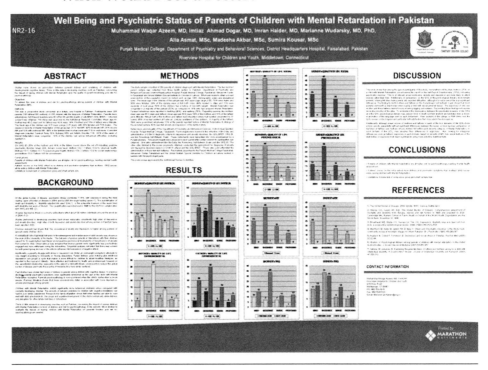

NOTE: This graphic illustrates the sections of a poster and how you may want to organize them.

SOURCE: http://www.psydep.com/blog/?p=115

Professional conferences almost always attract more people who want to present their research than can be accommodated as speakers. Rather than giving an oral presentation, many researchers opt for a poster presentation. A poster is a great way to begin presenting at conferences.

Ask your instructor about any undergraduate, graduate, or professional research conferences in your area then apply to present a poster there. This usually involves submitting an abstract of your poster.

What Happens During a Poster Presentation?

Once your poster has been accepted for presentation at a conference you will be notified of the time and place it is to be displayed, as well as any information on preparing your poster. Poster presentations are often done in large ballrooms that can accommodate many posters at one time. Interested people will have seen the abstract or title of your poster in the program book and will plan to come by and look at it. At your assigned time, you hang your poster in the designated spot, and wait for people to come by to discuss your research with you. Plan to stay with your poster throughout the session. Be prepared to answer questions about your project, listen to new interpretations of your findings, meet other researchers with your same interests, network, hobnob, and generally have a good time talking about research. It is a good idea to bring copies of a handout describing your poster so interested people can take a copy with them. Alternatively you could collect email addresses and email a copy of the poster.

How Do You Get Started and
What Information Goes On the Poster?

One easy way to create a poster is to use a PowerPoint template. You can find many templates available free online. For example, see some of the options at http://www.wakehealth.edu/Creative/Posters/PowerPoint-Templates-for-Large-Format-Posters.htm {suggested search term *powerpoint poster template*}. Look through the illustrations of scientific posters here and elsewhere online. Focus on posters presenting scholarly scientific research (or whichever ones your instructor recommends). You will not need a trifold format posterboard like you used when you presented at a science fair. You will need a poster that is around 36 inches x 48 inches. At some conferences, posters must be no larger than 8 feet x 4 feet. The conference's website will likely tell you the maximum poster size that is allowed. It should have a title banner, names of authors and authors' affiliations (see if your institution has a logo you can copy and paste into the banner). Include at least an abstract, introduction, method, results, and discussion or conclusions. The same sections included in a manuscript are used on a poster, but they are very brief. The length of each section will be determined by available space and the nature of your research project. Your instructor will give you more specific details about your poster. You can copy and paste from a word processing file or type directly into the poster. Remember to type the tables out—don't copy the ones from the SPSS output. A poster is less formal than a paper, so you can use bullet points. You need to give enough information for the reader to follow what you did and what you found, but you'll have to be concise and hit just the most important points.

How Should the Poster Be Organized?

Posters are intended to be read as people walk by. Your poster, therefore, must be in large type, so it can be read from a distance of about 4 to 8 feet. One fourth of an inch might be the minimum size. I prefer to use a sans serif font such as Arial. Headings are slightly larger than the text, but that's not a rule. You have a limited amount of space, so every word, figure, or table must be necessary and concise. Since people will be reading as they walk by, organize your information from left to right so it can be read with one pass.

PREPARING AN ORAL PRESENTATION OF YOUR FINDINGS

An oral presentation contains all the parts of a lab report. The length of your presentation can vary considerably depending on the situation. Try not to read a paper or slides to your audience—that's boring! You are telling a story about a topic that is interesting to you, so share your findings with enthusiasm. Your report should include the following:

1. A quick review of the most relevant literature, leading up to your hypotheses or research question. Explain the theory that frames your research project. You want the logic of your literature review to lead up to your study; by the time you

get to the end of this opening section, you want your audience to be clear on why your study was the next logical step. End with the purpose and hypotheses.

2. A Method section in which you describe the participants, materials used, procedure, and plan of analysis

3. Your findings should test your hypotheses. Present the most relevant statistics. Use tables, figures, flow charts, models—anything to help your audience visualize your findings.

4. End with your interpretation of your findings, how your findings relate back to the larger literature on the topic, whether your findings supported the theoretical framework for your study or not, conclusions, and your study's strengths and weaknesses

Some points to keep in mind when planning and presenting your oral report (adapted from *Learner-centered assessment on college campuses* by M. E. Huba & J. E. Freed, 2000, Needham Heights, MA: Allyn & Bacon):

1. Is the presentation clear, logical, and organized? Can the reader follow the line of reasoning?

2. Does it contain all necessary elements as listed above? Is the material accurate (do you have all your facts straight)?

3. Have you matched the level of detail in the presentation to the type of audience? Give enough detail that your audience knows everything needed to follow your talk, but not so much detail that you put them to sleep.

4. Dress professionally, speak loudly enough for everyone to hear, use good posture, and look enthusiastic!

5. Use some form of communication aid to help you and your audience stay on task. Your visual aid (e.g., PowerPoint slides) should not include a lot of words—keep it at the level of an outline that highlights the most important points. Make sure the material on the visual aid is large enough for everyone to see.

6. Allow time at the end for your audience members to ask questions. Encourage them to do so. Don't be offended if someone disagrees with something you said. Respond respectfully and learn from whatever they have to offer.

Use the information above and prepare a 20-minute (or however long your instructor requires) oral presentation on the data you collected for your individual research project. Present this to your classmates.

CLOSURE

By now, you are experienced at writing APA-style papers. If, when you complete your research project and hand in your final paper, you think your paper turned out to be pretty good, consider repeating the study (this time after obtaining approval from your IRB), then submit the resulting paper to one of the journals devoted to publishing undergraduate or graduate student papers. For example, see http://psych.uncc.edu/undergraduate-programs/undergraduate-journal-psychology or http://www.kon.org/CFP/cfp_urjhs.html {suggested search term *undergraduate* (or *student*, or *graduate student*) *journal* (*your discipline area here*)}. Also check with the website of your discipline's professional organizations. Alternatively, you may want to investigate preparing a poster or oral report on your data. By way of caution, if your research project was not approved by an IRB, then you may not be allowed to present it outside of your class. If you want to present your study to a wider audience, you should obtain IRB approval first. If you are not sure whether you can present your data outside class, check with your IRB. Ethics always matter!

IF YOU WANT TO GO FURTHER . . .

The Publication Process: What to Expect When You're Submitting

You've done it—you completed your research project and are pretty darn excited about the findings. Go you! You've decided you would like to submit the paper to a journal for publication or a conference for presenting (but remember you may need to repeat the study after obtaining IRB approval). If you've already selected a conference you would like to attend, review the organization's website for deadlines for submission and formatting requirements (page limit, style of writing, etc.). If you want to submit to a journal, let's talk first about what a peer-reviewed journal actually is.

The American Psychological Association (APA; 2010) states that "the peer-reviewed literature in a field is built by individual contributions that together represent the accumulated knowledge of a field" (p. 225). This statement can easily be applied to many different disciplines. Journals serve as a major hub for research experts in a particular field to not only disseminate new information and research findings, but to perform quality control on the *type* of research that is being shared. Every peer-reviewed journal has an editor, who is charged with looking over every manuscript that is submitted to the journal to check for relevance (is it consistent with the aim of that particular journal?), content (does the manuscript significantly contribute to the field?), clarity and conciseness of the paper (is the paper well-written and clearly describing the study?), and commitment to required formatting guidelines (does it fit within the journal's page limit, contain all required sections, follow the set writing style such as APA?). If the editor deems the manuscript worthy of review, the manuscript is sent to a panel of reviewers. Who are these reviewers, you ask? They are your research peers—other graduate students, professors, medical professionals, for example, who specialize in your content area.

Reviewers who agree to review the manuscript are given an allotted amount of time (it may be weeks or months, depending on the journal) to complete and submit the review. Also depending on the journal, the review process may be blind (all names removed) or not (your name and/or the reviewers' names are provided). The reviewers will make comments and edits on the quality of the paper, the significance of the findings, the methodology, accuracy of results and interpretations, and other appropriate areas of the manuscript. The reviewers will then make a recommendation for the manuscript to be rejected, revised (based on given feedback) and resubmitted, or accepted. Sometimes a journal may require a manuscript to be revised several times before being accepted, but once the final acceptance is made, the manuscript enters into the production phase of publication (yippee!).

So, now that you know how the process works, here is a suggested to-do list to prepare you for the journey. Remember, if you are co-authoring the manuscript, all authors will be involved in this process.

1. **Pick a "journal home."** This sounds easy, but it can take some time to research all of the possible journals out there that would be a good fit for your manuscript. Start by asking your advisor or instructor if they have any recommendations. Then look at the journals where articles you have included in your literature review were published. Make a list of these journals. In fact, I recommend keeping a running list of these journals if you are a student intending to become a researcher or professor. Search the names

of the journals and find their websites. Examine the types of articles they publish, their mission statements (sometimes listed as aims and scope), and their impact factor (high numbers are better!). An impact factor of a journal is the number of current-year citations divided by the source items published in the journal during the last two years. Basically, this number shows how much and how often researchers are citing articles from that journal. Different institutions may place more or less emphasis on the impact factor. Sometimes the most appropriate journal for your article has a low impact rating or may not be rated at all. Let your instructor guide you on this.

| About the Title | Manuscript Submission | Aims & Scope | Abstracting/Indexing |

SAGE Open publishes peer-reviewed, original research and review articles in an interactive, open access format. Accepted articles span the full extent of the social and behavioral sciences and the humanities.

SAGE Open seeks to be the world's premier open access outlet for academic research. As such, unlike traditional journals, *SAGE Open* does not limit content due to page budgets or thematic significance. Rather, *SAGE Open* evaluates the scientific and research methods of each article for validity and accepts articles solely on the basis of the research. This approach allows readers greater access and gives them the power to determine the significance of each article through *SAGE Open's* interactive comments feature and article-level usage metrics. Likewise, by not restricting papers to a narrow discipline, *SAGE Open* facilitates the discovery of the connections between papers, whether within or between disciplines.

SAGE Open offers authors quick review and decision times; a speedy, continuous-publication format; and global distribution for their research via SAGE Journals Online. All articles are professionally copyedited and typeset to ensure quality.

SOURCE: http://www.sagepub.com/journals/Journal202037/

Something else to note here—there has been a recent increase in "predatory" journals, that is, journals that have not yet met standards of credibility and may allow authors to "buy" a spot in their journal. Check out Beall's list of predatory journals at http://scholarlyoa.com/publishers/ (search for the one of the current year, as the list changes rapidly) and be sure you do not submit to any journals that may be fishy. However, journal status may change over time, so again, be guided by your instructor here. There are very legitimate journals that are "open-source" for which the authors must pay to publish, so don't rule out a journal just because there is a publication cost. Pay attention to these charges, however, as some can be quite expensive.

Once you've made a list, check the possible journal homes against criteria you have set—do you want to submit to a smaller journal that is specific to your topic, or a major name in your field? Ask colleagues or members of your department about the reputations and competitiveness of journals you are considering. Then, make a list of your top three. Submit to your top journal first—if you get rejected without the option of revising, move on down the line.

2. **Tailor your paper.** Now that you've picked your targeted journal, you need to craft your paper to fit the journal's style, formatting, and content requirements. Now, we are NOT redoing your entire research project here simply to fit a certain journal; you should pick a journal home where your topic and findings are well-suited. However, you want to make sure that your manuscript meets all formatting requirements and highlights areas that are important to the journal. For example, perhaps the one you choose really values practical implications—you can spend more time discussing the application of your research findings in the Discussion section.

| About the Title | Manuscript Submission | Aims & Scope | Abstracting/Indexing |

SAGE Open is an open access publication from SAGE. It publishes peer-reviewed, original research and review articles in an interactive, open access format. Articles may span the full spectrum of the social and behavioral sciences and the humanities. *SAGE Open* seeks to be the world's premier open access outlet for academic research. As such, it evaluates the scientific and research methods of each article for validity and accepts articles solely on the basis of the research. This approach allows readers greater access and gives them the power to determine the significance of each article through *SAGE Open's* interactive comments feature and article-level usage metrics. Likewise, by not restricting papers to a narrow discipline, *SAGE Open* facilitates the discovery of the connections between papers, whether within or between disciplines.

SAGE Open requires authors to pay an Article Processing Charge (APC) of $195 for publication. The APC is payable upon acceptance.

For general information on Open Access at SAGE and Open Access FAQs, please visit this page.

Manuscript Submission

Before submitting your manuscript, please ensure you carefully read and adhere to all the guidelines and instructions to authors provided below.

SAGE Open receives manuscript submissions online through SAGE Track, powered by ScholarOne Manuscripts™. Authors should register for an account at http://mc.manuscriptcentral.com/sageopen, where they will create a login ID and password. SAGE Track will serve as the center for editorial staff to communicate with authors, editors, and reviewers electronically, and it will function as the platform for the review process.

Peer Review

There should be an "Author Guidelines" link on the journal website that is very useful for this step. Make a checklist of

- The journal requirements, including page limits
- The required sections (Introduction, Hypotheses, etc.)
- The writing style (APA, AMA, etc.)
- Citation requirements (Is there a limit? Are citations numbered or alphabetical?)

- Table formatting
- The submission process (Is it online? Do you need to register an account? Is there a submission fee?)

Revise your manuscript accordingly. Once you have a final draft . . .

3. **Ask a friend, colleague, or advisor for one final read-through.** You want to put forth the best possible version of your manuscript, so ask a trusted colleague or faculty member to read through your final paper for edits and comments. Once you have your final FINAL version . . .

4. **Submit—and wait.** The waiting process can be a pain, but just expect that the process can take two to three months, or more. Typically journals will give you an estimated timeline for how long it will take for you to receive word on the status of your submission, so keep that estimated number in mind. If the journal told you it would three months and it has been nine, certainly touch base with the editor! Otherwise, be patient. When you finally hear back . . .

5. **Read the review, then put it away.** You've gotten your manuscript back and . . . it was rejected. Or, it was a revise-and-resubmit with a million harsh critiques. Speaking from experience, the best thing to do is read through the review once and then put it away for a day or two. Even if you get a revise-and-resubmit, it is likely that reviewers made a lot of comments and critiques, and this can feel hurtful or make you angry that someone is tearing apart your paper that you worked so hard to write! But remember, this is all part of the peer-review process. If you received back a manuscript with nothing but rave reviews, I would worry about the quality of that journal. No research project is perfect, and expert reviewers are bound to find at least a few areas that could be improved. Try to view the entire process as a learning experience to make you a better writer and to make your manuscript top-notch. Once you have taken a few days off . . .

6. **Tackle the feedback.** If the manuscript was rejected, still go through the feedback to see what the reviewers felt needed to be improved. If these reviewers picked up on some problems in the manuscript, it is likely the next round of reviewers will too, so go ahead and amend your manuscript as needed. Once you have a revised version you feel comfortable with, submit it to the next journal on your list. Caution: It would be a bad idea to ignore reviewers' comments and send the manuscript out to another journal without making changes. Many people review for a

number of different journals, and it is very possible the manuscript will wind up being reviewed by the same person. Said person will be very annoyed if you didn't consider the suggested changes!

If you received a revise-and-resubmit, take special note of the timeline in which they are expecting you to submit the revisions. Plan your time accordingly! Usually journals expect you to create a document of all the reviewers' comments, and you will go through and respond to each one, stating how you addressed their critique in your revised manuscript (e.g., adding in a paragraph to the Discussion, redoing an analysis) or providing a detailed and compelling justification for how or why your manuscript should maintain its original format or content. Once the revision process is completed (and potentially repeated several times), you will hopefully receive an acceptance! Congratulations!

Assignment: Whew, it is quite a process, but having your research published and sharing your exciting findings with the world is rewarding. To help you get the process started, complete the following:

Create a list of journals where you could potentially submit your manuscript. Pick one and answer the following questions:

1. What is the scope of the journal?

2. What are the page limits?

3. What are the required sections (Introduction, Hypotheses, etc.)?

4. What is the required writing style (APA, AMA, etc.)?

5. Are there any specific citation requirements (Is there a limit? Are citations numbered?)?

6. What is the submission process (Is it online? Do you need to register an account? Is there a submission fee?)?

Think about what changes would need to be made to your manuscript in order to be submission ready. Consider submitting a manuscript to your targeted journal or another journal on your list.

REFERENCES

American Psychological Association. (2010). *Publication manual of the American Psychological Association* (6th ed.). Washington, DC: Author.

LAB 15

Tables and Figures

Objective

The purpose of this lab is to provide experience in creating APA-style tables and figures. Instructions on using both Excel and SPSS to create figures are described. Additional material discusses additional figures (stacked bar charts, pie charts, error bars, multiple independent variables [IVs] and dependent variables [DVs]), author notes, appendices, and web-based supplemental material.

Target Article

Payne, J. D., Schacter, D. L., Propper, R. E., Huang, L., Wamsley, E. J., Tucker, M. A., . . . Stickgold, R. (2009). The role of sleep in false memory formation. *Neurobiology of Learning and Memory, 92*(3), 327–334. doi:10.1016/j.nlm.2009.03.007. Retrieved from http://ac.els-cdn.com/S1074742709000835/1-s2.0-S1074742709 000835-main.pdf?_tid=23438b44-cbf9-11e4-a3be-00000aacb 35f&acdnat=1426523342_d2561d64fa3631635db8f940ea727a4e {or search on the title of the article}

Researchers have repeatedly shown the importance of sleep in accurate memory consolidation, but less work has examined whether sleep can influence the development of *false* memories. False recall is an important topic of study, particularly for research of eyewitnesses in the court system and to the study of memory functioning. Jessica D. Payne and colleagues (2009) conducted a two-group experiment in which they compared memory recall between a "wake" group, who remained awake for 12 hours between the word task and recall, and a "sleep" group, who slept for a full night between the tasks. Results showed that participants in the sleep group showed a higher veridical (accurate) recall, as well as a higher false recall on one of the tasks. The researchers concluded that under certain circumstances, sleep can promote false memories just as it appears to do with veridical memories.

TABLES

While graphs are great for presenting visual aspects of data, tables create a simple format for presenting descriptive data or analyses with lots of information and estimates. It would be boring, confusing, and a poor use of space to list means, standard deviations, and ranges for each study variable within the body of our writing. Researchers also use tables to present demographic information (see Table 1 on p. 330 in the PDF version of your targeted article for an example of a table presenting descriptives; also see Table 1 in the following sample paper [http://www.apastyle.org/manual/related/sample-experiment-paper-1.pdf {suggested search term *APA table format*}. The tables are placed after the references (all tables followed by all figures).

It is tempting to simply copy and paste the SPSS output table right into the paper. Do not do this! The SPSS output format is *not* in APA style. This applies to figures, too.

In general, tables should be simple, clear, only include horizontal lines, and should explain all abbreviations. Tables should be labeled consecutively (Table 1, Table 2, etc.), but the label should go *above* the table (while labels for figures are presented at the bottom of the graph! Go figure.). Tables can also include notes, located at the bottom of the table, which explain abbreviations and exactly what the table is presenting and the nature of the data. Additionally, you must *always* refer to your table or figure in the text. For example, on page 330 in Payne et al. (2009), the Methods section states that "a summary of the sleep measures is provided in Table 1." Although the tables are referred to in text, APA formatting of manuscripts (doesn't apply to articles once they have been typeset) requires them to be located at the end of a research paper, following the References section. For a list of more APA table guidelines, see https://owl.english.purdue.edu/owl/resource/560/19/ {suggested search term *APA table format*}.

You can create tables in Word, Excel, PowerPoint, and many other programs. For example, you can create one in Excel by simply typing the labels and data into the spreadsheet, creating horizontal borders as you see fit, highlighting the data, and using copy and paste to transfer into your Word document. You may also use PowerPoint by clicking *Insert, Table,* and choosing the cell height and width of your table. You can then type directly into the table created, and copy and paste into your Word document. If you use Word, you can type in horizontal lines, use the underline feature, or insert a table. For example,

Figure 15.1 Descriptive Data (N = 315) for All Covariates, Predictors, and Outcome Variables

	M	SD	Range
Age	48.65	6.51	32–67
Average Hours Sleep	6.90	.69	4.57–8.57
XYZ IQ Score	94.71	13.32	63–134
# Trials to Reach Memory Threshold	1.47	2.13	1–5
Correct Recall	123.19	13.98	90–173
False Recall	80.57	9.57	54–120

Average Hours Sleep = [(Typical weekday sleep x 5) + (typical weekend sleep x 2)]/7

Abbreviations: SD = standard deviation. IQ = intelligence quotient (standardized $M = 100, SD = 10$)

If you choose to insert a table, you will have to hide some of the borders since APA Style doesn't include vertical lines or internal horizontal lines.

The content of the table will depend on the type of analyses you did. Descriptive data usually includes sample size, means, standard deviations, and range. If you have categorical data, report the number and percentage of each category. See the regression lab for examples of the resulting tables.

FIGURES

Presenting numerical data in a table or figure is often an efficient and visually appealing way to present information to your reader. The purpose of a figure is to provide data in the simplest, clearest form possible. A figure can visually demonstrate results in a way that is much easier to understand. When deciding what type of table or figure to use, consider the nature of your data. Line graphs or scatterplots are typically used to present relationships between variables (see Figure 3 on p. 331 of your target article for an example of a scatterplot). You can also use a line graph to illustrate changes over time or changes within multiple groups. A bar graph is often used to compare means or counts between groups (see Figure 1 on p. 329 of your target article for an example of a bar graph). For a description of various types of graphs, see https://owl.english.purdue.edu/owl/resource/560/20/ {suggested search term *figures APA style*}. This website also provides a "Figures Checklist" you can use to make sure your figure is in APA format and being used appropriately. Per APA style, your figures should be labeled consecutively (Figure 1, Figure 2, etc.) and the title is placed underneath the figure. You can also include notes below the figure to describe the data being presented.

Take into consideration whether a figure adds new information or not. Unless you have a reason to do so, you don't need to duplicate information in a figure if a table would have worked just as well.

TRY IT YOURSELF

Canned Data—Creating a Table

Let's suppose you are looking at whether sleep after learning affects recall. The outcomes are veridical (true) recall and false recall, with higher numbers indicating greater recall. Sleep Group is a between-subject variable, and Type of Recall (veridical and false) is the within-subject variable. There are two IVs (sleep group and type of recall) with two levels each, making this a 2 x 2 mixed-factorial design. Pretend you want to create a table indicating whether recall varies as a function of sleep after learning. We'll let 1 = no sleep after learning and 2 = sleep after learning. You can go ahead and enter these data in an SPSS file—we'll use it later.

Sleep_Grp	Type of Recall	
	Veridical Recall	*False Recall*
1	221.00	204.00
1	197.00	173.00
1	187.00	179.00
1	163.00	175.00
1	129.00	106.00
2	240.00	196.00
2	203.00	162.00
2	188.00	142.00
2	177.00	140.00
2	155.00	126.00

Use the following descriptive information to create a table.

Report

Sleep_Grp		Veridical_Recall	False_Recall
1.00	Mean	179.4000	167.4000
	N	5	5
	Std. Deviation	35.02570	36.51438
2.00	Mean	192.6000	153.2000
	N	5	5
	Std. Deviation	31.75374	27.15143
Total	Mean	186.0000	160.3000
	N	10	10
	Std. Deviation	32.27658	31.24473

All we need to consider for the moment is the descriptive information. Take the information provided by SPSS and create a table displaying the means and standard deviations. Somewhere in the Results section, the author would have said something like "See Table 1 for descriptive data on groups."

Remember to include

- Table numbering in bold
- Title in italics
- Horizontal lines only
- Enough information for the reader to understand what is presented in the table
- Notes at the bottom of the table if needed
- Double spacing
- (For future reference) Each table and figure goes on a separate page after the references

Create your table *without* looking at the example below then compare and revise your table as needed. Make sure you communicate the same information as indicated below, and that your table is arranged in a way that is easy for the reader to follow. You can report sample size for each mean, or just once in the title or note. You may organize the data a bit differently than I did below. Try to think about how you can best organize the information to help your reader quickly process it.

HOW DO I CREATE A FIGURE?

There are several ways you can create a figure. You may use Excel, PowerPoint, SPSS, or other types of programs available. I'll show you examples in Excel and SPSS.

Figure 15.2   Mean Veridical and False Recall as a Function of Sleep After Learning

	Veridical Recall			False Recall		
	M	SD	N	M	SD	N
No Sleep	179.40	35.03	5	167.40	36.51	5
Sleep	192.60	31.75	5	153.20	27.15	5

NOTE: Type of recall was a within-subjects measure.

Excel

Let's pretend we were interested in the association between veridical and false recall. We hypothesized that those with higher correct recall would have lower false recall. We want to demonstrate the *relationship between two quantitative variables (i.e., a correlation),* so we will use ... yep, you got it! A scatterplot. Using the data from above, create a scatterplot that would create a visual of the relationship between the two types of recall:

Copy and paste the data from SPSS (or this document) into an Excel file.

1. Highlight the recall data (not the sleep group)

2. Click *Insert, Charts*

3. Click *Scatter* then click the first box presented

Excel will create the following figure (titles have been edited in the picture below):

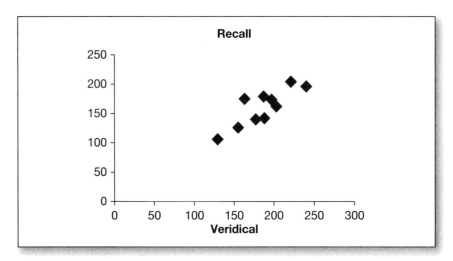

From here, you can right click various areas of the figure to change the title, add a label to the *y*-axis (the vertical line, which would be false recall) or *x*-axis, change the units of the variables, and more. You can also right click the data points and choose *Add Trendline* (click *linear*) to add a regression line running through the data points. As you can see, our hypothesis that high veridical recall would associate with low false recall (a negative correlation) was *not* supported. In fact, the opposite is true: People who recalled more correct words also recalled more false words (a positive correlation).

Still in Excel, let's use the sleep group x type of recall data above that lets us examine whether participants who sleep after learning will have greater (1) veridical and (2) false recall in comparison to a group who stayed awake after learning. We want to *compare means between two groups*, so we will use—a bar graph! To graph this, we need to type in our variable names and group means into Excel as follows:

	Veridical Recall	False Recall
No Sleep	179.40	167.40
Sleep	192.60	153.20

To create a bar graph, a visual of the group means for each type of recall, you would

1. Highlight the data and variable names

2. Click *Insert, Chart, Bar*

3. Click *Column* then click the first box presented

Excel will create the following figure:

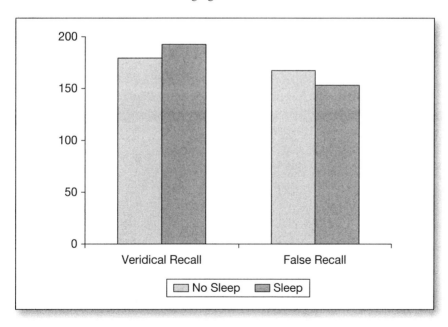

Again, you can right click various parts of the figure to change labels, axes, and so on. Voilà!

USING SPSS

Be aware that the instructions in these labs are developed using SPSS 21. Exact wording of commands may vary depending on which version of SPSS you use.

Let's practice creating graphs in SPSS. We will practice with between-subject variables and within-subject variables.

When the IV Is a Between-Subjects Variable

Continue to use the sleep group x type of recall data from above. At the moment, let's ask whether there is a sleep group difference in the Veridical Recall condition.

1. Click *Graphs*

2. *Legacy*

3. *Bar*

4. *Simple*

5. *Summaries For Groups of Cases*

6. *Define*

7. *Other Statistic* (You would select other statistic because we are reporting means instead of counts.) Select *Veridical Recall* and move it to *Variable Box*. Select *Sleep Group*, move it to *Category Axis*.

8. *OK*

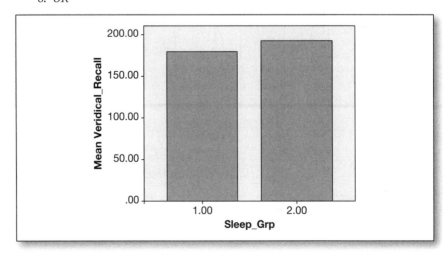

When the IV Is a Within-Subjects Variable

Using the same data, let's ask whether there is a difference in Veridical versus False Recall.

1. Click *Graphs*

2. *Legacy*

3. *Bar*

4. *Simple*

5. *Summaries for Separate Variables*

6. *Define.* Move the two variables to be compared to the box labeled *Bars Represent* then

7. *OK*

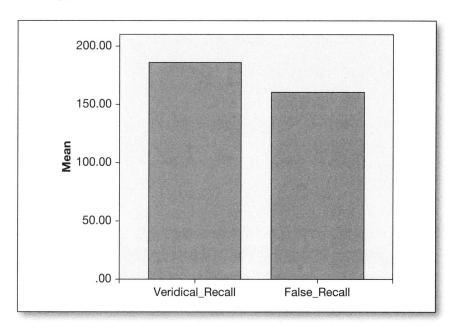

Let's create a figure that is a bit more complicated. Still using the data above,

1. Click *Graphs*

2. *Legacy*

3. *Bar*

4. *Clustered*

5. *Summaries for Separate Variables*

6. *Define*. Move *Sleep Group* to the *Category Axis* box, the two recall variables to the *Bars Represent* box

7. *OK*

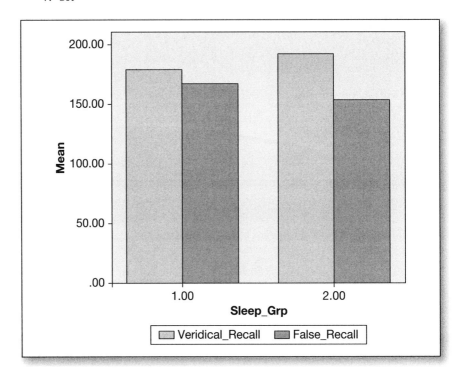

How would you interpret this figure based on your eyeball examination?

One more figure. Use the data below. For this example, we are looking to see if recall in general is different as a function of typical sleep duration (hours slept).

Hours_Sleep	Recall
6	5
10	10
7	7
5	4

Hours_Sleep	Recall
8	6
7	6
6	4
9	8
10	11
7	8

1. Click *Graphs*

2. *Legacy*

3. *Line*

4. *Simple*

5. *Summaries For Groups of Cases*

6. *Define.* Move hours_sleep to the *Category Axis* box, recall into the *Variable* box (you may need to click *Other Statistic* first)

7. *OK*

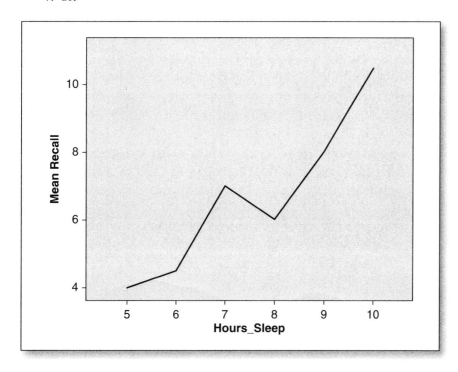

How would you interpret this figure?

As average time slept increased, _____ [mean recall also increased]. This may remind you of a scatterplot; the difference is in this case the association is not linear, and we may not have caught that in a simple scatterplot.

IF YOU WANT TO COLLECT YOUR OWN DATA . . .

You can measure false memory easily. Look up the following article:

Roediger, H. L., III, & McDermott, K. B. (1995). Creating false memories: Remembering words not presented in lists. *Journal of Experimental Psychology, 21*, 803–814. doi:10.1037/0278-7393.21.4.803

You can find the article online by searching the article title (for example, http://courses.washington.edu/passr101/Activities/ThanksForTheMe moriesMcDermott/Roediger%2520and%2520McDermott%25201995.pdf. Multiple lists of words you can use to test false memory are included in an appendix. Let's say you hypothesize that people who get more sleep will recall more veridical and false words. If your classmates are willing, randomly assign people to groups who will get 5 to 6, 7 to 8, or 9 to 10 hours of sleep for three nights in a row. If you just want two groups you could compare 5 to 6 hours to 9 to 10 hours. Participants can keep a sleep diary to document their time in bed each night. Those of you in the low sleep group—remember being sleepy can be dangerous! Don't drive or engage in dangerous activities until you are well rested. Everyone needs to do their best to sleep for their assigned amount of time for three nights in a row. You can pretest memory, then do a posttest using different lists. Counterbalance which lists are used pre- and posttest. After three nights of sleep, a designated experimenter can administer the recall task, calculate correct and veridical recall, and then record each person's average sleep across the three nights and correct and false recall. Analyze the data and create a figure or table to present the data.

IF YOU WANT TO GO FURTHER . . .

Scatterplots, line graphs, bar graphs, oh my! Let's learn a few more graphing skills to keep in our toolbox. We will learn how to create stacked bar graphs, pie charts, error bars within bar graphs, and graphs with multiple IVs. We will also use a feature of newer versions of SPSS called *Chart Builder*.

Stacked Bar Graph

A stacked bar graph can be a great way to display the relationship between two nominal or ordinal variables. This type of bar graph still uses rectangular boxes to represent categories of Variable A (on the x-axis), but now these boxes are broken into smaller segments that represent percentages of cases that fall within categories or scores of Variable B (on the y-axis). Let's say we gathered information on gender (male, female). A stacked bar graph could essentially provide the breakdown of who's who in regards to race and gender. The graph could show us how many participants were female Asians, how many were male Asians, how many were Black females, and so forth. Enter the data below and run a stacked bar graph in SPSS. In this example we coded race categories as White = 1, Black = 2, and Asian = 3. We will code gender as Male = 1 and Female = 2.

Enter the data below.

Race	Gender
1	2
2	2
1	1
1	1
3	1
2	1
1	2
1	1
1	1
3	2
1	2
3	1
1	2
3	2

(Continued)

(Continued)

Race	Gender
2	2
3	2
3	2
2	1
2	1
1	1

After entering the data, click the *Variable View* button at the bottom left of your screen. Click the cell under the column *Values* and click the blue ".." in the right side of the cell. Enter 1 for Value and *Male* for Label, then click *Add.* Then enter 2 for Value and *Female* for Label then click *Add.* Then press *OK.* This has set your value labels so SPSS "knows" what each score represents when graphing and can present it as such in the graph. Repeat this to enter value codes for Race. Lastly, look at the second-to-last column labeled *Measure.* Make sure this is set to *Nominal.* To run a stacked bar graph, variables must be either Nominal or Ordinal. Now click back to the *Data View* screen. ***Note—depending on your version of SPSS, the dropdown menu will be slightly different.*** From here,

1. Click *Graphs*

2. *Chart Builder* (if another box pops up asking about defining variable, click *OK*)

3. Click *Bar*

4. Choose/Drag *Stacked Bar* (for newer versions, the third picture graph)

5. Choose/Drag *Gender* for the *x*-axis variable

6. Choose/Drag *Race* to the top right dotted box

7. Click *Element Properties* if this box does not automatically pop up to the right

8. Under *Statistics*, choose *Percentage (?)*. Click *Set Parameters* and choose *Total for Each X-Axis Category*. Click *Continue*, then *Apply* then *OK*

Your graph should be presented in your output. From here, double click the graph and a *Chart Editor* will appear. Click the *Data Label Mode* on the left (see screenshot below).

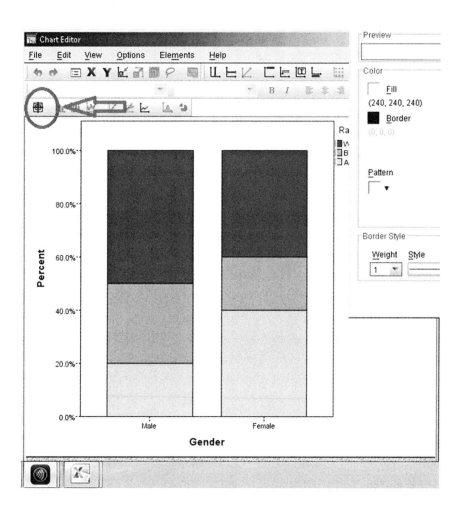

Now click on each colored segment—a box should appear displaying the percentages for each segment. Your final stacked bar graph should look like this:

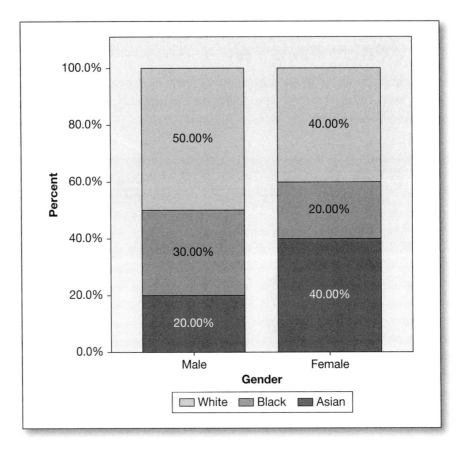

Feel free to play around with the Chart Editor to change colors, patterns, and labels on the graph. Get as fancy as you like!

Pie Charts

A pie chart can be used to display proportions of cases in each category of a nominal variable. Pie charts can be visually appealing and a simple way to display proportions. Using our same example as above, we could present the proportion of participants in each race category in a pie chart.

1. Click *Graphs*

2. *Chart Builder* (if another box pops up asking about defining variable properties but you have already set your value labels as we did above, then click *OK*)

3. *PIE*

4. Choose/Drag *Race* to the bottom box (set color)

5. Click *Element Properties* if this box does not automatically pop up to the right

6. Under *Statistics*, you can choose *Count* or *Percentage* (?) depending on whether you want to display the number of participants in each category or the percentage. Click *Continue*, *Apply*, then *OK*

7. When your graph appears, you may double click it to bring up the Chart Editor, click *Data Label Mode*, and click each pie slice to display the count/percentage. Here is an example of a pie chart of our race categories:

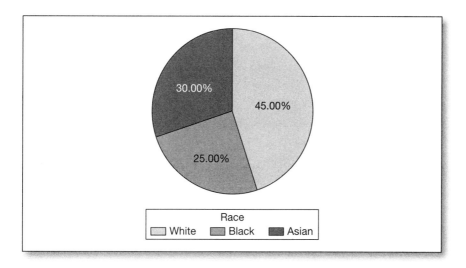

Error Bars

Error bars can be added to bar charts or line graphs to visually present variability in the data. With descriptive error bars, graphs and charts can visually show either the *range* or *standard deviation* of the data that is not captured if a graph simply presents means. With inferential error bars, graphs can visually present *standard errors* or *confidence intervals*. Remember that confidence intervals give us a range of values that serve as estimates of the true (but unknown) population parameter. The level of the confidence interval (e.g., 95%) tells us the probability that our range has captured the actual population parameter (e.g., we could be 95% confident that our confidence interval captured the true value of our variable that exists in the entire population). For example, let's say we are testing the effects of a new pharmaceutical drug on weight loss in comparison to a control group. I present the results in a graph:

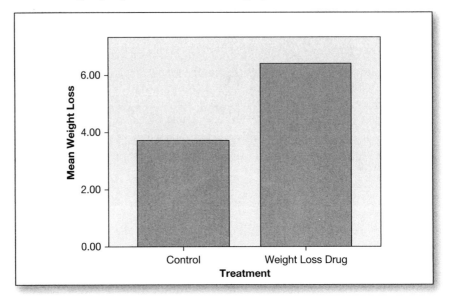

As you can see, the means of the control group and weight loss drug group are compared, and it appears that the experimental group lost about 1.5 times more weight than the control group. However, look what happens when we add error bars representing a 95% confidence interval:

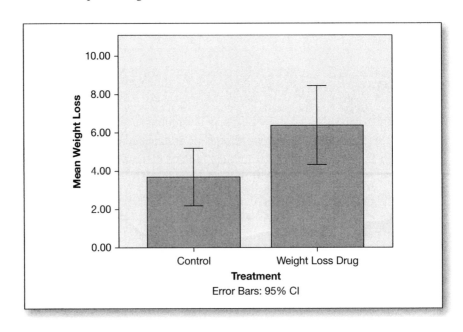

We now see that while the means are different, their confidence intervals overlap. This means that our range in which we expect the *true* population mean to fall (if every single member of the population was in the experimental group, how much weight would be lost) overlaps with the confidence interval for the control group. We would want to be cautious in interpreting the effectiveness of the weight loss drug.

When reporting error bars, you always want to state what your error bars represent to ensure data are not misleading. Note how at the bottom of the chart above, it states "Error Bars: 95% CI" so our readers know what the bars indicate.

When using SPSS, it is very easy to add error bars to a graph; simply click OPTIONS, the *Display error bars* under the *Element Properties* window. See below:

Try It Yourself

Go back to the lab on two-group designs and open your data set for the between-subjects *t*-test we ran. You should have a column of data for condition (double letter = 1, concrete = 2) and a column of data for recall. Using these data, create a simple bar graph. You can use the legacy dialogue option (review the instructions for SPSS above) or the chart builder (you may need to change the statistic designation from *value* to *mean* to get it to work). Add in error bars for a 95% confidence interval. *Note—in newer versions of SPSS, you will need to specify your continuous variable as* Scale. *You can do so by going to the* Variable View *screen and clicking* Scale *under the* Measure *column on the right.).* Create your graph and interpret it. What do you notice about the error bars? We'd like for them to NOT overlap. Once you've brainstormed interpretation of the graph, check your graph and responses against the answers below.

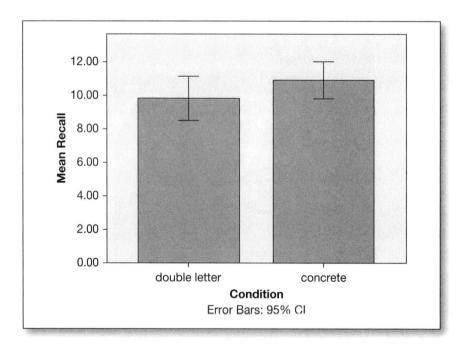

Does your graph look like this? Good! We notice here that the confidence intervals overlap, indicating it is likely the means for each of these conditions in the *true* population fall within the same range. Are we surprised by this?

No—not if you remember that these group means were not significantly differ-ent according to our *t*-test.

Graphing Factorials

The last type of graphing we will practice is plotting results from a facto-rial design. If you recall from the lab on factorial designs, we learned how to analyze designs with two or more IVs. Let's learn how to plot the results of factorial designs to visually present an interaction. Let's use our example from the factorial lab where we examined a 2 x 2 between-subjects (not mixed or within-subjects) design to test whether witness attractiveness or type of cloth-ing might sway jurors' perception of the believability of that witness's testi-mony. Open, enter, or copy and paste your data from the previous lab. Remember, our IVs are attractiveness and clothing. Then,

1. Click *Analyze*

2. *General Linear Model*

3. *Univariate*

4. Move the two IVs into the *Fixed Factors* box and the DV into the *Dependent Variable* box.

5. Go to *Options*, and click the box to the left of *Descriptives* and *Estimate of Effect Size*.

6. *Continue*

7. Click *Model* and click *Full Factorial*. Be sure to check *Include Intercept in Model* at the bottom. Click *Continue*

8. Click *Plots*. Select *Attractiveness* as *Horizontal Axis* and *Clothing* as *Separate Lines*. It actually does not matter which way the variables are plotted; it just depends on which variable you want on which axis. Use your own judgment as to which way makes the most sense.

9. Click *Add, Continue, OK*

Your output graph should look like this:

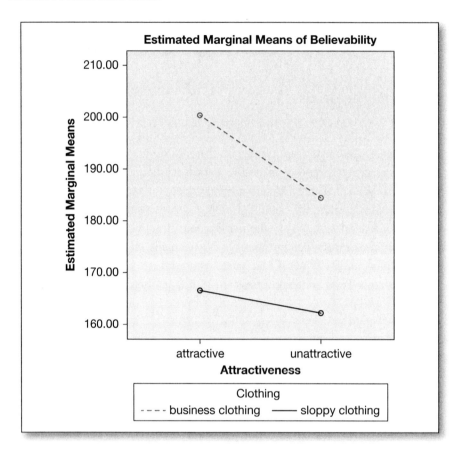

As you can see, the graph provides a helpful visual in understanding how the believability of a witness's testimony depends on both attractiveness and clothing; we can plainly see that believability was higher for witnesses wearing business clothing, but the level of believability *depended* on attractiveness (i.e., being attractive AND wearing business clothes yielded the highest level of believability). Plotting interactions can aid your reader in understanding the results and help you, as well! Just remember that if you include your plot in a research paper, double click on the graph in the SPSS output and edit as needed for clean, simple titles and axis labels.

A FEW MORE (OPTIONAL) THINGS

Author Notes

An author note is a small paragraph included on published articles that provides information about the first or corresponding author(s). It is always included on the title page or first page of the publication. An author note is typically not included on class papers, theses, or dissertations but may be required depending on your instructor's requirements. An author note should include the following:

First line: Departmental and institutional affiliation (i.e., the department and university or institution where the author works or attends school)

Second line: Changes in affiliation, if any (Did the author switch jobs or change graduate programs? This is helpful for readers to know so authors can be contacted if necessary.)

Third line: Acknowledgments, funding sources, or special circumstances (Often this is where authors will acknowledge grants that funded the research project.)

Fourth line: Contact information, usually university or institution mailing address and email (not your home address or personal email)

Author notes may also be used to report changes in affiliation, acknowledgments, conflicts of interest, and special circumstances. You can read more about this on pages 24 and 25 in the *Publication Manual of the American Psychological Association* (6th ed.).

Take a peek at the Payne et al. (2009) article from this lab for an example of an author note. You will see this paragraph on the bottom left corner of the first page. There are two corresponding authors for this article, and the author note provides their university and medical center addresses and emails.

Appendices

In a research paper, sometimes there are materials that are meaningful to your research but would be distracting or too lengthy if put within the body of the text. Examples could be a very large table, a list of words, a questionnaire used in the research, or a detailed description of equipment. This information can be included in an appendix, located after the reference section and before tables and figures. Each separate appendix material should have its own page and its own title. If you only have one appendix, label it *Appendix* (no quotations or italics). If you have several, title the first appendix *Appendix A* (no quotations or italics), the next appendix is titled *Appendix B*, and so forth. Order the appendices in the same order they are mentioned in the body of the paper. If you are including several tables or figures, these will be labeled *A1, A2, B1, B2* (no italics) and so on. As with regular tables, you must refer to the appendices within the body of the paper. See the following for an example:

> http://writingcenter.waldenu.edu/Documents/How_to_Format_and_
> Cite_an_Appendix_in_APA_Style.pdf {suggested search term *format
> appendix APA style*}

Also see the sixth edition of the *Publication Manual of the American Psychological Association*, starting at page 38, for more information.

Understandably, information included in an appendix should be somewhat brief and easy to present in a print format (i.e., it shouldn't be 50 pages long or cost the publishers an arm and a leg to print—assuming the journal still puts out a hard copy). Materials that are difficult to include in print can sometimes be presented as web-based supplemental materials.

Web-Based Supplemental Material

Some materials are valuable to a research article but difficult to provide in print. Luckily, the age of technology provides an alternative way to present this information to readers. Web-based supplemental materials can be provided via a URL link on the first page and online version of an article. The link(s) can provide access to materials in a variety of forms, such as Word or PDF documents, tables in Excel or HTML, and audio or video files. According to the *APA Publication Manual*, supplemental materials should only be included if they somehow assist the reader in understanding, evaluating, or replicating the study. Some examples of suitable web-based supplemental materials include computer coding, lengthy mathematical models, oversized tables, audio and video clips, color figures, and additional details of intervention protocols or methodology. Note that all supplemental materials are held to the same ethical and copyright standards as printed materials, and these materials are peer-reviewed along with the rest of the manuscript.

To read about the potential impact of supplemental materials and to see an example of web-based supplemental materials, see the article by Jeremy Kenyon and Nancy Sprague (2014).

REFERENCES

American Psychological Association. (2010). *Publication manual of the American Psychological Association* (6th ed.). Washington, DC: Author.

Kenyon, J., & Sprague, N. R. (2014, Winter). Trends in the use of supplementary materials in environmental science journals. *Issues in Science and Technology Librarianship, 75.* doi:10.5062/F40Z717Z

IN CONCLUSION

Y ou're just about done! It was a lot of work, but you made it through a challenging class on research. You've learned some valuable skills that will serve you well no matter what kind of career you choose. For example, you can

- ✓ Identify a problem or research question.

- ✓ Critically read the background literature on that issue and summarize it, then develop a research question or hypothesis.

- ✓ Think of a way to address the questions by designing or finding appropriate measures. You know about issues of validity and reliability of measures.

- ✓ Collect, analyze and interpret data.

- ✓ Write about the project using APA style and/or formally present your findings. No matter what your career, never underestimate the importance of good writing and speaking skills.

You can highlight these competencies on your resume. Now, reflect on your experiences in this class. Write your answers to the following questions:

1. What did you learn in this class that was or will be helpful in your future plans?

2. What would you have done differently?

3. If you were to continue your line of research, what would be your next research question?

4. What skills did you develop or strengthen in this class that you can use in other careers?

5. What suggestions would you make that could increase students' learning experiences in this class?

©iStock.com/liravega

©iStock.com/PerfectVectors

INDEX